D0710420

Also by David Bret
The Piaf Legend

The MISTINGUETT Legend

DAVID BRET

St. Martin's Press
New York

Library of Congress Cataloging-in-Publication Data

Bret, David.
The Mistinguett legend / David Bret.
p.   cm.
ISBN 0-312-05471-8
1. Mistinguett, b. 1875.   2. Singers—France—Biography.
I. Title.
ML420.M538B7   1991
782.42164'092—dc20
[B]   90-48331   CIP

First published in Great Britain by Robson Books Ltd.

First U.S. Edition: January 1991
10 9 8 7 6 5 4 3 2 1

This book is for
Roger Normand
and Louis Rookx

N'oublie pas. . . .
La vie sans amis
c'est comme un
jardin sans fleurs

Contents

Acknowledgements

Writing any book is never easy. Writing a book about an outstanding artiste . . . and Mistinguett was never anything less . . . would be doubly difficult if it were not for that indefatigable group of people listed below who helped, and above all offered me their sincere friendship during what became a laborious task. I shall never be able to thank them enough.

Michel Guyarmathy . . . my dear Monsieur Folies-Bergère! You were a busy man, yet you graciously afforded me time and considerable patience. In the realm of the music-hall you remain King. Long may you wear your crown!

Roger Normand . . . you yourself know that mere words may not express my love and respect for you. You were and always will be that vital corner-stone adhering to the bastion of the music-hall!

Louis Rookx . . . a dear friend without whose help none of this would have been possible. Bravo!

Barbara and Marlène Dietrich . . . two cherished friends who, perhaps inadvertently, gave me confidence when confidence was hard to find! *Je vous offre mon coeur!*

The Mayor of Enghien, Philippe Suer; *Le Contrôleur d'Etat Honoraire d'Enghien*, Jean-Paul Neu; Madame Gambier and the staff of the Bibliothèque d'Enghien; the people of Enghien . . . admiration mingles with tears that you have decided to name a street in honour of your famous daughter. I shall never be able to thank you enough. Part of my heart will always remain in Enghien. God bless you!

Thelma Ruby . . . a marvellous actress and a dear lady who so wonderfully brought Mistinguett back to life again. I am so very grateful that you did, Thelma. Bravo!

I should also like to thank the following for their loyal support and assistance:

Pierre-Yves Garcin, of EMI/Pathé-Marconi, for allowing me access to invaluable documents and recordings of the French music-hall.

Kevin Daly of EMI London, and Delny Ingle of Conifer Records for assisting me with my research and supplying me with many rare songs of Mistinguett.

Topham Picture Library, for giving me access to some very rare photographs.

The staff of *The Times*, *News of the World* (England) and *France-Dimanche*.

Claire Hudson of the Theatre Museum, London

The extracts published throughout this book, for which I gratefully thank the publishers, are from:

Mistinguett – *Toute Ma Vie* (Editions Juillard, 1954)
Roger Peyrefitte – *Manouche* (Grove Press, New York) 1974

The MISTINGUETT Legend

Introduction

Enghien stands on the N14 some twelve miles north of Paris, between St Ouen and Montmorency. It is a quaint, pretty village with an assortment of Anglo-Norman cottages, a pseudo-Gothic castle, a spa for respiratory ailments and arthritis, a lake and a casino.

Historically, Montmorency may have a greater if not less interesting claim to fame for it was here, within the building known as the Montlouis, that the great philosopher Jean-Jacques Rousseau completed several of his more important works, including *Le Contrat Social* and *Emile*.

Enghien, on the other hand, is renowned for a most remarkable woman who was not merely famous, but infamous. A woman who was in many ways a very special kind of philosopher . . . a woman of singular talent whose fortitude and courage of conviction would hold Paris spellbound for the best part of sixty years. To the honest, hard-working men and women of Enghien she was known as Jeannot. Her full name was Jeanne-Marie Florentine Bourgeois, but to the world she was known simply as Mistinguett.

She was a goddess of love to many, and the scourge of the music-hall to more than a few. She was a woman with few scruples, boundless energy, reckless abandon and will-power. She loved with limitless passion and was revered in return. When crossed, she hated with a fervour second to none. Her faults by far outweigh her qualities, yet to this day she remains an enigma, and the world will never see her like again. She was the undisputed Queen of Music-Hall, a fact which not one single person in France would deny.

The Duc D'Enghien's
Unclaimed Bastard

She was born on 5 April 1875, and for many years she was the only child of a couple whose forebears were renowned locally for having hordes of children. This lack of progeny has often been blamed on her mother. Madame Bourgeois was a seamstress and feather-dresser whose dream of an acting career had been shattered following a nasty fall soon after Jeanne's birth. For the rest of her life she would walk with a limp, and for many years – until the birth of her second child, Marcel – she would remain housebound. Her incapacity, however, did not prevent her from being a workaholic: it was Madame Bourgeois who kept the family's head above water in times of strife and not her hard-drinking, erratic husband. Monsieur Bourgeois was a big, burly Belgian who made and stuffed mattresses, and who employed a small force of workers in his Montmorency workshop, though quite often the administration of his business was left to his wife . . . and, a little later, his daughter.

Jeanne Bourgeois was a determined, wilful child. When she was three years old a distant cousin asked her to be bridesmaid at her wedding . . . for the occasion, Madame Bourgeois decorated her dress with tiny feathers, and two important precedents were set. Jeanne would become a famous actress . . . when this happened, she would always perform with an abundance of feathers.

Lively Jeanne may have been, but initially boys were never a problem. When she was five her mother enrolled her at a convent school within which the Sisters of Providence were particularly strict, threatening to bring the wrath of God upon any girl who so much as looked directly at a member of the opposite sex. The nuns also tried

– and failed – to drill it into her that normal girls did not aspire for a career on the stage, which was in those days considered not just decadent, but pernicious.

Subsequently, whenever Jeanne could not have all her own way – which was often – she would threaten to run away from home in order to 'seek her fortune' in Paris, which could be only too easily reached from the Pointe-Raquet railway station just down the road from the *maison de famille*.

It would appear that Jeanne received very little love during her childhood. Her mother tried to keep her at home, and in check, only because she was a vital addition to the combined family business. After school she worked her so hard that the Sisters of Providence and the local priest became increasingly concerned about her health, though their protests were always ignored. Whenever it rained, Jeanne had to help out in Monsieur Bourgeois' workshop, and she also had to cook meals and clean out the workers' rooms. If it was fine, she was sent out with the trolley to pick up mattresses from neighbouring villages. Her only respite was Sunday, when Enghien would be visited by one of the several travelling circuses which toured the region. Alternatively, she would play truant from school and go off with her friends to steal apples or engage in a spot of shoplifting. It was a mania which would stay with her for the rest of her life, and she was never caught once!

After her son Marcel was born, Madame Bourgeois became almost impossible to live with. Suffering from post-natal depression, for some time she refused to have anything to do with the child and he was placed in Jeanne's care. This came as a great relief; she had begun to develop round shoulders through pushing the heavy trolley around, and she was allergic to the stuffing which went into the mattresses. Her mother's temporary indisposition meant that besides looking after her brother and running the household, Jeanne also had to deliver hats and organize the family budget. For Jeanne this was the ideal situation . . . she began fiddling the books, and meeting so many wealthy clients only fuelled her desire to tread the boards.

There then occurred the first major tragedy in Jeanne's life, though she would later say that it was a blessing in disguise. Soon after Marcel's birth the family moved and took over a café and grocery store on the rue du Départ in Enghien. The new home was a modest cottage behind the main building, surrounded by a large garden within which a previous owner had planted a small orchard of apricot trees. Monsieur Bourgeois cut some of these down to construct a chicken-run, and his anticipated enterprise wherein the family would make a little extra cash by selling eggs ultimately cost him his life. One day, whilst he was cleaning out his chickens, he gashed his arm on the wire. Tetanus set in, and one week later the family had laid him to rest in the local cemetery.

During the next few weeks, Jeanne kept a watchful eye on her mother, particularly as the doctor had proclaimed that she may have been on the verge of losing her mind. Madame Bourgeois was in fact as relieved as anyone that her husband was out of the way: since moving house he had lost all interest in his work, and Madame Bourgeois had found it too much of a strain trying to run both businesses and keep an eye on her wayward daughter at the same time. Thus the mattress workshop was closed down, Jeanne was made to supervise the seamstresses – setting another precedent, for as Mistinguett she would have all her fabulous dresses cut out and sewn up under her own roof and would never leave the room until satisfied that they were perfect – and extra help was enlisted from the village to look after the house and store. Mistinguett remembers her mother fondly in her autobiography, *Toute Ma Vie*, which she wrote in 1953, less than three years before her death:

> My mother spent most of her time visiting relatives. She was very fashionable and liked to wear enormous hats . . . with these and her wavy hair, she was a dead-ringer for Louis XV. She gossiped a lot and was forever talking to herself, pretending that she was on the stage. The thing is, she would have made a very good actress. I am what I am today only because of all the things I picked up from my mother.

These relatives were exclusively on the maternal side, and they all lived in or near Enghien. Madame Bourgeois had four brothers. Hippolyte, Corneille and Henri ran a removal firm and also rented out horse-drawn carriages. The fourth brother . . . he is not named in Mistinguett's memoirs . . . was the black sheep of the family because he was hunchbacked and unable to do manual work. Most of his time was spent playing the violin, and as he was keenly interested in the music-hall, needless to say he was Jeanne's favourite uncle. Apart from him, the most important member of the family was Tante Florentine. She was a formidable old woman who ran the local second-hand shop, and with whom Jeanne would stay during the school holidays. It was with Tante Florentine that she shared the happiest moments of her childhood. Occasionally she would accompany her aunt to the horse sales at Les Halles, and through her she got to know a little about Paris and its seamier side.

It was whilst staying with Tante Florentine that Jeanne was inaugurated into her first vital lessons about men and women, or rather the differences between the two, as she later put it.

The maid was having a passionate affair with the gardener: on Sundays after mass the couple would sneak into the cellar and charge the local children two sous to watch them making love. Also, when she was about twelve, Jeanne became leader of the local gang which rapidly became the scourge of the neighbourhood. The boys were terrified of her because she could fight as well as the rest of them. A favourite haunt was the bridge at Enghien, and as if Jeanne had not learned enough about the male anatomy from her aunt's gardener, what went on under the parapet of Enghien Bridge would have deeply shocked the Sisters of Providence, who were fighting a losing battle to keep their most troublesome pupil pure now that she had reached puberty. During one of her shop-lifting expeditions Jeanne had stolen a ruler from the haberdashery store, and after a few similarly-filched bottles of *vin-rouge* the ever-eager boys were made to drop their trousers whilst Jeanne got to work with the ruler, though for the time being her sexual interests did not progress beyond this adolescent fancy.

Her first sexual encounter took place when she was aged about fifteen, and brings to mind an interesting, if not typical, anecdote. The priest, ever-conscious of Madame Bourgeois' fragile health, had also begun to take a lively interest in her children, taking them on outings and bringing them gifts. One of these was a pet rabbit, which was promptly installed in the fatal chicken-run. Jeanne and the priest had gone into the meadow to collect some hay, and one of the local farmhands had tagged along. Even as a girl Jeanne was quite pretty, and the young man had begun showing off in front of her. Ultimately he had fallen into the river, and only the priest's speedy actions had saved him from a watery grave. The young man had been laid on the river bank, and the priest had irresponsibly ordered Jeanne to remove his clothes and keep him warm whilst he himself fetched the doctor. One would assume that Jeanne did this quite innocently. . . She placed the young man under a pile of corn-sheaves and the inevitable happened. Many years later Mistinguett said that losing her virginity had been a forgettable experience made memorable only by the fact that she had been chewing liquorice root at the time and had not known where to spit. Sadly, the young man died soon afterwards in a fairground accident, though his descendants still live and work in Enghien to this day.

The tragedy brought Jeanne to her senses. She realized that if she stayed in Enghien she would end up like her mother, tied to the family business, working her fingers to the bone and reaping too few rewards. Moreover, now that she had had a brief affair with one of them, the local boys no longer held any specific interest; the thought of settling down with a man like her father repelled her, and her brother Marcel was enough of a handful for her to decide early in life that she would never have any children of her own unless by accident, which of course is exactly what happened. Lusty farmhands may have proved more than adequate lovers for other girls in her station, and could always be found loitering around the bridge at Enghien once the day's work had been done. The village also had a number of prostitutes who plied their trade more or less openly. . . Jeanne was familiar with them all, and somehow managed to keep a tally of who was sleeping with whom. Her first lover may have sworn to have eyes for her alone: no doubt he had said exactly the same thing to dozens of other girls, and this made Jeanne cautious.

She was a devout Catholic who had committed carnal sin, and it seems likely that she would have been brazen enough to have confessed the whole affair to the priest, who himself does not appear to have been in any way celibate. What the Church had to say about her amorous activities would never bother her . . . she always maintained that whatever she did in life, God would be on her side because He was afraid of being otherwise! Hers was the bizarre religion of the *fille de joie*, wherein love is the profound virtue whether one is married or not. This somewhat bizarre philosophy worked well later on for Edith Piaf and it would suffice for Mistinguett, who had made up her mind that if she was going to have a man, the man himself would not matter much providing he was young, handsome and very, very rich!

Inspiration was always close at hand. Madame Bourgeois had always been gullible, and liaising with the priest, Jeanne somehow managed to persuade her doctor to convince her mother that whilst routine housework never did anyone any real harm, too much of it whilst a child was still studying at school was apt to have a weakening effect on the bladder. Jeanne therefore made a point of wetting herself whenever she carried anything heavy, such as a crate or barrel of wine from the cellar. The ploy worked. She was 'assigned' to lighter duties, which in effect amounted to little more than delivering hats to rich customers in the surrounding villages. Not only did Jeanne amend the bills to include her delivery charge . . . such was her cheek that she was often asked to stay to tea!

Most of Madame Bourgeois' clients were in their dotage. Some had *chevalier-servants* – today they would be called toy-boys; handsome young men who were sensible enough to know when they were onto a good thing. Quite a lot of these gigolos were also homosexual, setting yet another precedent, for when famous as Mistinguett, Jeanne would have an extraordinary penchant for men who, if they were not actually practising homosexuals engaged in affairs with other members of her company, were extremely effeminate. She even dressed her brother in girl's clothes when taking him to school, and was threatened with expulsion for doing so.

Jeanne Bourgeois therefore added another clause to her quest for the ideal man, in that sex and sexual preference would not precede a well-filled wallet and a healthy bank balance, and by the time she left the convent school she had already begun her search for that elusive millionaire who would crop up in one of her most fêted songs.

C'est facile d'être chic
Quand on a beaucoup d'fric!
Je cherche un millionaire
Qui m'dirait froidement:
'Mon or est à toi!'

(It's easy to be chic

When you've got lots of dough!
I'm looking for a millionaire
Who'll tell me coldly:
'My gold is yours!')

By around 1890 Madame Bourgeois had added another string to her bow – that of interior decoration. One of her very first commissions had been to refurbish the villa of Anna Thibaud, who lived in Enghien at the time. Anna Thibaud was an eccentric *chanteuse* who performed in the café-concerts of Paris and the provinces. She was a forerunner of Damia and Fréhel, the most popular exponents of the *chanson* in France between the two world wars, and one of the earliest interpreters of Fragson and Vincent Scotto. She must have been very talented. Though no recording of her voice has survived, she was well-praised by her critics. It does come as a great surprise, however, to find that she was revered by the working classes. Her extreme arrogance and snobbishness went as far as holding tea-parties on the lawn in front of her house so that her upper crust guests might poke fun at the locals, and there were cages containing exotic birds on every table.

When the time came for Madame Bourgeois to collect the money for the refurbishing of the villa, Jeanne was sent around with the bill. Anna Thibaud observed the girl's clothes and trodden-down shoes, and decided to add spice to the occasion by asking her to stay to tea. Jeanne could hardly refuse, for never in her life had she seen such a gathering of handsome young men, most of whom had slept with the *chanteuse*. . . or each other. One of these dandies asked Jeanne what she would like to be now that she had left school, and her reply caused more than a ripple of amusement. Anna Thibaud declared that no actress worthy of her name would ever venture onto the stage in trodden-down old shoes and with her fringe plastered down with soap. The clothes she could not rectify there and then, but she did send her maid into the villa to fetch a bowl of hot water, towels and a phial of expensive shampoo which was alleged to have been imported especially from some far-off land.

Anna Thibaud herself washed and set Jeanne's hair, which must have been rather noble of her considering that it was but a part of her cruel game. A mirror was held in front of Jeanne, and she was asked if she still considered herself fit for the theatre. The response was the same as it had been before, to which came the reply that even with pretty clothes and clean hair, Jeanne Bourgeois would still be the ugliest girl in Enghien, if not in the whole of France. Anna Thibaud then added, scathingly, that even without this apparent deformity there was still the question of her background and hideous reputation. Jeanne Bourgeois was not just working-class as her father had been, Anna Thibaud declared. Quite simply, she belonged in the gutter!

For a moment, Jeanne hovered on the brink of tears whilst she surveyed the sea of mocking faces. Then she found the courage to single out one man in particular, and exclaimed, 'I'm just as good as anyone here. That man over there is my real father. I'm the Duc d'Enghien's unclaimed bastard!'

The statement was made often during Mistinguett's career, and there is now absolutely no way of proving it one way or the other. Mistinguett liked to add to her own legend by making up stories, but even the wildest of her fantasies contained some element of truth. Madame Bourgeois certainly had been in the habit of visiting the castle before Jeanne's birth, and she neither admitted nor denied the fact when, a few years later, Mistinguett began scribbling the statement across publicity photographs.

After the humiliating incident *chez* Anna Thibaud, however, Jeanne Bourgeois was certain of one thing. No one would ever make her look a fool again.

Still very much the leader of the local *voyous*, Jeanne formed her own 'repertory' group and began putting on plays and revues in her father's old workshop. If Tante Florentine's gardener and maid could charge two sous for what they got up to in the wine-cellar every Sunday morning, then Jeanne could charge twice that amount to put on a show of a more artistic if not substantially less educational nature!

Madame Bourgeois made the curtains and arranged the decor. Jeanne, as if already a great star, was content to sit back and watch as the boys who had chased her now put their hands to better use and erected a stage. Her first 'production' was *Le Médecin Malgré Lui*, in which she poked fun at Molière by writing her own script. The entire village turned out to support her: this would suggest that she really had turned over a new leaf, or that her actual reputation had not been as bad as has been made out. They were amused to find that Jeanne had dressed the female members of her cast in male attire. This, she said, was a reversal of the way Shakespeare had put on his plays, and was accepted by all but the Sisters of Providence, who were deeply offended. They went to see Madame Bourgeois after the show, but were promptly shown the door.

Madame Bourgeois was now firmly on her daughter's side, and convened a family meeting to decide what course of action to take. Jeanne's hunchback uncle – the only person she trusted, by all accounts – suggested that she should start taking violin lessons. Jeanne was delighted!

Then, as always, she was capable of thinking one step ahead of everyone else. There were no reputable music teachers in Enghien. . . only in Paris, where all the rich people lived! Though she had only visited the city briefly with Tante Florentine, she knew everything about it. She knew that once she got there she would be able to work things out for herself and achieve the mighty career she had so far only dreamed of!

The music teacher was Père Boussagol, at that time eminent with the Opéra de Paris. His classes were held in the Impasse Vivienne, which lies between the Boulevard Montmartre and the rue du 4 Septembre.

Jeanne was one of three pupils who boarded the train for Paris at Pointe-Raquet, and she stuck out like the proverbial sore thumb because her mother could not afford to dress her the way she would have liked. In fact, Madame Bourgeois' financial situation was so bad that Marcel had had to be placed temporarily in a children's home. Neither did the budding star get on with the other girls in her class; most of them were snobs, and of course Jeanne had absolutely no airs and graces, which only added to her special magic later on. She also confessed that the only enjoyable part of an otherwise insufferable experience was the time she spent waiting in Père Boussagol's waiting room prior to her lesson . . . its walls were hung with hundreds of portraits and photographs of all the big stars in Paris. The lessons themselves she found both boring and difficult; holding the violin strained her shoulders and neck which were already weak after pushing her trolley, and she found the scales tedious. When Boussagol told her that in order to reach concert platform standards one had to rehearse for anything up to ten years, she decided to give it up as a bad job. She left Boussagol and, without telling her mother what she had done, enrolled for singing lessons. She also changed her name: Jeanne Bourgeois became La Princesse de la Pointe-Racquet, after the local railway station! The name was not as ridiculous then as it seems today; some years later there would be a Môme Moineau and a Môme Fromage, and a popular circus act called The Little Willies!

The singing lessons were short-lived. Jeanne thought that operetta left much to be desired, and in an amateur production of *Le Petit Duc* she crooned her way through 'La Rondo de la Paysanne' with her hands planted on her hips like a café-concert *chanteuse*. The producer was so annoyed that he fired her.

Ultimately, Madame Bourgeois discovered that her daughter had been duping her, and there was a nasty confrontation at Enghien. Jeanne's excuse for opting out of violin lessons – which on the face of it does sound plausible – was that she was afraid of becoming hunchbacked like her uncle. She was also suffering from fatigue and probably on the verge of a nervous breakdown – her mother's insensitivity in working her too hard whilst at school had probably seen to that. Madame Bourgeois therefore sought advice from the Sisters of Providence and the priest: incredibly, she was stupid enough to believe anything this irresponsible, interfering group of people told her. When they suggested again that Jeanne's behavioral pattern was due to puberty, Madame Bourgeois followed their instructions to the letter. Jeanne was put on a diet of oysters and liver juice and, astonishingly, hot spinach poultices were applied to her breasts. There is little wonder she rebelled by going on a hunger strike for a week, and the thought of her child starving herself to death because of what the nuns had told her suddenly brought Madame Bourgeois to her senses. This time everything would be above board: Jeanne was enrolled with a Monsieur Roche, who ran a school for dramatic art not far from the Champs-Elysées.

It was whilst working with Roche that the famous episode with the hat took place. Mistinguett told the story often; each time it was amended slightly, and it is hard to tell what happened exactly, though the version recounted by Manouche in her autobiography should be reliable.

Manouche had been born Germaine German, and was so different from Mistinguett in temperament and upbringing that it seems

incredible that they should have met at all. Not only this. . .
Mistinguett unofficially became her godmother, and Manouche was
one of the few people she trusted, even though in her memoirs, ghosted
by Roger Peyrefitte in 1972, Manouche is often crude and unkind to
the woman who only ever treated her with the utmost affection and
loyalty, at a time when she probably did not deserve it.

This was an age when practically every woman in Paris wore a
hat, even drama students, and Jeanne had of course made up her
mind that she would have a show-piece to rival even the best of her
contemporaries. One of Père Boussagol's assistants, a large lady, had
turned up one morning in an astrakhan creation trimmed with real
silver, and Madame Bourgeois agreed to make a similar hat for her
daughter. It was then that Jeanne found out that her mother had been
engaged by the enemy – for Anna Thibaud was also fond of astrakhan
and silver!

Jeanne decided that the best course of action would be to make the
hat herself, and it is here that the story differs. She herself said that
after sewing together the main body of the hat she went into the
market and bought two mousetraps. These she placed in the garden
under an apricot tree, and by next morning she had caught a pair
of linnets. Manouche's was told differently: the birds were family
pets whose necks she had wrung. Another theory was that they had
been given to her mother by Anna Thibaud and that Jeanne killed
them in order to exact revenge on the *chanteuse*. In any case, the
birds were stuffed and mounted onto the hat; Jeanne wore it for
her singing lesson the next day, and all went well. The following
day she was not so lucky. It was midsummer and very hot. The
train into Paris was packed with day-trippers, and the windows of
the compartment were rusted up and would not open. When she
disembarked at the Gare du Nord, Jeanne found herself surrounded by
a huge swarm of bluebottles. There were ribald comments from some
of the commuters, but Jeanne refused to remove her hat. Making it had
taken ingenuity and a lot of hard work and it was, after all, different!

When she was not rehearsing with Monsieur Roche, Jeanne would
go off with her friends to the Jardin des Tuileries or the nearby Place
de la Concorde. Here they would entertain passers-by and tourists.
Street singers were all the rage, and would remain an integral part of
the French entertainment scene for another fifty years. Jeanne went

around with the tin after delivering her patter, and was pleasantly surprised how much money could be made out of amusing herself. The money was always shared out equally, but whereas her friends wasted their portion, Jeanne held onto hers. The desire to get away from her mother was now stronger than ever, and if she spent anything at all it was at a little bistro in Montmartre where waffles were the house speciality, or at the ice-cream parlour near Les Halles which she had discovered with Tante Florentine.

Alternatively, Jeanne would stroll up the Champs-Elysées and stand outside the café-concerts listening to the singers. One of her favourites was Amiati, for whom the popular poet Paul Déroulède had written 'Le Clairon qui Sonne la Charge'. Another artiste who was all the rage in 1892 with a semi-comic song called 'C'est dans le Nez que ce M'Chatouille' was Thérésa, but the establishments where these two artistes performed – the Alcazar and the Folies-Marigny – were well out of Jeanne's price-range, and if she ever went inside a café-concert it would be the Ba-ta-clan or the Eldorado.

It was probably at the Eldorado that she first saw one of the most celebrated entertainers in Paris. Her name was Alice Ozy, and she was something of an all-rounder; besides being a singer and actress, she had an extraordinary talent when it came to mimicry, and she also danced and played the flute. The first time Jeanne watched her perform she was moved to tears, and decided that she would have to meet her. For several days she hung around the dressing room door, but was ignored. Great artistes were not then in the habit of speaking to the public in the street or signing autographs. This did not deter Jeanne who spent a whole afternoon sitting on the lawn in front of Alice Ozy's house; the coup paid off handsomely. The woman and the girl became friends.

For the first time in her life Jeanne Bourgeois had found a person genuinely interested in her from an artistic angle, and when she informed her that she wanted to become a star, Alice Ozy did not ridicule her the way Anna Thibaud had done. Though an extremely busy woman working several venues concurrently, she managed to set aside a little time each day to put Jeanne through her paces, offering valuable lessons in deportment and teaching her a few basic dance routines whilst accompanying her on the flute. It was Alice Ozy who eventually introduced Jeanne to her first impresario, Monsieur

Saint-Marcel, a man of considerable influence in Paris at the turn of the century. Between them, they managed to persuade her to change her name. The idea for the new pseudonym came from the operetta in which she was playing at the time, in which one of the leading characters was called Miss Helyett.

Though Miss Helyett had practically no impact on her Parisian audiences – simply because she was still singing the wrong songs and appearing in the wrong shows – she very quickly became the rage of Enghien. Boys fought amongst themselves to accompany her from her home on the rue du Départ to the railway station, and they were always there to meet her off the train with bunches of flowers. In their eyes, she was a celebrity already!

The local *voyous*, however, were not her only admirers. The famous fashion designer, Poulbot, saw her leaving the Gare du Nord one morning in her infamous hat and craved permission to do a few sketches. Jeanne complied . . . many years later he would present them to her at the Casino de Paris! She soon learned to her disadvantage, however, that not all well-dressed gentlemen were blessed with honest intentions. One morning – it was raining heavily and she had left her umbrella at home – Jeanne was hurrying along the rue Lafayette when a carriage pulled up alongside her and an elderly man asked if she would like a lift. Jeanne accepted. The next day the carriage was again waiting for her outside the Gare du Nord. This time the old man offered her money for sex and actually fondled her. Sex did not take place. Since the tragic affair with the farmhand, Jeanne had decided to hang onto what was left of her virtue until her millionaire came along; but she did snatch the money and that night spilled the whole story to Tante Florentine, who in turn hatched a plan with Madame Bourgeois. When the old man's carriage drew up outside the Gare du Nord the next morning, these two formidable women dragged him out into the street and beat him senseless with their sticks!

In spite of what had happened, Jeanne was allowed to continue her studies. It is quite likely that after confronting the old man, she insisted upon her mother and aunt meeting Alice Ozy, simply to prove that everything was above board. It also seems probable that at some time the actress offered her some kind of financial support which was politely turned down, and which heralded yet another adventure that was pure Mistinguett!

It came to her notice that the casino at Enghien was planning a gala night, and this gave her an idea. Her stubborn pride may have prevented her from accepting hand-outs from friends such as Alice Ozy, but this did not mean that she was averse to making a little money which would swell the coffers for when the time came to pack up and leave home for good: she had already begun looking for a room in Paris. Now, on the spur of the moment, she decided that she would earn what she could by selling flowers at the casino.

As in later life, Jeanne acted without thinking. After she had picked every single flower in her mother's garden, she climbed over the fence and raided the neighbours' rose-bushes. Shoving the flowers into two milk pails, and still wearing her ghastly hat, she headed for the casino where she demanded to see the manager. Within the foyer she was accosted by the concierge, who threatened to throw her out. Jeanne pushed past him into the auditorium, where dozens of important guests were about to sit down to dinner. The manager was so astonished by Jeanne's audacity that he allowed her to set up an impromptu stall outside the casino entrance!

Until just before the Second World War, most theatres, music-halls and cabarets engaged flower-sellers, though no establishment had ever seen the likes of Jeanne Bourgeois. Business was so good that night that she was allowed to return, and as the wealthy gamblers entered the building they were not asked if they *wanted* to buy flowers . . . Jeanne walked straight up to them and pinned them in the men's buttonholes, and such was her cheek that she never had a dissatisfied customer.

By this time she had invaded every garden in her street. When all the roses were gone she stole dahlias, which she sprayed with insecticide to kill the earwigs. When these eventually ran out she sold sprigs of privet and boxwood and told her customers to pretend that it was Palm Sunday.

Then, when a handsome young man who had hitherto been down on his luck won a fortune at the black-jack table, her success was assured. The young man had arrived in the company of the *chanteuse* who was performing at the casino, and Jeanne was invited to her dressing-room. For Jeanne it was like entering another world, and when the chanteuse gave her a complimentary ticket for the next performance of *Les Chouans* at the Théâtre l'Ambigu, she was more than delighted. The actual evening was a disaster: one scene in the play was so dramatic that Jeanne burst into tears and wailed so loudly that she was evicted from the theatre.

Finally, it happened. Courtesy of Monsieur Saint-Marcel, Jeanne was given the break she had dreamed of. Alice Ozy arranged the meeting; in her memoirs Mistinguett said this took place on the train from Pointe-Raquet to Paris, though it is more likely to have taken place at Alice's home. Saint-Marcel was in the middle of writing a revue for Fagette, which would later presented by her at the Parisiana. Though largely forgotten today, even by the most serious music-hall enthusiasts, Fagette was one of the biggest names in Paris before the War, and was nicknamed La Boléro de Diamants. Her big number in the show, which may not be adequately translated into any other language, was 'La Vertinguette':

> C'est la vertin-quoi?
> C'est la vertin-qui?
> C'est la tinguette,
> La vertinguette!

A *guinguette* was a popular dance hall much favoured by the lower and working classes of France, and could often be found standing next to a river or canal. It was an institution which began in about 1880 and which flourished until the beginning of the last war. Critics may argue that there are still a few *guinguettes* in Paris . . . this is a matter for conjecture. Like the present *Moulin Rouge* and *Folies Bergère*, what claims to be authentic music-hall is nothing of the kind, but an attempt to woo tourists with an abundance of bare breasts and Americanized chansons. The real *guinguettes* were of the sawdust and spittoon variety, smoky, rowdy, rough and ready. The entertainment on the other hand was usually first-class. Many superstars of the *chanson* began their careers in these establishments. Damia and Fréhel sang songs about them. Jeanne Bourgeois was so fascinated by the word *guinguette* that she told Saint-Marcel and Alice Ozy that she was thinking of changing her name to Miss Guinguette.

Saint-Marcel came up with a better idea. By amending the name slightly, he baptised her Mistinguett, and for the next sixty years she would answer to nothing else.

A Den of Thieves

Mistinguett's debut at the Casino de Paris occurred towards the end of 1893, when she was just eighteen. Monsieur Saint-Marcel secured her the engagement, and Madame Bourgeois made the costume . . . a flouncy checked skirt with matching bib which complimented the comic number she had been given to sing and which raised more laughs than had been anticipated.

> Je suis La Môme du Casino!
> Fraîche comme un coquelicot,
> Mais galbeuse et rieuse,
> Et toujours rigolo!
>
> (I am the Casino Kid!
> Fresh as a poppy,
> But shapely and laughing,
> And always having fun!)

Each night she would go on stage at eight; by nine she would be back in Enghien, two francs richer and that much more content because she was now able to give her mother a little money towards her keep, and this ultimately enabled her brother to be removed from the children's home and returned to the family fold. The Casino, however, was not the be-all and end-all that she had anticipated. There were complaints from the galleries that her voice could not be heard above the orchestra and the clamour of the young men who clustered around the stage bawling innuendos. Many of these would gather around the stage door after each show with bunches of violets . . . Mistinguett always preferred these to the larger bouquets, but for the time being the young men were always sent packing.

Mistinguett was unusually honest about her debuts:

> I loved watching all the great artistes, especially when they made mistakes. Most of them imitated each other, but I had no intention of copying them . . . if I was a second-rate star, at least I was myself. I even had a weakness for a woman called Violette, who was a gay. As for the real stars of the music-hall, I would never dare criticise them because they were in my opinion the gods. And in any case, we did not have much in common. I was young, with principles . . .

The word 'gay' did not have quite the same misconstrued meaning as it has today. However, in the context of Mistinguett's memoirs it would suggest that her experiences with the farmhand and the elderly gentleman did make her think twice about any involvements with men, thus precipitating her towards a close friendship with the artiste, Violette, of whom absolutely nothing is known. Critics who have suggested that it may have been a lesbian relationship are wholly unfounded in their conclusions, however, and it would appear it was nothing more than platonic, as the relationship with Alice Ozy had been . . . especially when one considers what happened next.

Mistinguett was working the Casino every night, but during the afternoons she was also gaining vital experience in some of the café-concerts. Most of these put on the usual variety acts – a mixture of singers, circus acts and comedians and the evening always ended with a miniature revue. Saint-Marcel included her in his shows at the Casino Saint-Martin and the Parisiana, where she interpreted his songs and others which she had borrowed or stolen from Thérésa and Harry Fragson.

This enigmatic young man, the son of an Anglo-Belgian brewer, had been born in London in 1869. Though unfortunately ignored by most British music-hall directories, he should not be, for it was he who wrote and introduced 'Hello, Hello, Who's Your Lady Friend?' Though not quite at the height of his popularity when he met Mistinguett, he soon would be, and during the next decade would remain the biggest male entertainer in France, launching and helping many artistes, the most famous of whom was Damia, with whom he had a passionate affair. At the Parisiana, Fragson gave Mistinguett permission to sing his latest success, 'Adieu Grenade ma Charmante'. Though she recorded most of the songs from her early reviews later in her career, this one was never committed to shellac, probably in respect for Fragson's memory. The last time they appeared together was in a gala benefit at the Ba-ta-clan, just a few days before Fragson was shot dead by his father during a heated argument over a chorus girl.

Another legendary figure of the music-hall at this time was Polin, who died in 1927. His speciality was to appear on stage dressed in a railwayman's uniform, and whenever an obscene word or phrase was about to crop up in one of his songs he would pull from his pocket a checkered handkerchief which he would wave as a signal for the ladies and prudes amongst his audience to cover their ears. His success at the time was 'Situation Intéressante', and it was on the strength of this that he was invited to top the bill at the Trianon in 1897, with Fragson as his *vedette-américain* . . . this is the artiste, of secondary importance to the *vedette*, who closes the first half of the show. Fragson, in turn, insisted that Mistinguett should be given a spot in his half of the show, and in a short black dress fashioned by Madame Bourgeois she performed two songs. One of these, 'Les Espagnoles', was so ridiculous that it is almost a blessing that she never sang it again:

> Je ne suis pas de ces Espagnoles
> Qu'on va voir l'jour des Batignolles,
> Je suis née entre deux boléros,
> Un jour de courses de taureaux!
>
> (I'm not one of those Spaniards
> That you see on Batignolle Day,
> I was born between two boleros,
> On the day of the bullfight!)

When she sang the song on the evening of her première, her voice still did not reach the gallery. Someone in the audience yelled, 'Higher!' Mistinguett hitched her dress up as far as her thighs and shouted back, 'How much higher do you want it to go?' In those days when it was considered daring for a woman to show her calves on stage – and Mistinguett had already outstepped the rules of decency by wearing a short dress – many people thought her so vulgar that they walked out of the theatre in disgust. For the ones who stayed, this was the beginning of a new era. Instead of firing her, the director gave her a spot further up the bill and increased her salary! Her contract with the Trianon, initially for one week, lasted several months.

The Sisters of Providence, however, had been right when they had accused the music-hall of being a den of thieves, vice and corruption. Fragson himself was a notorious womaniser, and was not renowned for being kind to the fairer sex. This is perhaps why the young Mistinguett steered clear of him when they were not working together, though the company she was keeping offstage certainly left much to be desired. Polin was a respectable man, but some of his followers were not. One of these was an up-and-coming young entertainer called Louis Leplée . . .

Leplée is of course famous for the fact that it was he who discovered and launched Edith Piaf in 1935. The following year his brutal murder made headline news throughout Europe, and Piaf herself was questioned and admitted to knowing little about her protector's private life. This makes very grim reading. Leplée took advantage of the fact that he was the great Polin's nephew, and could often be seen hanging around stage doors picking up men. In his younger days he was what would today be called a rent boy, and his promiscuity made him dangerous when it enabled him to become a part of the shady Parisian underworld, dealing in drugs, contraband and male prostitution. Eventually, it was this fascination for the sordid which cost him his life.

Leplée and Mistinguett had worked together at the Parisiana: he had just begun working as a drag-artiste, which she found fascinating, especially when he turned up at a café-concert wearing a dress and wig. Leplée was also a friend of the famous impressario Oscar Dufresne, another promiscuous homosexual who ended his days as the recipient of an assassin's bullet, and in this respect he would have been an important contact for a young woman whose ambition was to make it to the top, by unscrupulous means if need be. Dufresne had also been on extremely friendly terms with the director of the Casino.

It was probably Louis Leplée who persuaded Mistinguett to stay in Paris rather than return to Enghien every night, for after her second week at the Trianon she had already become part of his clique of transvestites and *voyous*, frequenting some of the sleaziest bars and clubs imaginable in the heart of Pigalle. In later years Leplée would take over the management of perhaps the most infamous of these . . . Liberty's. Mistinguett, Maurice Chevalier and Charles Trenet would be regular visitors, and the star of the show would often be Kiki de Montparnasse, whose act was the filthiest that has ever been seen on a French stage. It was after one such evening that Mistinguett missed the train home to Enghien, and in all probability it was Louis Leplée who found her, at short notice, a room on the rue Condorcet, within a stone's throw of the Place Pigalle.

Though never a prostitute, the nature of Mistinguett's work meant that she was constantly plagued by men, and like many artistes she found it essential to employ the services of pimps. Thirty years on, Piaf would do the same, though as could only be expected of Mistinguett, she went one step further and moved her 'bodyguards' into the room with her. On some nights there would be as many as six. They would wait until the concierge had retired for the night, then sneak in through a downstairs window. Those who were not homosexual would then draw lots to decide which of them was going to sleep with the star; the unlucky ones would camp down on the floor. Sometimes they would fight over her, and if this happened she would offer to sleep with the most effeminate member of her clan . . . she was convinced, even in those days, that she was capable of converting even the most committed homosexual to what she considered was normality, though she apparently had little success. Her clan waited on her hand and foot. Every morning they rose with the lark to steal bottles of milk, food from shop-fronts, or flowers, and when the concierge found out what was happening he was paid a commission to keep his mouth shut.

Not all these young men were drop-outs and thugs. One was a very respectable student, the son of Esther Lekain, who along with Yvette Guilbert was one of the innovators of the *chanson-populaire*. Another, Bébert, was such a thoroughly bad lot that he was eventually guillotined for murder.

Saint-Marcel, probably at times wishing he had never brought

Mistinguett to Paris in the first place, and remembering the promise he had made to Madame Bourgeois and Alice Ozy to look after her, was so horrified by his protegé's activities that towards the end of 1897 he took her away from the Trianon and sent her on her first tour of the provinces. The first engagement was at Clermont-Ferrand. She travelled overnight to get to the town in the heart of the Massif Central, and spent the better part of the day trying to locate the theatre; this was called La Concordia, and if Mistinguett was expecting it to be another Casino, she was sorely disappointed. It turned out to be little more than a glorified bistro in a dirty back alley, and the name of the establishment was not written in neon but in chalk above the door. Furthermore, when Mistinguett asked the owner what he had done with the posters and publicity photographs which Saint-Marcel had sent on ahead of her, she was told that posters were still in their envelope because the establishment had run out of glue, and the photographs were in a frame on the salon sideboard because the owner's wife thought them those of a long-lost relative!

In her memoirs Mistinguett is cautious not to give too much away about her tour. Though totally unknown outside Paris, and thoroughly miserable because she had left her boys behind, she realized that as an apprentice she would have to accept whatever offers came her way. She was still singing ridiculous songs, though for the time being the public were not interested in an over indulgence of drama, and in any case she would never become a *chanteuse réaliste*, or even a *diseuse* like Yvette Guilbert. One song which went down very well in Clermont-Ferrand and elsewhere on her tour was by the *chansonnier*, Montel.

> J'ai commencé par engueuler le patron,
> En lui disant: 'Vous n'êtes qu'un sale cochon.
> Les travailleurs, il faut les respecter,
> J'm'suis en grève et j'ai tout plaqué!'

> (I began by bawling out the boss,
> Telling him: 'You're nothing but a dirty pig.
> You've got to respect the workers,
> I'm on strike and I'm pissed off!')

The tour ended. Mistinguett returned to Paris to take up where she had left off. The room on the rue Condorcet still resembled a scene from Dante: the concierge had allowed the *voyous* to stay, not simply because they had kept up the payment on the rent, but because he had been terrified of doing otherwise. Surprisingly, Mistinguett had been missed by her admirers at the Trianon, and as she had been on her best behaviour whilst out of Paris, Saint-Marcel experienced little difficulty finding her work. For six months she did the rounds of the café-concerts and minor music-halls, and there were engagements at some of the classier establishments such as the Alcazar d'Eté and the Cigale. This was the height of La Belle Epoque, though she was not interested in the Great Exhibition with its moving pavement, Big Wheel, and multitude of sideshows, and she absolutely hated the Metro! She became friends with the great choreographers and dancers of the day, including Liane de Pougy and La Belle Otéro. Anyone who did not belong on her show business side of the fence left her cold. She disliked the acid-tongued Colette and her husband, Monsieur Willy. Oscar Wilde, who once breezed into her dressing room with a basket of flowers, was dismissed as a fat, slovenly Englishman.

Liane de Pougy was, in fact, even more despicable than Louis Lepée and some of the other characters with whom Mistinguett fraternized in the early stages of her career. Born Anne-Marie Chassaigne in 1870, she was the most notorious courtesan of her day ... both a promiscuous lesbian and an expensive whore. She was at this time the lover of the American heiress, Natalie Barney, who at the age of sixty would become the lover of Dolly Wilde, niece of the famous writer. At the time she met Mistinguett, de Pougy was also keeping a young man called Herbert Pollitt, an English transvestite actor who often danced with her at the *Folies Bergère* under the pseudonym of Diane de Rougy! Many years later, de Pougy would repent of her deplorable ways and enter a convent, whence she became known as Sister Mary Magdalene of Repentance. That she actually had a brief affair with Mistinguett is almost certain, even though the singer was involved with a wealthy young Brazilian known to posterity only as Monsieur de Lima.

When Mistinguett became pregnant at the turn of the century — the exact date is not known — it may seem incredible that under the circumstances of her then regime she could fit a name and face to the prospective father. All her life she maintained that this was de Lima, and there is no reason for us to believe otherwise or that the pregnancy was not a mistake. This was, after all, the most crucial stage of her developing career, and a baby would have been regarded as nothing but an encumbrance. We do know that Mistinguett performed right up to the sixth month of her pregnancy during which she visited Britain. When the baby was born he was christened Léopold, and took his father's surname and not his mother's. De Lima was also on hand to whisk his child back to Brazil, where they both stayed until Mistinguett was sufficiently well-known – and wealthy enough – for them to return to France. And in order to make up for her loss, Mistinguett summoned her brother, Marcel Bourgeois, to the hotel room on the rue Condorcet.

Mistinguett was suitably impressed by the British and their way of life, though for the time being the feeling was not in any way mutual. In London, she attempted to win the confidence of the producer C B Cochran, but succeeded only in obtaining a few minor engagements in suburban theatres. In spite of this she vowed that she would return to Britain, and when she did, some years later, she would take London by storm!

Toute La Belle Epoque!

Mistinguett regarded the Eldorado theatre as a convenient stepping-stone between the Casino and the truly great music-halls of Paris at the turn of the century, the most important of which was La Scala. Doubly convenient, from Mistinguett's point of view, was the fact that both theatres were under the direction of a formidable lady called Madame Marchand.

Having dispensed with the services of Saint-Marcel – setting yet another precedent, which was that once a man had overstayed his welcome and outlived his usefulness, he was almost always dropped like a hot brick – Mistinguett herself approached the director, and she was engaged to open the show. Though she only sang one song, she was an instant success and within a week had been moved up the bill. Once more, her mother made her dress . . . a knee-length creation of pink silk, edged with tiny feathers and silver spangles. It may be said that this dress made her, for her voice still was not strong enough to carry beyond the first few rows of the stalls, and the song was utter rubbish:

> Je suis Mam'zelle sans façon,
> Je rigole, je batifole,
> Et j'adore le rigodon. . .
>
> (I'm Mam'zelle, without fuss,
> I laugh, I fool around,
> And I adore a joke. . .)

Mistinguett hated the song so much that she would sometimes change the words and direct them at a member of the orchestra, providing he was handsome enough. Occasionally they would be directed at Harry Fragson, prompting her from the wings and making vulgar gestures. Fragson was the *vedette-américain*, and though he was not interested in having the little singer from Enghien as a lover, no doubt because he would not have been able to knock her around as he did his other women, he was trying to draw her away from the voracious Liane de Pougy, who every night after her performance plied her with chocolate and flowers. Fragson had also developed a somewhat nauseating habit of his own. After matinées he would take Mistinguett for a stroll through the Bois de Boulogne, where they would always find themselves surrounded by admirers. Mistinguett would dole out the chocolates which Liane de Pougy had given her, but as soon as she offered one to Fragson he would pull a face and declare that chocolate was bad for the figure. Then he would walk up to the nearest pile of horse-droppings, select the best morsel for himself and swallow it whilst Mistinguett shrieked with laughter. But this was not all. Fragson's mania for sick jokes went as far as sending 'chocolates' to his enemies, ones which he had fashioned from his own faeces. This was one habit which repulsed even Mistinguett.

Another acquaintance at this time was Yvette Guilbert, claimed by most authorities to have been the greatest *diseuse* of all time. She had been born in Paris in 1867, just two years before Fragson, her male counterpart in France, and with whom she had absolutely nothing in common. She had made her début at the Casino de Lyon in 1886, whence she had been whistled off the stage by an almost exclusively male audience because of her flat chest. In 1889 she had been engaged at the Eldorado, and this had been tantamount to disaster when her audience began bombarding her with cherry pips and orange peel: indeed, she had been so unpopular that for two months the theatre had been picketed. Then she had discovered the songs of Léon Xanrof, in particular 'Le Fiacre' and 'Maîtresse d'Acteur', and success had more or less come overnight. Prior to Mistinguett's arrival at the Eldorado, Madame Marchand had been in a quandary as to who should be topping the bill – Yvette Guilbert or Fragson – and after some deliberation she had decided upon the latter. The Eldorado was essentially a theatre which served the working classes. Fragson was a snob, a member of the society Mistinguett hated and often ridiculed and attacked in her songs.

Mistinguett had begun her stint at the Eldorado in 1897. Two years later, whilst at the height of her popularity, Yvette Guilbert collapsed on stage . . . the doctors diagnosed kidney failure, and for the next ten years she would be in and out of hospital for a series of major operations, before making the most spectacular comeback at the Casino de Nice. At the time of Yvette Guilbert's sudden indisposition, Fragson had been working at the Alhambra. He now returned to top the bill at the Eldorado, and Mistinguett asked Madame Marchand if she might occupy the position of *vedette-américain*. Madame Marchand knew that she was not yet up to this, and offered a compromise . . . a fifteen minute spot at La Scala. Mistinguett was delighted; Polaire, the greatest *chanteuse-réaliste* of the day, was in the middle of a sell-out season there!

Polaire was Mistinguett's favourite singer, but when they met for the first time at rehearsal the great star, no doubt aware of her reputation, refused to acknowledge her. Incensed, Mistinguett decided that she would have her revenge. She went to see the wardrobe mistress, pretending to be Polaire's maid, and was given the singer's dress. In those days Polaire had an eighteen inch waist, and was one of the prettiest women around: twenty years later she would put on weight and look like a gypsy. Mistinguett, an expert with needle and thread, let out the seams and covered the gaps with pieces of silk. Then she immediately set off in pursuit of a reputable music publisher. Until around 1940, few artistes had songwriters of their own. New songs were lodged with publishers, some of whom exercised great discretion by allowing only established entertainers to audition them. Others were corrupt and could easily be bribed. One such man handled the affairs of Polaire.

The actual song is not known, and how Mistinguett went about getting it may only be surmised. The evening when she sang it, however, was an embarrassing disaster. Polaire arrived at the theatre just as Mistinguett was about to go on stage, and the wardrobe lady told her what had happened to the dress. They marched into the wings whilst the orchestra was playing the introduction to Mistinguett's first song, and Polaire was horrified to learn that this too was her's. Mistinguett saw her . . . when she opened her mouth, nothing came out and she ran off the stage in tears, only to be collared by the angry singer. Eventually, Polaire and Mistinguett became the best of friends, though not until a great deal of water had passed under their respective bridges. For the time being, the great *chanteuse*, once she had recovered from her initial shock, persuaded Madame Marchand to re-engage Mistinguett at the Eldorado. It was here that Fate stepped in again, for Dranem was topping the bill.

It is a great pity that Dranem never really became known outside of France. He was something of an all-round entertainer – clown, comedian, raconteur-extraordinaire, exponent of the *chanson idiot* – and lived between 1869 and 1935. His real name was Armand Menard, which is of course Dranem spelt backwards, and until scoring a massive success in 1895 at Paris's Concert-Electrique, had earned his money as a jeweller, working part time in the café-concerts. His most popular songs at the Eldorado were 'Les p'tits pois' and 'Pétronille', all sung at some time or other by Mistinguett. His most famous song of all was Mireille's 'Papa n'a pas Voulu', which he recorded towards the end of his life. Dranem would charge onto the stage as though the theatre was on fire, then stop suddenly without ever once falling down. His jacket would always be several sizes too small, his unlaced shoes several sizes too big. On top of his bald head would be a tiny hat, which he would raise constantly whilst delivering his patter. Nothing was too ridiculous for him to sing, and unlike Mistinguett in her early years, he was always laughed at for the right reasons. When he opened at the Eldorado in 1899 he especially asked for Mistinguett to appear with him in *La Tête à L'Huile*, the hilarious sketch which he had devised to close the show. It was a role in which she truly excelled, and when Dranem eventually left the Eldorado in 1903, she took over as top of the bill.

At about this time she gave up her room on the rue Condorcet and moved to an apartment on the rue de la Fidélité, not far from the Gare de l'Est. During the transfer she managed to shrug off some of her hangers-on, though the new friends which she made in this slightly more opulent quarter of Paris were infinitely worse than the ones she had left behind. She became a regular visitor to the Cabaret Fischer, an establishment frequented by kings, princes and heads of state, and which was morally no better than the flea-pits of Pigalle. Edward VII, before and after he became king, always made a point of stopping off here. The first time Mistinguett went there was with her butcher, a man called Androt who spent all his money buying her a barrel of the best house wine. Mistinguett turned it down . . . drink was not a vice then, and never would be, for she would always be figure-conscious. The next night, he brought her a handsome young gigolo and afterwards picked up the tab! Many years later Mistinguett declared that if she could have married any man of her choosing, she would have selected her butcher . . . the astonishing thing is, she was not joking.

It was at the Cabaret Fischer, in 1904, that Mistinguett met, and formed an attachment with, Boni, the marquis de Castellane. He was the most outrageous snob imaginable, who later wrote in his memoirs: 'I am an exile, not from my country but from my epoch. I amused myself by living in another age, as much from a taste for beauty as from a distaste for my own times!' In 1897 he and his American millionaire wife had bought Le Marais, an impressive château in the Orge Valley, near Versailles. The château had been built by the architect Barré in 1770 for his uncle, but Boni de Castellane transformed it into a pleasure palace, wherein his wife was forced to turn a blind eye towards his succession of lovers of both sexes. His preoccupation was to ride through his woods in an open-topped carriage, wearing just his underwear, whilst his homosexual lackeys panted after him on foot, wearing nothing at all. Mistinguett was often entertained at Le Marais, where Boni commissioned a suite of mignonette green for her . . . unlike most of her fellow artistes she was not overtly superstitious.

Though Mistinguett never became Boni de Castellane's lover, she did accept his patronage when offered a tour of Russia. Many years later she would deny that he had paid for the trip, maintaining that she had only travelled to Russia in order to please a female lover, who had also wanted to see the country. This woman was, in 1950, still a famous singer whom Mistinguett refused to name in her memoirs, and whom she said still caused her to shiver whenever they met in the street. To this day, Mistinguett remains one of only a handful of French entertainers to have even considered singing to the Russians. Charles Aznavour and Gilbert Bécaud still go there. Edith Piaf was immensely popular there – so much so that on the day of her funeral the people of Moscow held a two minute silence in Red Square – but she would never have dreamed of singing there in person.

The first port of call was St Petersburg. It was also the last.

I was really looking forward to seeing Russia, that frosted fairyland of grand dukes. Most of the time, all they did was go around smashing plates, but some of the dandies offered me furs and jewels. There were so many gifts that I could have filled the entire compartment of my train. But it wasn't very funny. That woman treated me like a prisoner. She said that she was trying to protect my virtue! Every night she made me eat soup in our room, and once she made me dance barefoot on top of a pile of banknotes. I sang one song, and one song only. All of a sudden I no longer wanted to become famous in Russia.

Mistinguett returned to Paris and the Eldorado, where she was again *vedette-américain* to Dranem. Her repertoire still left much to be desired. She had no songs of her own, and the usual comic numbers did not go down too well because most of them belonged to the star of the show. Dranem did not object to anyone singing his songs because when he sang them they never sounded the same in any case. Mistinguett, however, did mind. She was painfully aware that over the last few years Paris had had more than its share of five-minute wonders, and she had no intention of being just another statistic.

The most important theatres in Paris at the time, so far as the musical revue was concerned, were the Bouffes-Parisiens and the Variétés − both are still going strong; but for some years these establishments had been rivalled by the Folies-Dramatiques, which was then under the direction of Richemond, an impressario not renowned for having much patience or for paying exhorbitant fees. Two operettas alone, *Les Cloches de Corneville and La Fille de Madame Angot*, had played over six hundred performances. It came to Mistinguett's attention early in 1905 that Richemond was casting for what many considered would be his finest production ever − *Coup de Jarnac*, written by Henri de Gorsse. Mistinguett attended the audition, and both the director and the writer were satisfied that she was right for the part. Only her reputation was against her; anyone who socialized with the likes of de Castellane and Liane de Pougy could hardly be expected to be granted any favours by a man as discerning as Richemond. Mistinguett came up with what she considered to be the ideal solution; in order to prove how good she would be, playing the lead, she proposed that she work for two weeks without being paid. This still was not acceptable to Richemond: no salary aside, Mistinguett was still more than capable of emptying his theatre with one of her filthy asides between songs! In fact, it was Henri de Gorsse who suggested the ideal compromise. Before, when things had got out out of hand, Mistinguett had been packed off on a tour of the provinces. Now, she was offered the leading role in another of de Gorsse's revues, *La Dame de Chez Maxim's*, after its star had dropped out of the production which was currently playing in Brussels. Richemond told her that if she did well for herself there, *Coup de Jarnac* would be hers for the taking. Mistinguett collected the script. The next morning she took the first available train to Brussels, and learned her part during the journey.

The revue was a terrific success. The Belgian press hailed her as the greatest star they had ever seen. Georges Feydeau was sitting in the audience, and became a friend. Richemond was so impressed that he offered Mistinguett a contract for three years, and asked her to leave the Eldorado at about the same time that Dranem left and Madame Marchand, the director, offered her top-billing! For some time, Mistinguett played both theatres; as soon as the curtain came down on *Coup de Jarnac* she would rush off to the Eldorado and perform in her own show, singing songs from the revue which at that time did not present any contractual problems – if there were any, she chose to ignore them. *Coup de Jarnac* also gave Mistinguett her first commercial success, for she recorded its main song, 'Petit frère à Fernand', which is today extremely difficult to come across.

The break from the Eldorado occurred towards the end of 1907. Staying at the Folies-Dramatiques, Mistinguett appeared in *Le Millième Contrat*, written by Henri de Gorsse and Louis Forest. Though the songs and the show itself would soon be forgotten, the run was not without its essential drama.

Mistinguett's lover at the time, if she had one, is not known. She was still socializing with Fragson and Boni de Castellane, and Liane de Pougy and her lost girls were never too far away. One evening a young man was ushered into her dressing room . . . unlike all the others he had not brought her flowers or gifts, but himself. Plucking up a Spartan courage, he asked her if she might like to go out with him, only to be told in no mean terms what to do with his offer. For more than a week the young man persisted, always with the same result, and Mistinguett never even bothered asking him his name. The final straw came when he tried to kiss her. She hated physical contact unless she was in the dominant role, and she bit his wrist so hard that he had to have hospital treatment. This was probably the first public exhibition of the ferocious Mistinguett temper, and would be by no means the last. One morning at the Gare du Nord, the young man gave her an ultimatum, just as she was boarding the train for Enghien to visit her mother. Again he was snubbed, and the next time he met her it was to give her a parcel, which he instructed her to open in the event of his death. A few days later it was not the young man who turned up at the Folies-Dramatiques, but his grief-stricken mother – her son had committed suicide by swallowing laudanum and flinging himself on a bonfire. He had left his mother a note, begging her to ask Mistinguett for a lock of her hair so that it could be placed inside his coffin. Mistinguett complied, but she still did not ask the young man's name, and when she opened the parcel he had given her she found it to contain his wrist-watch, ring and a silver charm . . . all inscribed with an ultimate message of love and the name of the woman who had rejected him.

Mistinguett can never be blamed even indirectly for this young man's death, and it has since been established that his mind had been deranged long before they met. Neither can she be accused of stringing him along, for she had told him only too clearly that she was not interested in having him as a lover. Quite simply, it was an unavoidable tragedy upon which she would sadly reflect for the rest of her life.

It was at this time that Mistinguett ended her friendship with Liane de Pougy, not because of the tragedy but because of the courtesan's recent involvement with Jean Lorrain, a man whose perversities defy description. He had been born Paul Duval in 1855, and though famous as a journalist at the turn of the century, much of his time was spent scrounging from wealthy friends such as Boni de Castellane and sleeping with sailors he picked up on his regular trips to Marseilles and Nice, and who he often employed as heavies when exacting money from his enemies, of which he had many. Lorrain was very rich . . . most of his income came from shady business deals, but he was also involved in contraband and drugs, prostitution and embezzlement. For a number of years he was one of the most feared men in Paris. Mistinguett was terrified of him and was no doubt relieved when he came to a sticky end. He had been a regular visitor to the Cabaret Fischer, where he had performed a song which would later be sung by Mistinguett whenever she wanted to shock any unwelcome guests who happened to drop in at Bougival, her later home, expecting an evening of culture.

The words, set to one of Vincent Scotto's lesser known compositions, were usually sung in Americanized English:

> I spent the night between two fellas,
> Two fellas from the docks!
> Who took turns, took turns,
> And cured me of the hots!

Mistinguett ceased frequenting the Cabaret Fischer as soon as she learned of Lorrain's death. Her new haunt was the Café de Paris, and her dining companions were substantially better than the old ones had been. These included Georges Feydeau and Vincent Scotto, who was writing songs and directing shows for two now forgotten *chanteuses*, La Fornarina and Madame de Lilo. The latter was one of the first artistes to sing a very famous song by Crémieux, 'Quand l'Amour Meurt', later adopted by Marlène Dietrich in the film *Morocco*.

Vincent Scotto, who had been born in Marseilles around 1874, had arrived in Paris in 1906. In a career spanning more than fifty years he composed over five thousand songs, and practically every French entertainer has sung at least one of these some time during his or her career. His first big success was 'Ah! Si Vous Voulez de l'Amour', which was recorded first by a café-concert artiste called Neuzillet, then by Mayol, who immortalized it. When he met Mistinguett he had just begun an important association with the *parolier* Henri Christiné, which would eventually result in a number of truly remarkable songs which are as popular today as they were then. One such song, which first appeared in 1906, was 'Le Navigatore'. Ostensibly it was written for Polin, though this did not prevent Mistinguett from singing it, even when they were sharing the same bill.

Je connais bien l'Amérique,
L'Asie tant bien que l'Afrique.
Je suis navi-navi-navigatore,
Mais de ces pays joyeux,
C'est la France que j'aime le mieux!

(I know America well,
Asia as well as Africa.
I'm a navi-navi-navigator,
But of these joyful lands,
It's France that I love the best!)

The lyrics for the song were little better than most of the dross which Mistinguett had been singing for years, though of course it has to be remembered that even at the best of times she was not primarily a *chanteuse*, but a visual artiste such as Gaby Deslys, Harry Pilcer and Max Dearly. Almost a quarter of a century later Henri Christiné would supply another lyric for 'Le Navigatore' – not necessarily more sensible, but more memorable. As 'La Petite Tonkinoise' it would provide a vehicle for that other lady of feathers and ferociousness, Joséphine Baker, who like many contemporaries would be despised by Mistinguett, who was after all the undisputed queen of the musical revue. For the moment, however, Mistinguett set about nurturing the legend which she was beginning to create.

The next step up from the Folies-Dramatiques was the Bouffes-Parisiens, situated in the Passage de Choiseul, just off the Avenue de l'Opéra. The theatre was beginning to make a name for itself, putting on operettas and revues, particularly by Rip, who some twenty years later would help to launch that other *monstre-sacré* of stage and screen, Arletty.

In 1908 Mistinguett became so obsessed with appearing in one of Rip's fabulous revues that she asked him if he would write one especially for her. Rip said that he would, at a price . . . the casting couch. Mistinguett did not hesitate. In return, Rip commissioned Wilned and Lafarge, two of the best comedy sketch writers of the day, to furnish him with the script for 'La Môme Flora', which was included towards the end of his latest revue. Le Millième Contrat closed at the Folies-Dramatiques, signifying the end of Mistinguett's first career and heralding what can only be described as the mighty years.

The Bouffes-Parisiens also belonged to Monsieur Richemond, who did not mind revoking the contract for the previous show as the box-office receipts from a Rip revue were double those of anything that had ever been put on at the Folies-Dramatiques, with or without Mistinguett. His co-director, Abel Deval, was not too sure, for he and Mistinguett hated one another. Until now, most of her costumes had been made by Madame Bourgeois, but for the new show Deval considered one of the best fashion houses in Paris. Mistinguett opposed him in every way, and in the end he refused to have anything to do with her. When Rip showed her the script, she told him that it sounded ridiculous and vowed that she would write her own or drop out of the production. Rip was so besotted by her that he allowed her to do exactly as she pleased. This she would do for the rest of her life! As for the clothes . . .

There was little about Parisian low life which was unknown to Mistinguett, and what she did not know she found out for herself. As has been shown, a great deal of it was present within the echelons of the bourgeoisie. Though she disliked the upper classes – and had she not hated her real name because it had been Bourgeois? – she was only too fond of patronizing them once she learned that they were blessed with some kind of perversity. What many people would consider the real low life of Paris, namely the prostitutes, pimps and *voyous* was altogether another matter. Not only were they an integral part of the community, most of them had been forced into a profession which they might never have chosen had it not been for dire necessity. The same could be said for the music-hall and theatre. In 1908, prostitutes were not restricted to designated areas of the city as they are today, and a major source of trade was the section of the eighth *arrondissement* which surrounded the Madeleine. Accordingly, in order to 'research' her part, Mistinguett interviewed a number of the girls and made a detailed study of what they were wearing and from which shops their clothes had been bought. The most popular choice was the Galeries Lafayette which was on the nearby Boulevard Haussmann. Mistinguett made a list of her requirements and went to see the manager, but she refused to pay for anything, claiming that the revue would prove an excellent advertisement for his store. Incredibly, she managed to get away with it.

La Môme Flora was the first of Mistinguett's own creations and took the Bouffes-Parisiens by storm. Little is known of its musical content other than the fact that there was a rude song called 'Les Vieux Messieurs Font Comme Ca' sung to the tune of 'Sur Le Pont D'Avignon'. However, several photographs taken during the sketch have survived. Mistinguett is wearing a ripped tartan skirt with the hem let down, an old coat and cap, laddered stockings and boots which have no laces! She was also so successful at making herself look like one of the local girls that when she left the theatre each night after her performance, still wearing her costume, none of the usual hangers-on recognized her. And if anyone tried to pick her up on the way back to the rue de la Fidélité, it was generally woe betide them. Only once was she stopped and asked for her autograph, this was when she left the theatre via the foyer to be met at the door by none other than Edward VII. Though it may seem on the face of it a little hard to swallow, the king and the showgirl became friends. Similarly, the *chanteuse* Fréhel, herself renowned for a waspish tongue, later formed a bizarre alliance with the queen consort of George V. Mistinguett in her memoirs speaks fondly of the king:

> To begin with, Edward VII knew Paris better than I did. He preferred Paris to London, and always wept when it was time to go home. We used to go to the Jockey Club together, and one or two places that even I had never seen before! He used to take great interest in my future projects, and told me: 'One day you will represent Paris for the entire world!' He was so fond of Paris that, many years after his death, I dedicated my song 'Ca c'est Paris' to him . . .

To be seen in the auspicious company of an English king, albeit that the French knew little of his own reputation and antics back home, enabled Mistinguett to acquire a certain amount of respect from several influential people who, had she still been under the influence of Liane de Pougy and Boni de Castellane, would never have spared her the time of day. One such was the French poet and novelist Catulle Mendès, who had been born in 1841, and whose most revered works were *Le Roi Vierge* and a play *Sainte Thérèse*. The article which he wrote about Mistinguett in *Le Journal* was one of his last – he died in 1909 – but it certainly got her noticed:

> Mistinguett has one thing in common with Fredona Nalil . . . her lovely naked legs! If this revue one day celebrates its one-hundredth performance, it will be because of those legs! This revue affirms the definitive glory of Mademoiselle Mistinguett, with her exquisite naked legs!

La Môme Flora, Mistinguett declared, was not merely art but poetry. It was an idea which was shared by the writer-director Robert de Flers, who one evening brought her flowers and told her that he had begun writing a new revue, *L'Ane De Buridan*, especially for her and that he was hoping to stage the show at the Gymnase. This delighted her beyond belief. She ordered de Flers to get on with things and gave him a week to finish the revue, which of course he did. She then told Richemond and Deval that she was leaving the Bouffes-Parisiens. Richemond was indifferent; she was still under contract to him and as far as he was concerned it did not matter where she worked so long as the receipts were good. Abel Deval was not of the same opinion. He accused her of breaking her contract and tried to impose a fine of 4,500 francs. Mistinguett refused to pay, and he threatened to blacklist her throughout Paris. This did not work either, and when he told her that she would always have the debt owing to the theatre on her conscience, she remarked that she had never had a conscience, which was probably true. In order to prevent the rift between Richemond and Deval from deepening, a compromise was reached. The fine was waived and Richemond, who for the last few weeks had been partner to the Mistinguett couch of approval, cancelled the original contract and got her to sign a new one wherein she would appear in a revue at La Cigale for an open fee – ostensibly this meant that she would also take a percentage of the box-office receipts. Mistinguett then went behind his back and signed a contract with Alphonse Franck for the play at the Gymnase – not that anything she signed from now on would be worth the paper it was written on – and the revue at the Cigale never took place.

Little is known of *L'Ane de Buridan*, other than that it was an unqualified success, and that Mistinguett played the role of Vivette opposite Mathe Régnier, one of the leading dramatic actresses of the day. For the first time, her name appeared in large letters at the top of posters and in red lights over the entrance: she was well on her way towards becoming the biggest star in Paris and the most feared. From now on, the chosen few would address her as Miss. Her enemies, of which there were many in theatrical circles, would call her anything behind her back and go to inordinate lengths to stay on the right side of her. In future, to cross Mistinguett would be tantamount to signing one's own death-warrant.

Max Dearly, Damia
and the Chaloupée

La valse chaloupée, or the apache-dance as it became known in England and America, ostensibly became Mistinguett's saving grace and opened for her and her equally difficult partner, Max Dearly, the gates towards immortal fame. She says,

> It came at that period in my life when I was pitched betwixt the theatre and the music-hall, at a time when I did not know which way to turn. The true music-hall no longer existed. I could say, the music-hall was me. It was born again, in effect, on the day that I met Max Dearly, a great artiste compared with whom I was nothing. . .

The meeting between Miss and Dearly was typical for both of them. Early in 1909 she had been engaged to play the part of a sewer worker in Syphon d'Asnières at the Gaîte-Rochechouart, and had been fired for curing herrings over the gas-mantle in her dressing-room. Dearly had been appearing in La Revue de la Femme at the Moulin-Rouge, directed by the impressario Samuel Louveau, known to his friends and enemies alike as Samuel the Magnificent. Samuel had caught Dearly in a most uncompromising position in his dressing room with his wife, the actress and dancer Eve Lavallière. Dearly had escaped by the skin of his teeth through a window, and had entered the bistro across from the Moulin-Rouge red-faced and with his trousers still in his hand. Mistinguett, sitting in her sewer worker's green vest and overall, had regarded this as perfectly normal.

Dearly had been born Lucien Rolland in Paris in 1874, but much of his youth had been spent in the south. Always an anglophile, he had joined the dancing-singing troupe Willi-Willi in Marseilles and had 'invaded' Paris at the turn of the century. As Rolland-Villary he had opened at the Ba-ta-clan in *Le Crime de Pierrot*, and had formed a bizarre attachment to a lady of that name, a dancer with a wooden leg. Afterwards he had toured the provinces, where one night he had doubled for a Scots actor, Mac Deely, hence his celebrated surname. Returning to Paris in 1900, he had opened at the Concert-Parisien with Eve Lavallière and the following year they had starred together in a revue at the Variétés, where he had introduced his celebrated English jockey routine. This had resulted in him signing a form of open contract with the theatre, though like Mistinguett he always refused to be tied down, and was so popular and influential that he could more or less please himself where he worked. For many years his greatest rival was Harry Fragson, especially where women were concerned; neither were in the least gentlemanly, and like Fragson, Dearly ultimately believed that the art of seduction was violence, as opposed to the conventional methods of courtship. That he was a sadist goes without saying. He also made a pun of Fragson's real name, Léon Pott, and combining this with one of the singer's less endearing habits, referred to him publicly, in English, as Shit-Pott. Mistinguett loathed him, and even at the height of their success Dearly never had a good word to say about her.

Eve Lavallière was no less bizarre. Born Eugénie Fenoglio in 1866, she was a neurotic, extremely possessive bisexual who often appeared on stage dressed as a man, though unlike Liane de Pougy she did not air her sexual preferences publicly. There was a sound reason for this. Lavallière was an agoraphobic, for whom the brief distance between her apartment and the pavement where the taxi was waiting to transport her to the theatre was a monstrous ordeal. Though some of her stage costumes were stunning, away from the footlights she rarely took off her *peignoir* and always wore it to rehearsals. Her acute neurosis is thought to have stemmed from her harrowing childhood – whilst very small she had watched her father attempting to strangle her mother and had later watched him kill himself. It seems likely that this forcible acceptance of violence drew her towards Max Dearly in the first place, and it is equally likely that her marriage to the director Samuel was not just one of convenience but a grave mistake.

Like Dearly, Lavallière had been granted an open contract with the Variétés. Her first major success here had been as You-You, in Robert de Fler's *Le Roi*, which many years later was revived by Marie Dubas. From then on she worked incessantly until 1917, when like Liane de Pougy she entered a religious institution, in her case the Tertiary Order of Saint Francis, where she died in July 1929.

In the bistro in 1909, it was Mistinguett who persuaded Max Dearly to end his affair with Lavallière. For the first time in twelve years she was out of work, and hoped that if she could persuade him to fall in love with her instead, he might offer her a part in his next revue. Seeing her in her sewer worker's overall did absolutely nothing for his libido, but her candour and subtlety impressed him no end. He told her that he had just invented a sensational new dance routine, the *valse-chaloupée*, and that he was looking for a partner not for the first half of the bill, but for the finale. Mistinguett took him up on his offer without hesitation, probably dreaming of the not too distant future when she would be hailed as a new sensation, swathed in feathers and dripping with jewels. If this was the case, she would be sorely disappointed so far as Max Dearly was concerned. He told her that as a 'fille des classes ouvrières' she would have to dress accordingly, and that her only 'stones' would be cobble-stones. Had she known what she was letting herself in for, Mistinguett might never have agreed to meet him early the next morning for an impromptu rehearsal on a piece of waste-ground behind the rue de Clichy!

The *chaloupée* was a passionate piece wherein traditional dance steps gave way to sensual body movements, recreating Max Dearly's violent machismo so far seen only in the bedroom. The more his partner complained, the rougher the dance became. She turned up for rehearsal wearing a calf-length skirt and high-heeled shoes. When one of these came off, Dearly decided to leave it in the routine. When Mistinguett's skirt ripped, this too was included.

The action takes place in a low dive in Paris. Customers are clustered around the bar. The *fille de joie* enters. She has a fistful of money which she counts. Then, hoisting up her skirt, she tucks it into the top of her stocking just as the *voyou* enters. He looks menacing. Drawing his knife from his belt, he grabs the girl and demands the money. When she refuses, he beats her up. Beating her fists against his chest she attempts to get away and he swings her around and flings her to the floor like a rag. He drags her to her feet and they dance a little. She tries to get away again, and he tosses her over his shoulder, under his legs. Again they dance. She slaps him, then knees him between the legs. This infuriates him beyond belief . . . grasping an ankle and an arm, he spins her around and around in circles, up and down, missing the floor by a fraction of an inch, and this time when he lets her go, she crashes into the bar and scatters the customers. Finally, he tosses her over his shoulder, places his knife between his teeth and carts her off to face her fate, whatever that may be!

The savage movements of the *chaloupée* would often be accompanied by a tirade of insults and filthy words, not always drowned by the orchestra; and the violence, once the dance reached the stage of the Moulin-Rouge on 27 July 1909, was only too authentic. In executing the *chaloupée*, Mistinguett and Dearly only brought their intense hatred of each other to the fore, and the piece remains one of the most astonishing in the entire history of the French music-hall. What made it even more exciting towards the end of the Moulin-Rouge run was the fact that if Dearly was in a particularly nasty mood he would drag her off the stage by the hair! There is little wonder then that outside the theatre she would not even speak to him!

Off and on, Miss and Dearly danced the *chaloupée* for another ten years, by which time they were both forty and aware that even the huge fees they commanded hardly compensated for all the bruises and insults, and some theatre directors were even afraid that one day they would go too far and end up killing each other!

After the *chaloupée*, Miss returned to the Bouffes-Parisiens to play another season of *L'Ane de Buridan*. Compared to what her admirers had come to expect at the Moulin-Rouge, her performance was regarded as tame and she quickly transferred to the Hennequin-Weber revue at the Palais-Royal, *Tais-toi Mon Coeur*, where she created a burlesque dance of her own, which she called *Le Ribouldingue*.

She was now the most sought after artiste in Paris, reluctant to sign contracts, and generally creating havoc by dropping out of productions whenever a better offer came along. When she appeared in *Sauf Vot' Respect* at the Capucines she complained that the stage was too small for her to dance properly . . . the revue was transferred to the Marigny, and the show currently playing there was forced to close. Because she was so good, directors put up with her tantrums, and if having Mistinguett appear at their theatre meant ousting one or two lesser-known stars to make room for her, this was done with as much compassion as possible. Mistinguett's excuse was that she had made it to the top with a great deal of self-sacrifice and indifference from her peers, and that if these artistes had any talent at all, they would soon fight their way back to the top. Few of them did, and two starlets who fell by the wayside, overwhelmed by the power and popularity of this woman, actually took their own lives. Mistinguett of course must never be held responsible for the weakness of others; after all, the same thing could just as easily have happened to her, given a change of circumstance.

At the Marigny, Miss was approached by Samuel Louveau and his writer-friend Louis Artus. Some years before, Samuel had turned up at the Eldorado with a four year contract said to have been worth a fortune. The conditions of this had caused Miss to show him the door, *tout de suite*. Samuel had been in contact with her mother, Madame Bourgeois, and for some reason which has never been satisfactorily explained, both had been intent in getting her to change her name from Mistinguett to Gervaise. This time, however, Samuel was more than satisfied with her pseudonym and he again offered her the contract for four years. Miss signed it at once. Artus, famous at the time for his extravagant comedies – his best-known work was *Coeur de Moineau* – had written one especially for her, *Les Midinettes*.

Through Samuel and Artus, she entered the Comédie Francaise du Boulevard, a distinguished workshop which boasted the biggest array of acting talent in Paris at that time, including Albert Brasseur, Eve Lavallière, Jeanne Granier and Max Dearly, who is said to have been livid with Samuel for signing up the best partner he had ever had and his worst enemy. Though Mistinguett disliked almost everyone on her show business side of the fence, Jeanne Granier became a friend. Like many of the great French dramatic actresses, her career had begun in the café-concerts as a soprano performing the works of Paul Déroulède and others of his ilk. One morning she had woken up with laryngitis: after a few days this had gone, and so had her voice. During a visit to Paris, Edward VII had met her at Fischer's and had been so impressed by her graceful looks and charm that he had arranged for her to travel to London, where she had appeared at the Royalty Theatre in a somewhat controversial production of *The Education of Prince*.

It was in January 1910, when *Les Midinettes* was playing to packed audiences, that Miss and Dearly were approached with a very lucrative offer. A British impressario, on holiday in Paris, had by chance seen the couple dancing the *chaloupée*, and as a consequence they were offered a contract with the Savoy Theatre in London. Where money was concerned, Dearly would have been willing to sign away his soul, but coaxing an unwilling partner into performing a dance which, by and large, had been little more than a show of flared tempers was another matter. She turned him down flat, and when he vowed that he would find another partner she threatened to sue him . . . more than this, she swore that if any other woman ever danced the *chaloupée*, she would personally scratch her eyes out! Dearly was good to his word, and though Mistinguett never got around to exacting her revenge, she would always hate the young woman who had taken her place, even more so when she became just as famous as she was!

Marie-Louise Damien had been born on the rue Albert in the 13th *arrondissement* of Paris in December 1889, the daughter of a gendarme. In 1902 the family had transferred to Lorraine, then a part of Germany. For the rest of her life, Mistinguett would always refer to Damia as 'that fucking German', and in doing so would make herself many enemies, for unlike herself, Damia remained one of the politest and most respected members of French society and probably the most loved entertainer in France after Edith Piaf. Marie-Louise was never happy living in a village in Lorraine and at the age of nineteen returned to Paris to seek her fortune. Her career on the stage happened quite by accident. She had very little money, and as it was mid-summer decided to conserve what she had by sleeping on a bench in the Bois de Boulogne where she was discovered the next morning – incredible as it may seem – by Harry Fragson, out taking his constitutional. Fragson, not one to ignore a damsel in distress, and a decidedly pretty one at that, decided to offer what help he could and without asking for the usual favour in return. He loaned her money and arranged for her to stay with friends until such time as she had found herself a suitable job. Marie-Louise promised to pay him back when she got famous and but for another strange twist of fate the matter would have ended there.

Marie-Louise found a job working in a bistro; ironically, it was the same bistro where Mistinguett had met Max Dearly, and one evening the dancer and Harry Fragson dropped in for a night-cap. Fragson recognized her at once and she was invited to sit at his table. The establishment did not usually allow the staff to fraternize with the clients, but when those clients were as important as Dearly and Fragson, exceptions had to be made. When Marie-Louise offered to pay back the money she owed, Fragson waved it aside and asked her instead if she might consider doing a favour for an old friend. Instinctively, she told him that she was not that kind of girl, then Dearly himself announced that he was searching for a girl to partner him in the *chaloupée*. Marie-Louise declared that she did not know how to dance and Dearly retorted that neither had the last one!

The rehearsals for the *chaloupée* took place after-hours at the Alhambra, where Fragson was starring at the time. Dearly was astonished at the girl's subtlety and grace, and engaged her after the very first session. In reality, the *chaloupée* did not demand the talents of a professional dancer . . . most of the actual steps were executed by Dearly himself, leaving his partner with all the bumps and bruises, which were fewer now that he had a woman who did not loathe him. As Dearly and Damien, the couple opened at the Savoy in March 1910 in the revue *On the Stage*, and the *chaloupée* was just as successful in London as it had been in Paris.

Back in Paris, Mistinguett was marching around in a fury, making life unbearable for everyone at the Gymnase, so much so that Samuel Louveau threatened to tear up her contract and evict her from his theatre. Marie-Louise Damien, she declared, would be best to enjoy her success whilst it lasted, for she would never dance on a French stage! To a certain extent this prediction came true. One night, before going on stage at the Savoy, Marie-Louise was sitting at the table of the musical director, Gerald Du Maurier, who happened to mention that whilst on his last trip to Paris he had purchased a copy of the sheet music to Lucien Boyer's latest song, 'Les Goëlands'. Boyer had written the song at the turn of the century, but so far had been the only one to perform it. Marie-Louise announced that it was her favourite song and ventured a refrain. Du Maurier was so overcome with emotion that he insisted upon her singing the song that evening after the *chaloupée*.

> Ne tuez pas le goëland
> Qui plane sur les flots hurlants,
> Car c'est l'âme d'un matelot
> Qui plane au-dessus d'un tombeau,
> Et pleure, pleure . . .

> (Don't kill the seagull
> Which soars over the roaring waves,
> For it is a sailor's soul
> Which floats and cries
> Above a tomb . . .)

Returning to Paris, Dearly and Damien adapted *On the Stage* into French and staged it at the Théâtre de Chatelet. Still fuming, Mistinguett turned up at the theatre every night and handed out leaflets urging spectators not to go in and see the couple. This caused a rift between her and Harry Fragson, who had now taken Marie-Louise under his wing. He introduced her to the impressario Roberti, who was then married to a mannequin called Pervenche; a few years later, as Fréhel, she would be recognized as one of the greatest *chanteuses-réalistes* of her day. Roberti disliked Mistinguett – there did not have to be any specific reason for this – and he offered Marie-Louise a spot in the next Fragson revue at the Alhambra, providing she could find another song to go with 'Les Goëlands'. Fragson took her to a music publisher, and she was given 'Quand les Papillons', which some years later would become a massive success for the soprano, Yvonne Printemps.

Now that there was virtually no competition, Mistinguett and Marie-Louise almost became friends. Mistinguett anticipated that as soon as Marie-Louise moved to the Alhambra, she would be able to take up with Dearly where she had left off. This did not happen. Marie-Louise Damien monopolized the Théâtre de Chatelet – besides the *chaloupée* and her two songs, she took a leaf out of Mistinguett's book and invented a dance of her own. This she called the *danse-sinistre*, in which she appeared on stage like a long, lithe panther in a black sheath of a dress, gliding across the stage like a spectre. The idea, she later said, had come from the American dancer Loîe Fuller, with whom she would eventually form an attachment.

By January 1911, when they opened at the Alhambra, Marie-Louise and Fragson were lovers. She later said that in spite of his violent reputation he always treated her kindly, and that he would always remain the greatest love of her life. She also got him to mend his ways . . . from now on he would act the role of the perfect gentleman, and one of Marie-Louise's conditions for staying with him was that he no longer fraternized with Mistinguett. Fragson persuaded her to 'feminize' her name and she became Damia . . . as such she would become the greatest of all the French dramatic singers and would appear with great success all over the world to within nine years of her death in 1978. Mistinguett found herself appearing with Damia many times in galas and recitals, but she always refused to have anything to do with her and insulted her publicly whenever she could. Damia, on the other hand, always kept her comments to herself.

Mistinguett, meanwhile, closed at the Gymnase, and on 9 April 1911 opened at the Eldorado in *La Vie Parisienne*, by Meilhac and Halévy. For some reason she disapproved of the theatre . . . perhaps it reminded her too much of her early struggles, or more likely the money was insufficient for the life-style she had become accustomed to. Samuel transferred the revue to the Folies-Bergères, and this in turn led to the monumental meeting with the man who would transform her life . . . Maurice Chevalier.

Chevalier

Maurice Chevalier, a true *enfant du faubourg*, had been born in Menilmontant in September 1888, the son of a house painter. His mother, whom he affectionately called La Louque, worked as a braid trimmer. Like Mistinguett, Chevalier was primarily a visual *artiste*. Though he was an above average dancer early on in his career, his singing voice left a great deal to be desired, as did his acting talents. What made him a very great star, universally, was his tremendous personality, and a unique ability to convince audiences and peers alike that what he was doing was definitive, which of course it was not. Something of a child prodigy, and very much a mother's boy, he had made his debut at the Café des Trois-Lions, where his dance-patter had been recompensed by a bowl of soup. During his teens he had teamed up with his brother to form *Les Frères Chevalier*, a poor acrobatic act which had come to an abrupt end when his mother, sitting in the audience, had watched him take a nasty fall. In 1905 he had appeared at the Concert du Commerce and the Casino de Montmartre, where he had been billed as Patapouf . . . he would remember this many years later when meeting and launching one of his protégées, Henriette Rageon, who was thirty years his junior. She would become famous in France as Patachou, and more or less infamous in Britain as the cabaret star who occasionally stepped down from the stage to snip off the neck-ties of some of the men in her audience.

Soon afterwards, Chevalier had left Paris to tour the seedy clubs in the southern ports of France. He had scored a particular success in Marseilles when he had been asked to replace the immensely popular *chanteuse-réaliste* and political activist Eugénie Buffet: the Russo-Japanese war had just ended, and she had been evicted from the theatre for singing a song denouncing General Oku. Chevalier had returned to Paris in 1907 to be included in Dranem's show at the Eldorado, and after appearing at other establishments in and around Paris he had ended up topping the bill at the Alcazar d'Eté, with Damia as his *vedette-américain*.

Chevalier and Mistinguett had had their first encounter in 1909, during the run of *L'Ane de Buridan*. He had been but one of the many admirers who had queued up outside the door of her dressing-room with flowers, and she had not been impressed. She had even dismissed him as being gormless and effeminate. He had also appeared on the same bill which had included the *chaloupée*, but at that time she had been too involved in her on-stage feud with Max Dearly to take much notice. It was only when one of her 'spies' informed her that Chevalier was having an affair with someone else that she decided to strike, for she assumed that the other woman could only have been Damia.

For some reason, Mistinguett appears to have been frightened of Damia, though by now there was no professional competition, for Damia had given up dancing to concentrate on her search for the type of song which would ultimately revolutionize the music-hall. Like Yvette Guilbert, she had the uncanny ability to dig up long forgotten songs, such as Jean Richepin's classic 'Les Deux Menetriers', and make them her own. One evening Miss and her heavies turned up at the Alcazar d'Eté to 'interrogate' the singer, only to be set upon themselves by a very irate Harry Fragson who made it more than clear that for the time being, Damia was his exclusive property.

Ultimately, the third party was unmasked. She turned out to be yet another dancer and café-concert entertainer who would achieve later recognition as one of the founder members of the *chanson-réaliste* tradition . . . Fréhel.

Fréhel had been born Marguerite Boulc'h in 1891. According to the legend, she chose her celebrated name in 1920 because her family had originated from Cap Fréhel in Finistère, and as Fréhel she was the only woman on the music-hall circuit capable of out-vulgarizing Mistinguett. She had begun singing in local bars at the age of five, accompanied by a blind accordionist. At the time of her affair with Chevalier she was known as La Pervenche, after the periwinkle-blue of her eyes. This name appears on her first shellac recording, 'Comme une Fleur', which she cut in 1912 and which was a cover version of a Mistinguett song, thus only adding insult to injury. Though a few years on she would become immensely fat, in the years leading up to the Great War she was fêted as one of the most beautiful débutantes in Paris, though her self-confessed respectability had not prevented her from getting pregnant at the age of fourteen. Fréhel had later married the father, Roberti, who was then the agent of Damia and Chevalier. Almost inevitably, there had been a number of complications. Whether the child was born dead or aborted is not known. The fact is, Fréhel never got on with her husband and hardly ever lived with him under the same roof. Roberti was even more of a womaniser than Fragson. Fréhel, feeling lonely and rejected, found solace in Chevalier's arms, and a feud erupted between Mistinguett and Fréhel which would last a number of years and end in the most horrifying manner.

For the time being, the intervention of Fate prevented Miss from making a complete spectacle of herself by confronting the lovers and risking being spurned by the one man she wanted, by all accounts, more than any other. During the summer of 1911 she was offered an extremely lucrative contract with the Folies-Bergère, and such was her power by now that she was given full licence over the production, which meant that she was responsible for auditioning and engaging the cast, from the *vedette-américain* down to the chorus. She was also allowed to choose her own costumes and choreograph all the dance routines. Her methods were discerning, to say the least, and would remain so for another forty years. Mistinguett was never anything but a perfectionist, and only the best would be good enough. The chorus girls had to be beautiful, tall and leggy, and above all unattached. The boys had to be handsome, slim and strong . . . and if they were homosexual, so much the better. Homosexual men, she declared, were that much more reliable than the conventional kind in that whilst invariably there were 'in-house' relationships, they rarely got anyone pregnant. She was also entering that phase of her life wherein it became virtually a preoccupation to attempt to convert a gay man towards what she called 'the straight and narrow'.

Selecting the chorus for her new revue presented no problems, and Miss set about choosing her partner for a dance which she herself had invented – the *valse-renversante*. The director of the Folies-Bergère suggested Max Dearly and regretted doing so when

Miss threatened to boycott the production. She told herself that she wanted Chevalier and refused to settle for less. For several weeks she had him followed, monitoring his affair with Fréhel, to whom she sent threatening letters. Whenever he was appearing at a theatre other than the Alcazar d'Eté, she always made a point of going to see him. Donning a disguise she would buy a ticket for the gallery and worship him, as it were, from afar. Eventually she plucked up enough courage to wait for him in his dressing room after a show, and when she asked him to appear in her revue, he surprised her by saying that he would. The fee was not discussed and neither it seems was Fréhel.

That Mistinguett worshipped the very ground which Chevalier walked upon goes without saying – the sentimentality of her memoirs recounting this period of her life makes very poetic reading – though in reality the relationship was divided into two distinct phases from Chevalier's point of view. The first was unquestionably lust – any man good enough or indeed lucky enough to sleep with the great Mistinguett owned a certain prestige over his fellows, and almost always made it to the top in his section of the music-hall environment. The second phase progressed beyond the bedroom, although sex and success were inextricably linked. The current lover had to contend with the fact that he was not irreplaceable, and had to submit to his competition being flaunted in his face, both privately and in public. Mistinguett never made any secret of her taste for mean and moody men, even if they were homosexuals, and she was not ashamed of being called promiscuous. The current lover, however, had to swear to have eyes for her alone, in addition to which he had to put up with innumerable tantrums, intense jealousy, bad language and general humiliation. When the author interviewed one of these lovers a few years ago, he was told that Mistinguett's qualities by far outweighed her bad points, and that her extroverted public image was but a camouflage for the fact that, though rich beyond belief and always surrounded by a crowd of handsome hangers-on, at the end of the day when the curtain came down, she was just another lonely, sad old woman who desperately wanted to love and be loved for what she was, as opposed to what she possessed. The great *chanteuses-réalistes* of Mistinguett's generation, namely Yvonne George, Damia, Fréhel and Eugénie Buffet, drank heavily or took drugs in order to assuage their problems of loneliness. Mistinguett was always too health and figure-conscious to slide into the bottomless pit which engulfed and ultimately destroyed Yvonne George and Fréhel, and even Damia saw the error of her ways and lived to be eighty-eight. Mistinguett did not smoke and she hardly ever drank unless for medicinal purposes. 'Sex is the only bad habit I never wanted to give up,' she once said. 'It is good for the figure and the soul!' The fact that she, too, lived to be more than eighty whilst only looking half her age certainly proves her point.

Writing about Chevalier in 1953, she says,

> I still think about him when I am bent down, weeding my garden . . . that is when I hear the birds sing, and I look up and gaze through a kind of veil, back to the past. I forget that I am still alive, that once I was Mistinguett. Maurice and I shared exactly the same dreams. When I first met him, he squandered his money on silly things. I taught him how to be practical . . . now he is richer and more famous than I am! But I alone am living proof of his success, for he would never have got anywhere without me. My only regret is that we ruined our happiness by living too fast. . .

Mistinguett also credits herself with teaching Chevalier how to dress, how to eat and behave in public, and above all how to walk without mincing. In order to cast aside scoffs from contemporaries that she was old enough to be his mother – he was twenty-two and she thirty-six – she persuaded him to take her home to meet La Louque. She seems to have got on better with Chevalier's mother than with her own, and particularly enjoyed the family get-togethers around the dinner table which she described as an integral part of her second youth. What she did not know, of course, was that Chevalier was cheating on her behind her back, most likely with Fréhel.

The new revue at the Folies-Bergère was set to open on 15 December 1911. Two weeks prior to this, Mistinguett was given access to the theatre every morning for rehearsals. The *valse-renversante* was not as damaging to the partner as the *chaloupée* had been, although it was hazardous to whoever happened to be on the stage when it took place. The setting was a Parisian bistro . . . tables, chair, crates, the bar, and several spectators in street clothes. The dance began on top of a table with the dancer's feet sending bottles and glasses flying in all directions. Leaping down from the table, they would tear around the stage half-possessed, doing cart-wheels and leaps. Every item on the stage would be unceremoniously flung into the wings in their wake, including the spectators, until all that was left was the carpet. The dance would end with Miss and Chevalier at opposite ends of this, and after a final couple of somersaults they would fling themselves to the floor, and roll themselves up in the carpet. The first time this happened, Miss ended up with a split lip. During the next rehearsal, squeezed together in the dusty carpet and no doubt remembering what had happened with the farmhand in the cornfield at Enghien many years back, she got carried away; unbuttoning Chevalier's trousers, she attempted to find out if the rumours she had heard about his being 'well-blessed' were true. Chevalier is reputed to have called her a filthy little harlot, though needless to say he did enjoy the experience and over the next few mornings took it for granted that the same thing would happen again. Whether Mistinguett's confession is true or not – that she 'grabbed a handful' on the actual opening night in front of two thousand people – has never been verified, though few would have put it past her.

In spite of her passionate affair with Momo, as she called him, Mistinguett never lived with him, and during the next two years both spent most of their time furthering their respective careers, and even Fréhel was forced to occupy a back seat. It does seem likely, however, that Chevalier was still two-timing her, and she, too, had a 'reserve' . . . this was the young actor, Louis Verneuil, who was often seen in public with her until 1915. Eventually, he would marry the daughter of Sarah Bernhardt.

Early in 1912, Mistinguett opened in *Le Bonheur Sous la Main*, which was followed in June by the Rip revue, *En Avant Marche*, in which one of her plum lines was, 'Darling, are you aware that the princess shits herself?' By 3 November 1912 she was in yet another (un-named) revue at the Folies-Bergère, in which her co-star was Yvonne Printemps. Born Yvonne Wigniole in 1894, this talented youngster had first trod the theatre's celebrated boards in 1905, and ten years after working with Mistinguett she would make her name in Sacha Guitry's *L'Amour Masqué* and become the most famous French soprano of all time.

Two operettas followed. *Si J'Etais Roi*, of which practically nothing is known, was written by Robert de Flers and probably opened in January 1913. A few weeks later she was offered Barde and Carré's *Milord l'Arsouille*, which went on at the Scala. One morning, whilst rehearsing for this at her apartment, she was paid a visit by Vincent Scotto. This was unusual, for his works had never appealed to her in the past. Scotto offered her his very latest composition, 'Les Mômes de la Cloche'. Some years later it would be performed by Edith Piaf; it was, in fact, the first studio recording she ever made, and of course once it entered Piaf's repertoire it became synonymous with her name. Because of this, Mistinguett never recorded it herself during her numerous visits to the studio in the years leading up to the Second World War, which is a pity.

> C'est nous les mômes, les mômes de la cloche,
> Clochards qui s'en vont sans un rond en poche!
> C'est nous les paumées, les purées d'paumées,
> Qui sommes aimées un soir, n'importe où!

> (We're the kids, the guttersnipes,
> Tramps who roam around, broke!
> Outcasts, clapped-out outcasts,
> Loved for a night, no matter where!)

It was at the Scala that the girl from Enghien became La Grande Miss. Every night there would be no fewer than twelve costume changes. Though she had not yet incorporated the famous staircase entrance into her act, her dresses were the most fabulous Paris had ever seen. Mistinguett designed the early ones herself and even found time in her busy schedule to cut them out and sew them together at home. It was not simply a case of if a job is worth doing well, it is worth doing oneself. Each costume, she said, was like a bridal gown . . . it should be seen by no one until the night of the première!

Her co-star at the Scala was not a famous dancer, or even a beautiful man. It was the comic-illusionist, Morton, who had begun his career at the turn of the century as a conjuror's assistant, and who was now known as Le Coupeur de Tête because of a recent addition to his act. This was a form of armchair where a 'victim' selected from the audience would be invited to sit and resign himself to his fate:

> 'Ladies and gentlemen, for those of you who have never been guillotined before, I offer the ultimate sensation! The operation will cause no pain, and your head will be returned to you after the show!'

Before taking it to the Scala, Morton tried his routine on his friends, including Mistinguett. On the evening of the première, however, the stunt almost went wrong when the 'blade' ruptured the bag of red varnish behind the victim's neck before it should have done. The audience, thinking the man had been beheaded, rushed onto the stage to lynch the illusionist, who fled for his life to the comparative safety of Mistinguett's dressing room. Morton later perfected the routine and scored a massive success at the Scala when he returned a few years later to top the bill.

The Scala revue closed on 1 May 1913, and Mistinguett entered into one of the busiest and most bizarre phases of her career. Between May 1913 and the end of 1916 she appeared in no fewer than fourteen films. Most of them are forgettable, nine alone were made in the latter half of 1913, and it is impossible to say in which order they were made, save that the first was a brief clip with Chevalier in *La Valse Renversante*. It has been suggested that she also teamed up with Dearly again to film the *chaloupée* . . . if so, the clip has never come to light. One or two of Mistinguett's incursions into the virgin territory of the cinema are, however, worthy of a mention, as are her own comments regarding the medium:

> I don't much like making films. On stage I can seduce the public, or make them cry. It isn't so easy trying to do that to a machine with a glass eye! On screen I look like a magical corpse. The director is in control too much of the time, and not Mistinguett. When I'm on stage people clamour to touch me because it makes them feel good. They know that I'm real. Film directors are out of touch with the world. They're not satisfied with the money they've got . . . they always want more. And when you've made

a good film, if there is such a thing, the pianist always fucks it up at the end. . .

Les Miserables is, of course, a well-known story. Mistinguett played the part of Eponine. *Fleur de Pavé*, directed by Albert Capellani, had her playing the rags to riches story of a poor orphan who ends up on the stage, and was shot mostly in an improvised snowstorm. Her co-star was Prince, the hero of the silent cinema in France who, during his hey-day between 1910 and 1914, appeared in a different film every week!

La Glu – Mistinguett always referred to it by its English translation, *Bird Shit* – had a final scene reminiscent of Morton's 'guillotine' act, when her lover had to murder her by hitting her over the head with a hammer. The prop department supplied her with a ball of cotton wool to be worn under her wig in order to cushion the blows. The actor missed. Her head was split open and blood poured down her face, and to her horror the director asked for the scene to be shot again!

One film for which Mistinguett admitted a little fondness was *La Moche*. It was, of course, pure kitsch, and once more used the theme of the pitiful little waif cast out into the cold by cruel parents, only to be rescued by a handsome young man and employed by his rich family as a chambermaid. In this film, however, all did not turn out well in the end. The girl has a brother who, knowing nothing of her whereabouts, breaks into the house where she is working. She and her lover catch him trying to steal the silver. When her lover pulls a gun to shoot the intruder, she flings herself between them, is shot through the heart and dies in her lover's arms!

It was after this little melodrama, and after Chevalier had accused her of sleeping with her leading man, that Mistinguett decided to get away from Paris for a while. The most fashionable holiday resort in France in those days was Trouville. However, she opted for Deauville (which had yet to be 'discovered') because many of her more snobbish acquaintances had advised her to steer clear of it as 'ennuyeux à mourir'. Here, she set about arousing Chevalier's jealousy in such a way that she could have come close to losing him altogether.

At this point digression must be made to discuss one Félix Mayol, *interprète-extraordinaire*, who had been born in Toulon in 1882. He has variously been described as a genius and a turn of the century 'punk' because of his peculiar tufted hairstyle. Mistinguett had worked with him, off and on, for a number of years. At the Eldorado his big success had been the Breton-born Théodore Botrel's 'La Paimpolaise'. Later he had performed Scotto's 'Elle Vendait des Petits Gâteaux', immortalized in the sixties by Barbara. One of his most popular numbers at the time of his 'alliance' with Mistinguett was 'La Neige', which she also sang but never recorded.

> Les petits de froid engourdis,
> Pleurant leurs souffrances,
> Pendant que gaîment les riches vraiment
> Vont faire bombance!
>
> (The little ones, numb with cold,
> Crying their sufferings,
> Whilst the rich folk gaily and truly
> Have a good blow-out!)

What really suited Mistinguett down to the ground was that Mayol was a rampant homosexual, and like herself unashamed of making a public spectacle of himself. Like Cocteau, Reynaldo Hahn, Marc Allégret and others who were developing just before the Great War, Mayol belonged to a curious group of supposed intellectuals who had adapted the custom known as 'le privilège du cape'. The custom was genuine enough . . . any Frenchman unable to find a convenient *pissoir* would ask a gendarme to extend his cape so that he could urinate behind it. Mayol, often in the company of Mistinguett, would choose a handsome young gendarme, then pretend to be drunk so that he would be offered assistance with the buttons of his trousers. It was not just a form of great amusement, but a means of soliciting which would often pay off. If it did not, Mayol would simply shrug his shoulders, wet his victim's feet, and walk off.

When Mistinguett arrived in Deauville during the summer of 1913, Mayol had already agreed to take part in her devious scheme to bait Chevalier. Together, they set about spreading rumours that they had had a violent quarrel, and naturally the resort was invaded by the press hoping for some exclusive. What they were told there astonished them so much that they believed it could only be true. Mistinguett had arranged a 'press conference' at the house of a friend. This was in the form of a dinner, to which had been invited her current lover: Louis Verneuil still considered himself such, even though she had told him that one day she would marry Chevalier. Verneuil had brought along a few friends of his own, all hand-picked. Gaston Gabaroche was a well-known theatre director, actor and writer of revues and songs . . . he would later write songs for Damia, Marie Dubas and Edith Piaf. Lucie Delarue Mardrus was a poet and novelist who moved in society circles. Fyodor Chaliapin was the famous Russian bass who had recently taken a shine to Damia, and who was going through a bad patch because the media had accused him of taking advantage of Fragson's recent death: the hero of *La Belle Epoque* had been shot dead by his father during an argument over a chorus girl. Damia, of course, had not been invited to the gathering.

During the meal Mistinguett and Mayol glared at each other. Maurice Prax, the young journalist assigned to report what he had been told would be the scoop of the century, wrote that the atmosphere was decidedly uncomfortable because everyone at the table had a skeleton in their particular cupboard. Finally, Mistinguett banged her fist on the table and ordered Mayol to leave. Mayol then explained to his guests the reason for his quarrel with Mistinguett — it had been a lover's tiff! Miss, never less than a great actress, a-là-Bernhardt, promptly burst into tears and begged forgiveness, after which her 'lover' asked her to marry him. The act was so convincing that even Louis Verneuil believed it, and of course Maurice Prax's story appeared on the front page of his newspaper the very next day. . .

> Mayol and Mistinguett to Marry! Latest Sensation!
> Félix Mayol, the well-known artiste, has fallen in love with Mistinguett! What is more, the celebrated star claims that he has always been the man of her dreams! Sensational, perhaps, but nevertheless it really is true!

In effect, Mistinguett's plan backfired on her when Maurice Prax's Parisian contacts began interviewing her friends there, each of whom added his or her own little snippet of information regarding some of the less-conventional habits of her private life. For several days she found life at Deauville practically intolerable. She, who had always adored publicity but only when it suited her, found it impossible to leave her hotel room without being besieged by reporters. When she told the press that they had been victims of a practical joke, they refused to believe her. Mayol, of course, was not embarrassed at all, though he did agree to publish a 'letter' which he had written to his friend, Dranem, in a local newspaper. The style of this, however, was typically Mayol, and served only to make matters worse:

> My dear old chap! As one of the latest wonders of Tangoville, let me explain why I have decided to give up Mistinguett as a bad job. Mind you, I was willing at first. I bumped into this deliciously-alluring little creature at the Potinière, and we had the most tender conversation. Then I suppose I got carried away. We decided to get hitched . . . just like that! Then I reflected, and thought about my public. You know what they're like. They would have expected me to have kids. So I told her that I wanted to remain a young girl. She was so understanding, old chap! We're happy together, and I shan't be getting in the family way!

Mistingett, however, did not see the funny side of Mayol's announcement. Packing her bags in the middle of the night she returned to Paris – even Louis Verneuil was left behind. Angry beyond belief, she talked a director friend, Léon Poirier, into engaging her at the Comédie des Champs-Elysées. For her finale, she herself put together a pot-pourri of Mayol songs, but not before changing the lyrics to some of the most insulting ever heard on a French stage. Mayol's only reaction was to send her a sprig of lily of the valley . . . fashioned out of diamonds! She and Mayol quickly patched up their differences and remained close friends until his death in 1941. As for Chevalier, he had apparently taken no notice of Mistinguett's adventure, and their affair took up from where it had left off.

In the autumn of 1913 Mistinguett opened at the Théâtre des Variétés in Alfred Capus' *L'Institut de Beauté*. Two weeks into the run she collapsed with stomach pains . . . her doctor diagnosed appendicitis. She refused to believe this, and of course the show had to go on. Towards the end of the year she was offered *La Revue Légère* at the Olympia.

The famous theatre was at this time in its infancy. At the age of 28, Joseph Oller had inaugurated the very first Parisian horse-racing publication, *Le Pari Mutuel*, from his base on the Boulevard des Capucines. This had been banned in 1893, when Oller had decided to convert his office block into a theatre, Les Fantaisies Oller. Three years later the name had been changed to the Théâtre des Nouveautés, and for a time it had put on Feydeau farces. With the advent of the circus at the turn of the century, Oller had transformed his establishment into the Montagnes Russes. This had been demolished soon afterwards, and from its ashes had sprung the building which would eventually put on recitals by just about every famous name in the world of international entertainment. Mistinguett was one of the first. Her début at the Olympia, however, was not without trauma. During rehearsals for *La Revue Légère* she collapsed again and this time was rushed into hospital, where her inflamed appendix was removed. Joseph Oller, aware of her passion for practical jokes, refused to believe that she was genuinely ill, and issued her with a summons. Oller himself was summoned to her bedside – not by Mistinguett but by her doctor – and when told that it was more or less touch and go he relented and informed her that no matter how long it took her to get well again, the revue would still be put on.

Mistinguett's sojourn in hospital was not without its share of adventure. Though she was lucky to be alive, two days after her operation she rose from her sick-bed to help the nurses . . . the hospital was short-staffed because of a flu epidemic, and one of her young 'patients' actually died in her arms.

It was at this time that she learnt that Chevalier had been called up for military service. Discharging herself from the hospital, she spent a few days with his mother and even tried to visit him at the camp in Belfort. This of course was not allowed, though over the next few weeks the couple wrote to each other daily. Chevalier's saving grace at Belfort was in effect a twenty-two year old soldier, Maurice Yvain. Their friendship, which initially may not have been just platonic, would endure for many years, and Yvain would collaborate with Albert Willemetz on many of Mistinguett's greatest commercial successes. They also wrote for Chevalier. One song, in which he expresses his curiosity as a child, 'Dites-Moi Ma Mère' was conceived in the army barracks at Belfort.

> Quand j'étais petit
> J'étais naîf, j'étais gentil,
> Et chaque dimanche à mes sortis
> J'interrogais ma mère:
> 'Dites-moi, ma mère,
> Pourquoi les chiens dans la rue
> Se montent dessus?'

> (When I was small
> I was naive, I was a good boy,
> And on Sunday mornings
> I interrogated my mother:
> 'Tell me, mother,
> Why do dogs mount each other in the street?')

Whilst Chevalier and Yvain were giving impromptu recitals to their fellow soldiers, Mistinguett was going through yet another bad patch. Complications had set in after her operation and once again she was assigned to a hospital bed. It would seem that there were other problems too and that she was forced to have a hysterectomy. This gave Chevalier real cause for concern. Somehow he managed to transfer from Belfort, which was near the Swiss border, to Melun, and when Mistinguett left the hospital, she booked herself in at the nearby convalescent home at Bois-le-Rois, from where she worked behind the scenes to make sure that he could visit her. It is very probable that she knew Chevalier's commanding officer, if not personally then through an intermediary, but in any case few red-blooded males were able to refuse any request from the great Mistinguett. For a few weeks she was deliriously happy, and for once Chevalier stood by her. She said, 'Those brief hours were the most beautiful of my life,' and probably meant it. Her happiness, however, was short-lived. . .

On 28 June 1914 an otherwise inconsequential young man named Gavrilo Princip, one of many millions living in Austria-Hungary with a desire to cast off the Austrian yoke and return to his kinsmen in Serbia, assassinated Archduke Francis Ferdinand, the heir to the Austro-Hungarian throne, thus igniting a spark which would ultimately set fire to the world. Exactly one month later, Austria declared war on Serbia, who appealed successfully to Russia for aid. France joined the side of her ally, and early in August 1914 Chevalier's regiment left Melun to fight.

> La Louque and myself were there to see him off, but after all my catastrophes I could think of nothing to say. They allowed us one last kiss. Then, orders were given for the march to begin, and through eyes blinded by tears we watched them disappear into the distance. Maurice's handkerchief was still waving, and then I lost sight of him, and I knew that my soul had just died.

Returning to Paris, Mistinguett flung herself headlong into her work. *La Revue Légère*, at the Olympia, was not the success she had anticipated because her association with the theatre had begun badly, and during the winter of 1914–15 she took on engagements which normally she would have turned down flat, simply to take her mind off Chevalier who, it appears, was not as tough a man as has been made out.

What she could not have known at the time was that before very long she too would be fighting in the war, in her typical but nevertheless inimitable way.

The Great War

The music-hall continued to flourish during the early years of the Great War. Paul Déroulède had been attacking Germany in his works since the turn of the century, only to expire in 1914 when the real thing happened. The *chanson-revencharde* tradition which he had created was handed down to two of his disciples, Yvette Guilbert and Eugénie Buffet, who performed his songs up and down France, often instigating riots.

Fréhel, still threatened by Mistinguett, had taken advantage of Chevalier's absence and had left Paris to tour the south of France. Max Dearly was still appearing in revues. Damia, after a failed provincial tour, had sailed to America and was having no trouble at all working in the vaudeville theatres of New York, even though her specialized songs were not in keeping with the American style. The inspiration for the trip had come from the dancer Gaby Deslys, already a major star in France and now the latest sensation on Broadway. In Paris, Mayol was crooning 'Viens Poupoule', and titillating his audiences with a string of anglicized songs such as 'La Polka des English'. The men and women strolling the boulevards were humming Polin's 'Mademoiselle Rose', and the latest theatrical revelation, at the Renaissance, was *Fred ou Joujou d'Amour*, which starred Gaby de Morlay and a very young Marie Dubas, one of the few French artistes for whom Mistinguett would have a genuine admiration.

The latest inventions, automobiles and aeroplanes, were now the subject of some of the most ridiculous songs ever heard. In August 1906 Harry Fragson had watched Alberto Santos-Dumont, a Brazilian airship pioneer living in France, fly two hundred metres at Bagatelle in a machine built by the Wright Brothers, and this had inspired him to write the music to Henri Christiné's poem, 'Dans Mon Aéroplane'. In the Spring of 1915, Mistinguett was singing 'L'Aéroplaneur' to her bemused audiences at the Cigale.

> Si qu'j'étais aéroplaneur,
> J'enleverais ma femme sur mes deux ailes,
> Pour nous aimer près du Seigneur,
> On ferait ça comme les hirondelles!
>
> (If only I was an aeroplaneman,
> I would carry off my wife on my two wings,
> To love close to the Saviour,
> We could do that like the swallows!)

In the summer of 1915, Mistinguett was reunited with her son, Léopold. The boy was then aged about fifteen, though in the photograph taken at the time he looks much younger and rather frail in his sailor-suit. Nothing is known of the whereabouts of his father, Monsieur de Lima, though recent research suggests that he had returned to Brazil in 1914, leaving the boy with relatives who lived near Paris. What is certain is that the de Limas had been granted custody of him after proving somewhat illegally that Mistinguett had been an unfit mother. This is of course ridiculous; as the boy had been taken away from her a few weeks after his birth she had never been able to assert herself one way or the other, and her bitterness towards the handsome young Brazilian who had, in effect, used her is understandable. Why she never took his family to court is not known and never will be. Mistinguett often gave something away about herself in her interviews with the press but she always refused to speak about her son. In 1915 when she took him on holiday to Deauville, the boy had been conditioned by the de Limas into despising her, and it appears that someone was sent clandestinely to Deauville to keep an eye on her. This was not necessary. For the first time in her life since leaving Enghien, excepting the brief weeks spent with Chevalier, she was truly happy. Not only did she prove herself the perfect mother, when the time came for her to hand Léopold back to his 'guardians' the poor child was dragged off screaming.

Mistinguett, always the most resolute of women, was now on the verge of a nervous breakdown. Chevalier was no longer there to offer comfort: though not the most faithful of men, in the short time the couple had known each other intimately he had always been willing to listen to her confidences, and might have been able to lend a helping hand regarding her problems with the de Limas. Now, she had no one. The Liane de Pougy clan had deserted her, though this in itself was a blessing. Yvonne Printemps spent some time with her whenever her busy schedule allowed her to do so. There was always La Louque, of course, but seeing Chevalier's mother only made her more aware of her loneliness. She decided, ultimately, that the only way of coping with her depression was to leave France. She therefore accepted a tour of Italy, which was not yet involved in the war.

In Rome she was greeted like a prodigal queen. The director of the theatre provided her with a dressing room for herself and another for her flowers . . . the Italians were delighted when she called it her funeral parlour, though she was not joking. Italy, she later said, was the pits because she was paid next to nothing whilst playing to packed houses every night, and in theatres whose seats were dearer than the ones in Paris. After Rome, she played in Turin, Florence and Bologna, and by the time she reached Naples – the last leg of the tour – she had had enough. The theatre director had run up a long list of debts, and he tried to pull a fast one by only paying her half her fee! Mistinguett bawled him out to no effect. The director had an interest in a theatre in Palermo, Sicily, and he agreed to pay her the rest of the fee but only if she agreed to do the next engagement for nothing. When she refused to do this – for some reason she hated Sicily more than Italy – the director offered the engagement to one of her dancing girls. Mistinguett outwitted them both by taking the boat to Sicily, under cover of darkness like a spy, and hiring the theatre herself. After the show, she summoned a meeting of her troupe – there were thirteen in all – and demanded that her 'double' step forward and face her fate. Nothing happened so the next day Mistinguett decided to teach everyone a lesson. Instead of allowing her dancers to enjoy themselves on the beach, she told them that they were going to look around the catacombs and that unless the guilty party came clean, everyone would be locked underground! Still nothing happened and ultimately the plan backfired on her . . .

We went in, and all the corpses were staring at us. Soldiers and children . . . this was Italian passion at its best, and even I felt apprehensive. There was a woman in her wedding-dress, and when I touched this she fell on the floor in pieces. The girls weren't the only ones to scarper, I can tell you! Fortunately, the hotel barman revived us with vermouth. . .

The girl responsible for causing her *patronne* unnecessary anguish owned up and was promply fired. She fled back to the theatre director in Naples, and as soon as Mistinguett arrived there, ostensibly to board the train for Paris, she found herself shadowed and eventually threatened by his henchmen. They informed her that she still owed him money, and more or less press-ganged her into accepting a four day engagement in Milan. For the first time in her life she was afraid, and her ordeal was by no means over. When she arrived in Milan there were no publicity posters outside the theatre and the director had impounded her baggage – this included several large trunks containing her costumes, valued at more than a million francs. The director then declared that she would only get them back providing she paid off her original debt to his partner in Naples. She refused, even though she was not in any position to argue . . . she had very little money and her only clothes were the ones on her back.

A friend, whom she refers to in her memoirs as Monsieur Veischotte, came to her rescue. He had left France at the outbreak of the war, probably to evade being called up for military service, and had recently settled in Milan. It would appear that he had once been part of the Liane de Pougy clan . . . all that counted, so long as Mistinguett was concerned, was that he was immensely rich. Almost at once, he became her lover.

Mistinguett gave three recitals in Milan, wearing costumes which had been paid for by Veischotte. She then sent her troupe back to Paris and moved in with him for two months. Though he obviously carried a lot of weight in Milan, Veischotte was unable to retrieve her impounded baggage. The authorities informed him that Mistinguett's costumes would be auctioned towards the war effort, and though he had no reason to do so, Veischotte offered her compensation by financing two films. *La Double Blessure* and *Vanna* were shot in

October 1915, and were not unsuccessful in Italy and France. By this time Italy had entered the war as an ally of France and Mistinguett was acclaimed in Milan as an unofficial representative of her country. She sang 'La Marseillaise' on the balcony of the town hall, and was not afraid of shedding a few tears!

The next morning she left for Paris. Veischotte accompanied her to the railway station, where he presented her with a platinum ring set with diamonds. Mistinguett accepted the ring, but she politely turned down Veischotte's marriage proposal. The problems with her impounded costumes would drag on for more than two years, when the theatre director in Milan agreed to give them back on condition that Mistinguett signed a contract to appear at his establishment without pay. She surprised him, and her entourage, by accepting, which goes to show how much her fabulous costumes must have been really worth.

On 5 November 1915 Mistinguett appeared in a charity show for wounded soldiers at the Olympia, and for the first time in her life broke down on stage. This evening may justifiably be regarded as the turning-point in her career, emotionally and professionally. She was transformed from a vixen into a tender, warm-hearted woman, and even when she performed the semi-comical 'Je Me Fais Petite', all the emotion of the traditional *chanteuse-réaliste* was there. The audience, who had made her cry, now found themselves dabbing their eyes:

> Je me fais petite-toute-petite,
> On n'me vois pas,
> On n'sait pas qu'je suis là!
> Je comprends bien que sur terre,
> Y a pas d'soleil et lumière
> Pour nous pauvr's gens. . .

> (I become small-so-small,
> One doesn't see me
> Or know that I'm there!
> I understand well that on earth
> There's no sunshine or light for we poor folk!)

The soldiers were so moved by the song – even though Mistinguett admitted that she was only taking the mickey out of herself – that they asked her if they could take it back to the trenches and adapt it as their anthem! She was not sure about this. 'Je Me Fais Petite' was hardly in the same league as 'Roses of Picardy'! However, when one of the commanding officers told her that he had been approached by Damia with a request for permission to sing one of her creations, 'La Malédiction', on the actual battlefield in Flanders, Mistinguett changed her mind. This was perhaps just as well for the soldiers, for the Damia pastiche really has to be heard to be believed, and is considered so morbid that even today some radio stations will not play it on the air.

Since returning from America, the great *chanteuse* had found it hard to secure engagements in Paris, and consequently had opened her own establishment, the Concert-Damia in the heart of Montmartre. She was the first singer in France to perform with a spotlight directed on her face, and her reviews were nothing short of sensational. Mistinguett had been to see her out of curiosity – incognito, of course – but the only thing which had appealed to her about the Concert-Damia was the fact that it had been teeming with homosexuals. It was even suggested that Damia's lover, Fyodor Chaliapin, was having a secret affair with one of the stage hands!

Towards the end of November 1915, Mistinguett was approached by the writer Michel Carré and offered the lead part in his new revue, *Taisez-Vous, Méfiez-Vous*, in other words, Shut Up and Watch Out. The show opened on 21 December at the Scala, and in it she alternated between the role of a chimney-sweep called Jessy, and that of a drunken has-been café-concert *chanteuse*! The revue was very successful, and incredibly she found the time to make another film, *Mistinguett Détective*, which was one of her better silent films.

It was at the Scala, on 6 January 1916, that she was brought the distressing news that Maurice Chevalier had been wounded and·taken prisoner. She later said that she had 'died' on this day, and most ironically she *would* die on that same day, exactly forty years later.

There was absolutely no question of 'the show must go on'. Mistinguett cancelled her performance that night, only hours before curtain-up. She was not yet sure where Chevalier was being held captive, but she knew exactly what to do; it was as if she had anticipated something like this happening, and it mattered little to her that there were thousands of wives and girl friends throughout France experiencing the same anguish. The message told her, point-blank, that Chevalier had had his eyes put out and his hands cut off. She was sensible enough to realize that this was probably an exaggeration meant only to cause her consternation, but she also realized that Chevalier was not a regular he-man, and that if he had not been injured physically he may have been mentally scarred.

Furnished with the necessary documents, she set off the following afternoon for Geneva which, in addition to housing the headquarters of the International Red Cross, was a veritable hot-bed of double-dealing and espionage. It is quite likely that she had worked with the young Dutch-Javanese dancer born Gertrud Margarete Zelle, who as Mata Hari had been performing all over Europe, and especially in Paris where she had settled just before the war. Like the popular singer, Berthe Silva, she had developed a passion for riding in the Bois de Boulogne wearing the top hat and black veil of a bygone age, and she was almost certainly an acquaintance of the dreaded Liane de Pougy. When Mistinguett set off for Switzerland, Mata Hari's contacts with the German secret service were on the train, watching her every movement. However, when the train subsequently pulled up at a level crossing just outside Sens, it was boarded by French soldiers carrying bayonets and she was arrested.

Mistinguett was not afraid of admitting her mission, after all, Chevalier was a prisoner of war, and amongst her papers it appears there was a document bargaining for his release. The soldiers only ridiculed her. She was made to strip and given an old sweater to cover her blushes. Even so, she refused to give in and demanded to see the commanding officer, only to be told that he was busy playing poker. Barefoot, hungry and shivering, she was locked into a room and given no indication as to when she would be set free. When morning came there was still no sign of the commanding officer, and she was made to walk across the town, still in a state of semi-nakedness, to appear before the local *commissaire de police*. To a certain extent, Fate came to her rescue here, for the *commissaire* knew her personally . . . some years before, he had worked as a gendarme at Pointe-Raquet, and before transferring to Sens had been *commissaire* for Montmorency. Mistinguett's clothes were returned to her, and she was ensconced in a hotel for the night whilst the man made a few discreet enquiries. In effect, these amounted to little and she was advised to go back to Paris. The same soldiers who had arrested her escorted her to the railway station but she tricked them into believing she had had her handbag stolen, and when they chased after the 'culprit' she sneaked onto the train bound for Geneva.

In Geneva she was granted an interview with the director of the International Red Cross who agreed to help her. She was installed at the Hotel Beaurivage and told to be patient: patience, of course, was not one of her finer virtues and she was terrified of being recognized. Several days later Chevalier was located in a prison camp in Germany. Though not seriously hurt, he was reported to be on the verge of a mental breakdown, and simply having his address did not satisfy Mistinguett. She arranged for a food parcel to be sent to him and returned to Paris to take the matter further.

Emile Buré was private secretary to the cabinet minister Aristide Briand, whose ideology was that progress should not be made in winning wars, but in preventing them. It was Buré who suggested penning an appeal to the Spanish king.

Mistinguett and Alfonso XIII were already acquainted. He and his queen had visited Paris in the autumn of 1913, and one of the non-political highlights of the visit had been Mistinguett's revue at the Théatre des Variétés. After the show she had been invited to supper and had been much impressed by the handsome young king who had informed her, tongue in cheek, that his favourite pastimes included tennis, polo and making love to beautiful women. Alfonso also found time, during the course of the evening, to show her some of his battle scars. In all, he would survive thirteen attempts on his life, but the worst had been on his wedding day in 1906. His bride was Princess Victoria Eugénie, a grand-daughter of Queen Victoria. During the royal procession in Madrid a fanatic had tossed a bouquet of flowers containing a bomb into one of the carriages: seventy-five people had been killed, but the king and queen had escaped with cuts and bruises. Mistinguett did not like Victoria Eugénie, however, especially when she informed her that she preferred Feydeau farces to revues! And she was more than a little disappointed when, after their supper, Alfonso declined to accompany her back to her apartment!

Now, Alfonso did not hesitate. He wrote to her within a few days and informed her that 'Operation Villefleur' had already begun, and that news of Chevalier's release would be imminent. Mistinguett wrote her lover a long letter, but instead of sending it by courier she ultimately decided to deliver it personally. First of all, she sent for her mother and brother; they spent the night at her new apartment at 24 Boulevard des Capucines, whilst Chevalier's mother, La Louque, fetched Mistinguett's son from the de Lima household. The next morning she escorted her family to a villa she had rented at Paramé: the Germans were now within sixty miles of Paris, and there were rumours that the capital would soon be occupied. Outside Paramé, she was arrested for the second time. For some weeks the police had been searching for a female spy. All that was known of this woman was that she was a show business personality, and that she owned a grey car similar to Mistinguett's. In the light of what happened next, it seems likely that she was who everyone in the region thought she was. She was subjected to the most gruelling interrogation by the *commissaire de police* and forced to submit to a rigorous body search. She handled the situation well, and of course nothing was found and she was allowed to travel on to Geneva. Here, a message was waiting for her from Chevalier: Tell Monsieur De Villefleur That I Thank Him From The Bottom Of My Heart.

Operation Villefleur had succeeded, and Mistinguett was told that Chevalier would be released within a few weeks. However, her Geneva adventure was far from over. Whilst staying at the Hotel Beaurivage she was approached by a representative of the German ambassador, who attempted to press her into spying against France. It was the only way, he declared, that she would ever see Chevalier again. For twenty-four hours she hovered between becoming a traitor or losing the man she loved, and of course there was no question of either. Thus, under threat of death from the Germans, she confided in an agent from the Deuxième Bureau and accepted a better offer: whilst pretending to spy for the enemy, she would be working for France.

Absolutely nothing is known of Mistinguett's activities whilst working for the Deuxième Bureau, though evidence has recently come to light of the danger she was subjected to. One night she was invited to a dinner party given in honour of the German chief of counter-espionage, and it was here that she was exposed for double-dealing and arrested. Her trial was both clandestine and perfunctory, but the outcome was that she was sentenced to be shot. What saved her life was the fact that a number of Germans had been taken hostage by her fellow patriots in Geneva – these included the young wife and daughter of the Kaiser's secretary and two un-named agents of the German secret service. Mistinguett was allowed to return to Paris, and two weeks later, in October 1916, she was reunited with Chevalier.

Chevalier ought to have shown at least a little gratitude towards this remarkably brave woman who, though not in the best of health at the time, had put her own life on the line in order to save his. He did not. He had only been back in Paris a few weeks before he began revealing his true colours.

> I will never forget the train, and the railway station that day. My heart was a-glow, after twenty-six months of separation. Provisionally, we were no longer Mistinguett and Chevalier, but two reunited lovers. Then he asked me to leave him alone, and I thought I understood why. His captivity had broken his spirit. He knew that he would have to go back to square one with his career, and as he had no money he had no alternative other than to accept my hospitality. I never minded helping him, and I tried to ignore the fact that when he finally found the one thing he had been searching for, he would not be sharing it with me.

Had it not been for Mistinguett, it is extremely doubtful that Maurice Chevalier's 'second' career would have got under way. Few impressarios and theatre directors in Paris wanted to have anything to do with him, though there was apparently no reason for this. Damia's treatment by the same handful of insensitive people after her provincial tour has already been mentioned. During the latter part of 1916, Mistinguett turned down several promising revues because the writers had been against her idea of having Chevalier's name in letters the same size as hers on the billboards. She was told, bluntly, that if she was expecting such a thing, then by the time it happened she herself would be too old to stand on a stage. As a last resort, she went to see the directors of the one theatre she hoped might come up with a solution to her problem . . . the Folies-Bergère.

Léon Volterra and his partner, Beretta, had enough problems of their own without wishing to be involved in a wrangle with Mistinguett. They had just taken over the Olympia from Joseph Oller, and Volterra was talking of rejuvenating the Casino de Paris, whose popularity had slumped since the start of the war. Beretta was against the idea, and Mistinguett caught him in one of his worst moods, if this was at all possible. He flatly refused to have Chevalier anywhere near his theatre! Mistinguett knew that in persisting she would be tempting fate as far as her own career was concerned. She told Beretta that Chevalier was so hard up that he would be willing to work for three hundred francs a night. Beretta compromised by saying that he was worth no more than fifty. After more outbursts of temper, Mistinguett was given the go-ahead to include Chevalier in her next revue, and the fee was doubled. She herself made it up to four hundred francs, and Chevalier was never made any the wiser. *La Grande Revue Des Folies-Bergère* opened on 15 March 1917, and served to prolong the passionate side of the 'affaire Chevalier-Miss' for a few more months, though within a week of the première both were looking for new bed mates, and by the time it ended they were hardly on speaking terms. Mistinguett had by this time found a new way of incurring Chevalier's ire: he was not allowed inside her apartment on Boulevard des Capucines unless there was a scarlet ribbon tied to the railings of her balcony. Otherwise there was a printed notice which read 'Enter At Your Own Risk!' In spite of this, Mistinguett still admitted to her friends that she was head over heels in love with the man!

At the Folies-Bergère, Mistinguett was clearly riding on the crest of a wave. The directors of the theatre, however, were finding life together impossible, and during the run of *La Grande Revue* Léon Volterra moved out and finally took over the Casino. He then teamed up with the writer Jacques Charles, who had just completed a revue which he boasted would put all the others to shame. This was *Laissez-Les Tomber*, and though Mistinguett was Volterra's obvious choice, because she would not work anywhere without Chevalier, the leading role was offered to someone else.

Gabrielle Caire, later to take the name of Gaby Deslys, had been born in Marseilles in 1881, and until around 1905 had fared little better than being given walk on parts in the local theatres. She had then decided to take Paris by storm, and had proved such a nuisance pestering directors that one of these had packed her off to New York just to get rid of her. As shrewd as she was pretty, and no doubt because she was willing to sleep with anyone who would offer her work, she had ended up a major star across the Atlantic. Her début, in November 1911, had her playing a waif who wanted to sell herself in order to become famous in the theatre, and was based on one of Mistinguett's revues. It was in her dressing room, one night after her show, that she met the man who would change her life.

Because she was French, many Americans wrongly assumed that Gaby Deslys was more sexually liberated than their own women. Within weeks of her début in New York she had received a large number of marriage proposals. Manuel, King of Portugal, had pledged to give up his throne for her hand, but she had turned him down. On this particular occasion, some twenty admirers had crowded into her dressing room. Most had brought her huge bouquets of flowers and had been recompensed by a kiss. One tall, dark young man with a brooding disposition had brought only himself . . . Gaby had observed him standing in a corner, but as soon as she had approached him he had sloped off without saying a word. Intrigued, she had asked around and had been told his name – Harry Pilcer – and that he was currently appearing in a revue off Broadway.

The following night, it was she who was to be found waiting in Pilcer's dressing room. Pilcer smiled, and told her that he had been expecting her. Gaby was astonished by his charm, and the fact that he was the most handsome man she had ever seen. Moreover, he informed her that he had a gift, worth ten times more than all the flowers in the world. Nothing delighted Gaby Deslys more than receiving expensive presents. She had a massive collection of furs and jewels. Pilcer said that his gift was so special that it might be best to wait until they got back to his place before she unwrapped it. This made her suspicious . . . she demanded that it should be there, within the comparative safety of his dressing room, or not at all. Pilcer shrugged his shoulders and slowly removed his clothes. Gaby was surprised, but not shocked, that he had tied a pink bow around his private parts. . .

In spite of their unconventional meeting and his apparent machismo, Harry Pilcer was not all that he seemed. Though an American citizen, his parents had come from Budapest and until the age of

sixteen the young Pilcer had barely spoken a word of English. By
this time he had made up his mind to become a dancer, and in order
to pay for his lessons he began working as a male prostitute on the
street corners of Brooklyn. Soon afterwards he was picked up by an
impressario who told him that these were a waste of time. Pilcer had
a style of his own which was so remarkable that he was immediately
put into a revue on Broadway. In November 1909, when he was still
only 20, he travelled to Chicago and topped the bill at the Princess
Theatre in *Flirting Princess*. From then on he toured America with
tremendous success and eventually returned to New York, and his
meeting with Gaby Deslys.

In November 1911 the couple opened in *Vera Violetta* at the
Winter Garden, and though the star of the show was Al Jolson,
it was Deslys and Pilcer who brought the house down every night
dancing the Gaby Glide, choreographed by Pilcer himself to Louis
Hirsch's music, and there were over a hundred performances. The
Deslys-Pilcer-Jolson trio had another success at the same theatre in
June 1913 with *Honeymoon Express*. One night, when Jolson was
unable to perform, Harry Pilcer sang 'You Made Me Love You' to
a young man sitting in the stalls. In spite of his affection for Gaby
Deslys, Pilcer went off with him after the show and this resulted in
his theme tune, 'I'm Just Wild About Harry', being written several
years later in memory of a night of passion. It was included in the
1921 Broadway revue, *Shuffle Along*, whose chorus line contained
Joséphine Baker.

The really big Pilcer-Deslys revue was Irving Berlin's *Stop! Look!
Listen!* which opened shortly before Christmas 1915 at the New York
Globe. They danced the ragtime non-stop for thirty minutes, and as a
result of their success were offered a contract with the Globe Theatre,
London. Their success there was even more astonishing than it had
been in New York, and the news swept across the Channel like wildfire to reach the ears of Mistinguett and Jacques Charles, who was in
the middle of scripting a new revue.

Jacques Charles maintained that he had written *Laissez-Les
Tomber* with Pilcer and Deslys in mind, though this could not
possibly have been true, and insisted that they take on the lead roles
at the Casino. He and Léon Volterra travelled to London to see them at
the Globe, and were amazed at the transformation in Gaby Deslys. In

America she had discovered the jazz band, then unheard of in France, and though her songs still left much to be desired, they were full of Americanisms and innuendos and Volterra was utterly convinced that she would eclipse even Mistinguett. And Jacques Charles, astonished by Harry Pilcer's openness, immediately fell in love with the man, though he must have been sorely disappointed when Pilcer told him to his face that the feeling was not mutual. From now on he would only have eyes for his pretty little dancer. When Gaby Deslys died suddenly in 1920 she was still in her prime, and Pilcer became so ill that it was rumoured he would never dance again; only Mistinguett was capable of saving him from suicide. In Gaby's memory he constructed a chapel in his villa and filled it with her portraits. His most cherished one still hangs over the altar to this day.

Laissez-Les Tomber opened in the summer of 1917, and one of its most famous scenes depicted a line of ladders from which semi-naked chorus girls descended onto the stage, hence the title. Pilcer himself, whom one contemporary critic described as the most beautiful man in the world, wore a skimpy tunic . . . half-way through his spot he danced out of this to reveal not much underneath. The audience went wild, and after the night of the première he soon attracted a massive homosexual following. The most thrilling scene saw Pilcer in a tuxedo, dark hair sleeked back, dancing a series of complicated routines up and down the ladders with Gaby Deslys, who was drenched in gorgeous pink ostrich feathers. This went on for more than thirty minutes, and of course for Pilcer and Deslys a simple orchestra would have been grossly inadequate. Their finale was an extremely noisy affair, organized by Pilcer's brother, Murray, who had been brought over from Chicago to play the ragtime, complemented by the wailing of sirens, saxophone blasts and revolver shots. It ended with a number so ferociously sensual that many prudes in the audience walked out in disgust. This was 'Le Jazz-Band'.

> Y a du jazz-band partout, le jour et la nuit,
> Y a du jazz-band partout, bonjour Paris!
> Y a des jazz-bands qui rendent les hommes fou!
>
> (The jazz-band is everywhere, day and night,
> The jazz-band is everywhere, hello Paris!
> There are jazz-bands which drive men insane!)

Though Pilcer's and Deslys's popularity came close to that of Mistinguett, she was never jealous of their success. During the past twenty years she had watched a number of stars who had twinkled but for a moment before fading into obscurity. The word superstar had not yet been invented, but she herself would eclipse them all by being herself. Within Harry Pilcer she recognized a supreme natural talent ... even if he had not been quite so handsome, he could not possibly have failed to make it to the top. Gaby Deslys, on the other hand, she only recognized as a mere flash in the pan who had earned a lot of money and won many hearts because of her looks. Once the ageing process began showing up under the lights, Mistinguett said, Gaby Deslys would curl up and die.

In fact, this is exactly what happened, though in Deslys's case she was helped along by consumption. Shortly before her thirty-ninth birthday, she collapsed and died in Pilcer's arms. Mistinguett is reputed to have been devastated by the news of her death. For two years she had been trying to woo Pilcer into her bed, but in spite of his promiscuous past he had stayed faithful to Gaby Deslys. Eventually she had given up on him to focus her attention on Maurice Chevalier, who was apparently misbehaving himself again with Fréhel.

During the early years of the war, this young woman had given up modelling to concentrate on her career as a *chanteuse*. Her first record, 'Comme une Fleur', had been released back in 1912, and had actually been dedicated to Chevalier. Mistinguett sang the song a few years later, ostensibly to teach her how the song *should* have been sung, and in fact both versions sound equally dreadful. As *La Grande Revue des Folies-Bergère* was drawing to a close, much to everyone's relief, word was brought to Mistinguett that Chevalier had been sneaking back to the theatre after hours to meet Fréhel in his dressing room. She immediately hired someone to keep tabs on him, and when this contact knocked her up in the middle of the night she was so eager to exact her revenge that she left the apartment with a coat thrown over her night dress, under which she had concealed a meat-cleaver! Chevalier was caught 'in the act', and when the police arrived a little later they discovered her chasing him round the dressing room, threatening to emasculate him!

The gendarmes were so amused that they never even charged her, and out of gratitude she offered them free seats for the following evening's performance. Chevalier, of course, was pardoned for his part in the affair. He told Mistinguett that Fréhel had led him on, she believed him and the young singer was so terrified that a few weeks later she left Paris. It was during her exile, in 1920, that she was badly injured in a car crash, and when she eventually returned to the city she was no longer a threat . . . her weight had risen from eight to eighteen stones, and the fact that men no longer found her attractive endeared her towards Mistinguett, who became one of her best friends.

Towards the end of 1917, Pilcer and Deslys were offered a contract with the Folies-Marigny for a staggering two hundred thousand francs (Edith Piaf earned the same amount, but that was forty years later). Though the new revue was not scheduled to open until the following February, Pilcer was concerned for Gaby's precarious health and advised her to drop out of *Laissez-Les Tomber* and rest for a while, which she reluctantly did. Volterra was left with a seemingly unfathomable problem – the revue at the Casino was fully booked for the next few weeks, and only one star in Paris was capable of taking over from Gaby Deslys. This was Mistinguett. She was asked if she would dance with Pilcer but refused because she knew that if she did it would cause an eruption in her private life. Even though he was bisexual, and narcissistic to the point that he would spend hours before every performance gazing at his naked form in the dressing room mirror, she realized that he was twice the man Chevalier would ever be. Volterra then asked Pilcer to leave the show and this of course resulted in the most violent quarrel. Pilcer's temper was unpredictable, and though he had been a major star in Europe for less than a year he was thoroughly opposed to being upstaged by a man who, though by now possessed of a passable singing voice, could not dance. For the rest of his life, Pilcer would loathe him and make no secret of the fact. Occasionally, they would find themselves participating in the same revue. In 1936, at a gala benefit for the widow of the great clown, Antonet, they shared the same bill as Mistinguett, and actually ended up fighting in the dressing room. By this time, of course, she was no longer amorously interested in either of them.

Even so, Mistinguett was reluctant to allow Léon Volterra to monopolize her career, and before moving to the Casino she appeared with Chevalier in two minor revues at the Ba-ta-clan: *Mistinguett* and *Gobette of Paris*. In the latter she sang the most poignant little love song to a pot dog, which was meant to be a personal message to the alleged man in her life:

> Elle ne l'aimait pas, lui non plus,
> Quelle drôle de chose qu'dans l'existence
> Deux amants peuvent fair connaissance,
> Mais ils ne s'étaient jamais vus. . .
>
> (She didn't love him, he likewise,
> How funny that in life,
> Two lovers can be acquainted,
> But unable to stand the sight of each other . . .)

The new *Laissez-Les Tomber* almost eclipsed the Pilcer–Deslys triumph, though many of the dandies sitting in the front stalls were disappointed that they were seeing Chevalier and not Pilcer. Mercifully, perhaps, he kept his clothes on during the famous ladders scene. The night of the première was not without event. Whilst Mistinguett and Chevalier were in the middle of a duet, Paris was shelled by Big Bertha. Subsequently, the revue was nicknamed *BOUM!*

Although they were gradually getting to hate each other, Mistinguett and Chevalier did agree to appear together in the next major Jacques Charles revue at the Casino, *Pa-Ri-Ki-Ri*. There were so many rows during rehearsals that both the writer and the director seriously considered cancelling the production. Chevalier, boasting of his success in the previous revue, asked for his name to appear in letters the same size as those of his leading lady. For the time being the terms of his contract would not allow this, but he was nevertheless bitter and aggressive and attempted to intimidate her by threatening to walk out on her. This precipitated her involvment with perhaps the most bizarre of all her admirers . . . the costume designer, Gesmar.

When Gesmar met Mistinguett in 1918 he was still only seventeen years of age. A native of Nancy, he had arrived in Paris three years previously, armed only with a box of crayons and a head full of brilliant ideas. Andrée Spinelly had found his designs so fascinating that she had engaged him on the spot. Effeminate and neurotic, he had attempted suicide in her apartment after a lover's tiff and she had thrown him out. Mistinguett proved much more understanding. She missed her own son terribly, and Gesmar was able to fill this gap in her life without presuming upon her in any way. Whilst working with her on the designs for *Pa-Ri-Ki-Ri*, he poured out his lamentable life story, and soon afterwards she unofficially adopted him. For the next fourteen years she would hardly ever be seen in public without him trailing behind her like a faithful little dog. She found him an apartment in the adjoining block on the Boulevard des Capucines, and because of the way he fussed over her soon began calling him Maman', something which only angered Chevalier. All the same, it was Gesmar who attempted to keep the couple together, and he had almost succeeded in doing so when Chevalier offered Mistinguett an ultimatum. The incident, and what was said, was well-publicized:

Chevalier: Either I have my name in lights, the
             same size as yours, or I go for good!
Mistinguett: Fine! Don't forget to close the door
             as you leave!

On the political front, Germany's downfall was hastened by the collapse of her three major allies – Turkey, Austria and Bulgaria. On 3 November 1918 fighting broke out amongst the German fleet at Kiel and rapidly spread to a number of other ports. The socialists in Berlin ceased supporting the government and seven days later the Kaiser abdicated and fled into Holland. The following morning, in the Forêt de Compiègne on the banks of the Oise, the Armistice was signed in a railway carriage and the First World War ended four hours later.

Mistinguett's personal war, on the other hand, would rage on for another eight months – and there would be no talk of any Armistice.

'I'm Just Wild About Harry!'

There was absolutely no question of a reconciliation between Mistinguett and Chevalier. When she loved a man, everything else outside her career was swept aside. Hers was the divine right to cheat, of course, but when the roles were reversed, no amount of persuasion would get her to change her mind. Her praise of Chevalier in the first volume of her memoirs is both prosaic and passionate, and yet her reasons for seducing him initially, as has been seen, were nothing to do with love in the conventional sense. Physically, he was the least attractive of all her lovers. Colette, who met him in Lyons in 1908, and who used him the basis of her character Cavaillon, in *The Vagabond*, had not been very impressed:

> He is a tall young man who walks like a human snake, as if he has no bones, and whose anxious, wandering, pale blue gaze tells of acute neurasthenia. . .

This apparent neurosis was often discussed by Chevalier himself in his autobiography, *I Remember It Well*, which was published only a few months before his death in 1972, just after he had attempted suicide:

> I am a simple type . . . the man of my one-man shows. Anything that does not go along with this side of my character only makes me profoundly uneasy. When I go to noisy parties, I feel like a peasant at a palace reception . . . nervous, and tight around the collar. The only places I really feel comfortable are at home with

the people I trust, or all alone on the stage where people have come to see just me, my past and my present.

Though Chevalier ravished his public with his great magnetic charm and personality (frankly, he had little else to offer artistically), if Mistinguett's recollections are anything to go by, even this was suspect.

Chevalier's presence never brought me anything special, but his absence dominated the rest of my life. Was it my fault that he left me? Or was it because I couldn't stop thinking about the boy on the boulevard, trying to impress everyone in his first tuxedo? His head was so swollen with newly-found self-importance, yet he was incapable of scratching his own arse! It is true that he wanted to marry me . . . yet how could someone like me settle down with a man like that? Mind you, I don't think badly of him, even though he treated me badly. In our oasis of happiness, the grass was artificial, and the water always unfit to drink. I never found a single reason to justify loving him. He used me, and as soon as he got what he wanted, he dumped me.

Even so, there was one last attempt to get them to patch up their differences . . . this time it was her revue-writer, Jacques Charles, who inadvertently placed his head on the block. In May 1919 he was one of the privileged few selected to accompany her to her summer retreat at Villerville. The others included Albert Willemetz and Maurice Yvain, and the trio would later collaborate on some of Mistinguett's finest songs and provide others for Chevalier and Joséphine Baker. On holiday, Mistinguett usually liked to live life to the full, but at Villerville she suddenly lapsed into a deep depression. She was in fact suffering from pre-menstrual tension – it was a condition which had plagued her since leaving Enghien – but Jacques Charles was of course unaware of this, and assumed that she must have been pining for Chevalier, who was currently in between revues and staying with his mother. Chevalier was summoned, and though she flew into a rage the moment she saw him, she did take his advice when he suggested that a long sea voyage might assist her condition. She later admitted that this was the only sensible advice that her former lover had ever come up with. Immediately, she set about conquering the United States. After all, if Gaby Deslys had been successful on the other side of the Atlantic, why should not she?

Little is known of Mistinguett's first trip to America. The crossing was a bad one, but she enjoyed the roughness of the waves, probably because she was the only one of her company not to suffer from sea-sickness! She was not impressed, however, by some of her fellow travellers. Besides a group of American industrialists, there were several members of the English aristocracy. These people very soon attempted to befriend her, though she knew all the time that they were only laughing at her behind her back. As usual, she decided upon revenge by shocking them. . .

> I invented a little game. Chairs were arranged in a circle, and I selected a group of handsome young men. First of all I touched them up. Then someone tied a band around my eyes, and they sat down. The object of the game was to sit on the lap of each one, with my hands on my head, and recognize each man by rubbing my thighs against the bulge in his trousers. I have to admit that I won first prize every time. . .

The genuine passengers on the ship, of course, loved every minute of Mistinguett's company. In spite of her wealth, she was never a snob. When they asked her if she would sing them a song, she and her boys put on an entire revue!

Mistinguett's adventure in New York, however, began badly. After the mid-Atlantic revue, Jacques Charles had been given the task of packing her costumes, and it was only after he had locked her trunk that he realized he had forgotten to put some of the items back in! These included several pairs of silk stockings, a night-dress, and a pair of baggy bloomers which she used for one of her comedy routines. Needless to say, his luggage was checked by eagle-eyed customs officials and he was arrested! The reporters on hand to welcome the latest French import made a meal of the episode, and this influenced the Americans' first impressions of her. She returned to Paris in August 1919, probably asking herself why she had bothered going to America in the first place. Her disposition, during the homeward journey, was subdued. She spent much of the time in her cabin. Jacques Charles, when he was not being seduced by one of the ship's stewards, began working on a new revue. This one, he claimed, would be better even than *Laissez-Les Tomber*, and to prove the point he named it *La Grande Revue du Casino*. It opened just four weeks after Mistinguett docked at Le Havre.

La Grande Revue was not one of Mistinguett's favourite shows, probably because she had expected Chevalier to be present at the rehearsals, hoping for a slice of the action. He had, in fact, taken advantage of her absence to escort the British actress Elsie Janus around Paris during her visit to the city, and he had accompanied her back to London where they were appearing in a revue with the Dolly Sisters. Chevalier had learned English from a Durham miner whilst he had been in the army, which explains his accent, which was as curious as it was contrived and which would not improve during the next half century. Mistinguett may have been relieved to find Chevalier gone . . . she was certainly very angry when Léon Volterra brought in Max Dearly at the last moment to share top billing, which must have really rubbed salt into her wounds. It was at the Casino, in September 1919, that he partnered her in the *valse-chaloupée* for the very last time, and until his death in 1943 she never spoke to him again.

Paris qui Danse, which opened in November 1919, was even more of a disaster from a personal stance. Though the revue was immensely successful, Mistinguett was forced to share the bill with Chevalier, fresh from his London triumph. More than this, she had to kiss and serenade him on the stage!

The story-line for the revue was relatively straightforward, if not a little incredulous. The pupils of a boarding school, for some unexplained reason, have consulted with the Confédération Générale du Travail and subsequently gone on strike, and the dance teacher has decided to take his most promising student – which of course had to be Mistinguett, playing the role of Miss Touffue (whose English counterpart is Miss Involved) – on a tour of the world in his aeroplane! During the course of the journey the weather changes constantly, as do the parodies of the operettas and operas native to each country visited. Besides getting himself arrested during Mistinguett's first trip to the United States, Jacques Charles had managed to meet Florenz Ziegfeld, and the American showman had bought the rights to stage some of Charles' ideas in one of his famous Follies, at the New Amsterdam Theatre. In return, Ziegfeld had given Charles permission to use two of his numbers in *Paris qui Dance*. Before an Amsterdam windmill, a bride and groom did a jig whilst singing 'Tulip Time', then collapsed onto a bed of animated tulips. From a giant white grand piano, a succession of operatic heroines arose to a chorus of feathered girls and tuxedoed young beaux who sang 'A Pretty Girl is like a Melody'. The last of all was Venus, straight from the painting by Botticelli, but totally naked – the first time a full-frontal nude had ever been seen on a French stage. Finally, shadowed by the Acropolis, Miss Touffue assumed the identity of Helen of Troy. Mistaking a wedding for a funeral, she made amends by executing a tango with a scantily-clad Greek god!

Mistinguett only found one part of the revue actually humiliating. This was when she had to sing to Chevalier, for the song was 'Comme une Fleur', which had helped to cause the rift between them in the first place.

> Il effeuilla ma pudeur,
> J'trouvais qu'la vie était douce,
> J'en fichais pas une secousse,
> Et comme une fleur
> J'baignais dans le bonheur.

> (He stripped away my petals of modesty,
> I found life was sweet,
> And didn't mind the shock.
> Like a flower
> I bathed in happiness.)

When *Paris qui Danse* closed in the summer of 1920, Jacques Charles had already completed the sequel and Mistinguett was presented with the script. Chevalier had returned to London, and in any case she had already made it clear that she would never work with him again. Though Léon Volterra's offer of a rise in salary was tempting to a woman who was already beginning to develop an inordinate fondness for *le fric*, he was asked to keep the revue on ice. 'The public will have to do without me for a while,' she declared. 'Right now my friends need me more than they do.'

Gesmar, that most complicated of characters, had attempted suicide again because of problems in his love-life. Mistinguett drove him back from the hospital herself and installed him within the apartment on Boulevard Capucines, where with her usual flair for diplomacy she supplied him with a chorus boy to keep him company whilst she looked after Harry Pilcer, on the verge of total breakdown after the death of Gaby Deslys.

The Mistinguett-Pilcer affair is only mentioned briefly in her memoirs, no doubt because doing so caused her great pain. It now seems certain that he was the most important love of her life, even more so than Chevalier. A photograph has come to light since their deaths which displays Mistinguett wrapped in Pilcer's arms, and their expressions do not disguise their affection for each other. Pilcer was never condescending, and because he was as rich and almost as famous as she was, had no excuse for using her as a meal ticket. What he recognized in Mistinguett was not an abundance of feathers and wealth, but a desperately lonely woman who needed to love and be loved. It is true that the events of his disturbed and promiscuous youth do not always present him in a favourable light, and it is also true that Mistinguett once said that she had taken him away from Gaby Deslys in order to exact her revenge on Chevalier. 'I went to see Gaby because she had promised to loan me a dress,' she declared. 'I forgot about the dress, and came home with her man!' Pilcer himself denied this, and there seems no reason not to believe him, considering the way he carried on after Gaby's death.

For several weeks, Mistinguett and Pilcer shared a retreat near Paris, away from the prying eyes of the press. She was so concerned for his health that she barred even his closest friends from coming to see him. The only exception was when Jacques Charles and Léon Volterra arrived for the reading of Gaby Deslys's will . . . she had left every last franc to the poor of Marseilles. Pilcer then admitted that shortly before her death, he and Gaby had made a pact that if one died the other would commit suicide. Mistinguett ignored the remark. Pilcer was a big, tough man, and he was still only 28. She told herself that he would get over his loss. In fact, he was good to his word and a few days later swallowed an overdose of barbiturates which his doctor had prescribed for his depression. Mistinguett herself pumped his stomach, and never left his side for a moment. She, who had thus far in her life treated men like doormats, slept on the floor next to his bed every night, and when he was well enough to travel she took him back to her Paris apartment, where he was 'mothered' by Gesmar and his lover whilst Mistinguett set about organizing his comeback.

Mistinguett was now making records . . . like her former rival, Damia, this aspect of her career came late in life when her singing voice had developed in strength, but at a time when recording techniques were at their best mediocre. She herself would have been the first to admit that she was no singer, at least in the tradition of the *chanteuse-légère*. As has already been explained, she was far better seen than heard, and in some of her raunchier early numbers her voice sounds raw and off-key, which was of course her intention. Her greatest gift in this respect was that she was able to put a song across without paying too much attention to what she considered the inconsequential – key changes, timing and diction. The latter, too, was often made more confusing because her songs were delivered in Parisian argot, the equivalent of the English cockney. Edith Piaf and Fréhel adopted this unusual but astonishing form of dialect for the early part of their careers, but once they became more widely appreciated they changed. Mistinguett never did. This is why attempting to translate her songs into any language but their own presents innumerable difficulties, and one is only able to offer inadequate paraphrases which rob them of most of their effect. It is also a fact that many of these songs are not even transferable to any other singer in French. However, when Mistinguett interpreted a rare tender ballad, the effect was entirely different. Both diction and delivery were spot-on, and the sob in her voice was for real, putting her in the same league as her *réaliste* peers.

'Au Fond de Tes Yeux' may be regarded as the first of the truly great Mistinguett vehicles. It was dedicated to Harry Pilcer, and as such was a heartfelt proclamation of love. It was still in her repertoire in 1935 when Louis Leplée invited her to attend Edith Piaf's début at Gerny's. Mistinguett was horrified when the young singer opened her recital with 'Les Mômes de la Cloche', and would always pretend to dislike her. Even so, she admired Piaf's cheek when she asked her permission to sing 'Au Fond de Tes Yeux', and did not refuse the request. Needless to say, Piaf's respect for this woman was so immense that she never recorded the song.

Au fond de tes yeux,
Que je contemple avec ivresse,
Je devine mieux ce que tu penses.
Je vois un peu de peine,
Et même un gros chagrin.
Je découvre des pleurs parfois
Qu'tu retiens au fond de tes yeux.

(Deep in your eyes,
Which I study with rapture,
I make out your thoughts.
I see a little pain,
Or even a great grief.
Above all I discover the tears
You hold back deep in your eyes.)

Jacques Charles was touched no end by Mistinguett's devotion to Pilcer, and no doubt more than a little envious that the dancer was sharing her bed and not his. In America, Al Jolson was singing 'I'm Just Wild About Harry' and still worshipping him from afar. Jacques Charles made up for his disappointment by assisting Albert Willemetz with the lyrics for Mistinguett's new song, to be included in the revue which had been written some months before, and which was now amended to include several spectacular dance routines by Pilcer. The inspiration for the song had come from Francis Carco's *Mon Homme*, which Jacques Charles had been reading at the time of Gaby Deslys's death. He decided not to change the title because this and the new lyrics expressed exactly how he felt about Harry Pilcer. Many years later, after Pilcer's death in 1961, he wrote, 'He was tall, dark, mysterious and splendidly beautiful. He danced as naturally as most people breathe, and I only wish that I could have got to know him a little better!' Mistinguett was never told the truth, and may not have known that her lover was also attracted towards men. Some years later, Chevalier would tell a reporter, somewhat over-confidently, that he had been the inspiration behind Mistinguett's signature tune, particularly as the music for the song had been supplied by Maurice Yvain, his companion from his army days. There is absolutely no doubt, however, that when she introduced the song in *Paris qui Jazz*, which opened at the Casino in the winter of 1920, she only had eyes for Harry Pilcer.

> Sur cette terre,
> Ma seule joie, mon seul bonheur
> C'est mon homme!
> Quand il m'dit: 'Viens!'
> J'suis comme un chien,
> C'est comme un lien qui me retient.
> J'sens qu'il me rendrait infâme,
> Mais je n'suis qu'une femme,
> Et j'l'ai tellement dans la peau!

> (My only joy and happiness on earth
> Is my man!
> When he says: 'Come!'
> I'm like a dog,
> It's like a bond holding me back.
> I feel that he's making me infamous,
> But I'm only a woman,
> And I've got him under my skin!)

'Mon Homme' remains Mistinguett's most popular international success, and has sold millions of records. However, she was not the first to record it. It was translated into English and became 'My Man', and the original American Funny Girl, Fanny Brice, committed it to shellac in November 1921, seven months after *Paris qui Jazz* had closed in Paris. Mistinguett did not record it until 1938, though by this time she too had sung it phonetically in English, during her frequent visits to London and New York. Unlike many French songs which often lose out in translation, 'Mon Homme' sounds just as good in any language.

The highlight of *Paris qui Jazz* was Jacques Charles' tableau, 'Fashion Through the Ages', for which Maurice Yvain had composed the music. The costumes and designs were by Poiret and Erté (of whom more later) and Mistinguett was asked to play Rose, after the then fashionable Côty perfume. Her dress, one of the most stunning she ever wore, consisted of ten thousand pastel-coloured rose petals, ranging from full-blown to faded. The latter she disapproved of. She accused Erté of hinting that she was getting past her best and declared, 'I must have roses which are freshly-picked, with dew-drops still on them . . . dew-drops which are made from diamonds!' Poiret and Erté could only follow her instructions. Besides designing her stage clothes they also dressed her for private engagements and fashioned all her jewellery. The ensuing dress cost several millions of francs, but it ran away with the show against a backdrop which would today be financially impossible to stage. Pilcer played Charlie Chaplin, Sinbad the Sailor and Ali Baba to Mistinguett's Scheherazade, and in one scene she appeared as a frisky white filly with him putting her through her paces with a whip!

Mistinguett was now the hottest property in France and the highest paid female entertainer in the world. Yet within two weeks of leaving the Casino she would be catapaulted to unprecedented heights and take on a challenge which would prove as astonishing as it was successful.

Her friend Robert de Flers approached her with a message from the great classical actress, Réjane. This legendary lady, the darling of socialite Paris, had created the heroine of Victorien Sardou's play, *Madame Sans-Gêne*, shortly before the author's death in 1908. She had now decided to revive it, but as she herself was too ill to take on the demanding role, she specifically asked for Mistinguett, whom she considered to be the next best thing. Mistinguett was terrified, probably thinking that the critics would accuse her of emulation. Though she had appeared in a number of straight plays early on in her career, she had never considered herself to be a serious actress, and had witnessed countless young hopefuls fall by the wayside when attempting a medium far different from their own. Even so, the piece was not without an element of personal tragedy. She was given the script to read . . . this was full of unconventional prose, cleverly combined with argot, and was not easy to deliver even by an experienced tragedienne. For this reason, Réjane promised to attend each rehearsal to put her through her paces. Mistinguett waited patiently, but this never happened. When on the third day she visited Réjane's apartment to enquire if all was well, the maid told her that the great lady had passed away during the night.

Robert de Flers suggested cancelling the play, or at least holding back until after Réjane's funeral as a mark of respect. Mistinguett declared that as she already knew the part, there was no point in this. The play opened at the Théâtre de la Porte Saint-Martin, and before going on stage Mistinguett told her audience that the applause should not be for her, but for her famous friend. With Pierre Magnier interpreting the role of Napoléon, it was an immense success and ran for several months, though it did inadvertently cause a major upheaval in her personal life. Pilcer, neglected and agoraphobic, was on the verge of another breakdown. Gesmar was still living at the apartment on the Boulevard des Capucines, even though he had ended his relationship with the chorus boy, and he now set about effecting a cure of his own. Whenever Mistinguett was playing a matinée he would invite his friends over to a party, and Pilcer would be forced to grin and bear it. One of these was the entertainer Marie Dubas, and though Pilcer did not fall in love with her, she would remain a friend for the rest of his life, and always get on with Mistinguett. Another was a young dancer called Jenny Golder.

Jenny Golder was an up-and-coming young force who had more than a little in common with Pilcer. She was an American, and even more highly-strung than Gaby Deslys had been. She was also nearer to his own age than Mistinguett, and though not as talented, almost as attractive. The parties stopped . . . the cunning Gesmar had achieved his ambition, and he moved back into his own apartment, leaving the couple to make hay whilst the sun shone.

Mistinguett had decided not to accept another season of *Madame Sans-Gêne*, ostensibly because Jacques Charles had written another Casino revue, and Léon Volterra had upped her salary by fifty per cent.

The rehearsals for *Paris en l'Air*, which opened with a blaze of publicity on 29 October 1921, had everyone living on their wits. Pilcer had fallen in love with Jenny Golder, who was still visiting the apartment, but pretending to be Marie Dubas' companion. Mistinguett did not mind this. She wanted to get Marie on her side because she had just appeared in *Dans un Fauteuil* at the Casino with Chevalier. Mistinguett thought they might have been having an affair, so she asked Léon Volterra to give Marie a part in the new revue. Pilcer, not to be outdone, asked for Jenny Golder to be considered, and with Mistinguett's approval she was offered a non-singing role. Had Mistinguett foreseen what would happen she might have had second thoughts . . . Jenny Golder went on to steal the show!

Pilcer was asked to play opposite Mistinguett in the revue, but apparently declined on account of his health. This did not present any particular problem. During the run of *Madame Sans-Gêne*, Jacques Charles had spent a few days in London, a guest of Charles Cochrane, his British equivalent, and here he had been introduced to Earl Leslie, a handsome young dancer who had been starring in a revue at the Globe with the popular Dolly Sisters. Unable to resist a pretty face, especially a male one, Jacques Charles set about securing Leslie for his new revue. He and Mistinguett travelled to London to finalize the deal, and during their absence Harry Pilcer moved out of Mistinguett's apartment and into Jenny Golder's. It was a big mistake. In spite of her success in *Paris en l'Air*, she proved herself a hopeless entertainer with an acute lack of talent. In order to compete with Mistinguett, she made futile attempts at juggling and dancing, but could not sing. From behind her feathered fan she would wink and pout at her largely homosexual audiences, most of whom were perfectly willing to queue for hours in sub-zero temperatures to buy tickets to watch the lithe, sensual dancing of the real star of the show, Harry Pilcer. Not long afterwards the couple split up. Pilcer bought a villa in the south of France and moved in with a male companion. He declared that after his gruelling affair with Jenny Golder he would never trust another woman as long as he lived. Jenny went on to star in her own revue at the Folies-Bergère, and this was followed by a European tour which was not unsuccessful. Several months later, realizing that she was only a pretty face, and that such an asset is but a poor substitute for talent once the wrinkles start to appear, she shot herself. Meanwhile, Mistinguett had returned from London with Earl Leslie, and within a few weeks he had moved in with her.

Leslie's success in the revue was phenomenal. Between them, he and Marie Dubas created a dance called the Shimmy Dolls. To Maurice Yvain's music they played porcelain figures which climbed out of a musical-box shaped like a wedding-cake. Far from being jealous, Mistinguett encouraged the pair to become friends: her affair with Chevalier had taught her a valuable lesson in diplomacy. Within a decade Marie Dubas would be hailed as *La Fantaisiste des Années Folles*, one of the most famous and respected French singers of all time who was in many ways not unlike our own Gracie Fields. The song which made her in France was an immensely funny piece, 'Pédro', but she had an uncanny knack of switching from buffoonery to drama of the highest intensity. 'La Prière de la Charlotte' was her most celebrated song, and told the story of girl who begs the Virgin Mary to let her die so that her child might not suffer the way she has. Mistinguett rarely praised a fellow artiste, but when this song was released in 1933 she made a point of hurrying to the nearest radio station to put out a personal message of felicitation.

> Marie Dubas has created a veritable masterpiece. It is so sincere and lifelike that you can almost see the poor creature being carted off to heaven. Marie Dubas is the greatest singer in Paris today. I find it impossible to listen to her without bursting into a flood of tears!

Paris en l'Air proved so popular with the public that its run was extended several times: when it closed on 15 April 1922 there had been two hundred and fifty performances in less than two hundred working days. Besides dancing the Shimmy with Marie Dubas, Earl Leslie introduced a dance of his own which he called the Legomania. Mistinguett's most important sketch involved a train which she had prevented from being derailed . . . her skirt came off, of course, revealing her fabulous legs, and she and Leslie executed a high-kicking routine which all but brought the house down every night. Her most successful song, which would remain in her repertoire for another thirty years, was Maurice Yvain and Albert Willemetz's 'J'en ai Marre', which is so full of Parisian slang that parts of it are almost impossible to translate.

> N'croyez surtout pas qu'j'envie ceuss' qu'sont riches,
> Les autos, les bijoux, la grand' vie moi j'm'en fiche,
> Mais enfin tout est bien mal balancé,
> Et l'destin à quoi donc qu'il a pensé,
> Quand certains en ont tant et d'autres pas assez?
> De toujours manger d'la vache enragée,
> Moi j'en ai marre!

(Above all, don't think I envy the rich folk,
I don't care about cars, jewels and the good life,
But in a word, it's all badly balanced,
And what is Fate thinking about,
When some have so much and others not enough?
I'm fed up of having such a rough time!)

Mistinguett was indeed fed up. Earl Leslie may have been keeping her bed warm at night, but he was no substitute for the muscular, irrascible Pilcer, and she admitted herself that he reminded her too much of Maurice Chevalier. She had already been signed up for another revue at the Casino – this was *En Douce* – and was disappointed when the première had to be put off because the building was gutted by fire. As always, when at a loss in her love-life, she decided to go on tour. . .this time Italy and Belgium were too close at hand, and she decided to conquer South America.

Off to the Jungle to
Buy a Monkey!

Mistinguett's next revue at the Casino, *En Douce*, opened in the spring of 1923, almost a year since the last one had closed. Many people suspected that the fire which, because of the iron safety curtain, had gutted the stage but hardly touched the auditorium, was deliberate . . . the same thing had happened at the Moulin Rouge in 1914. Mistinguett, of course, believed that it had something to do with Chevalier wanting to get his revenge after the Pilcer affair, but this was just nonsense. Another suggestion was that the arsonist had a hatred of foreign stars invading French theatres . . . during his visit to the United States, Jacques Charles had signed a contract with the silent movie star, Pearl White, to appear in his production of *Revue aux Etoiles*. What he had not known at the time was that unlike Mistinguett, the celebrated idol of the *Perils of Pauline* had never performed her own stunts, and as many of these had been incorporated into the revue, Charles had found himself faced with the predicament of putting back the première whilst rewriting most of the tableaux. This had caused some consternation amongst her French co-stars, one of whom is alleged to have fired the theatre. Of course, there will never be any proof either way.

Jacques Charles' involvement with Pearl White won him few favours with Mistinguett. She said acidly, 'Why should we have her over here, when the Americans weren't interested in me?' In many ways she was right, though she later blamed herself for invading America when it was not quite prepared for her specialized form of culture! She told Jacques Charles that she would appear in *En Douce* only if he persuaded Léon Volterra to cough up for another tour of

America, ostensibly to prove to Americans that home-grown French talents were preferable to their counterparts on the other side of the Atlantic. One can only imagine her anger and disappointment when Volterra informed her that he was short of funds!

In fact, the revue went ahead as planned. Volterra put her in touch with Madame Rasimi, the director of the Ba-ta-clan, who offered her a contract to play in New York, provided she first of all accepted a tour of South America. Mistinguett signed up for forty five days. She told Léon Volterra, 'I'm off to the jungle to buy me a monkey. Perhaps it'll make a better job of handling my affairs than you!'

Mistinguett's costumes for the show had to be seen to be believed. One was a floor-length gown onto which had been sewn more than a thousand multicoloured silk handkerchiefs, and whose sleeves were twelve feet wide at the cuffs and trailed behind her like a train. In spite of this, she was upstaged by some of her co-stars, especially when the revue went into its second staging in May 1923. These included Damia, Yvonne George and Barbette.

For once, Mistinguett had nothing to reproach Damia for. It is true that on the first day of rehearsals she had turned up wearing a red velvet dress, a gold hat and enough cheap costume jewellery for Sacha Guitry, who happened to be there, to tell her to her face that she looked like a performing flea trainer, but she was no longer interested in dancing, and the Russian Fyodor Chaliapin had been replaced in her affections by the American choreographer-dancer and creator of the Dance of the Seven Veils, Loïe Fuller, with whom she was living in the heart of Montmartre. The fact that she may have been lesbian – something which she always strongly denied – earned her a certain amount of respect from Mistinguett, who still, though, refused to speak to her. Damia followed Sacha Guitry's advice, and encouraged by her manager Paul Franck, the director of the Olympia, she changed into a black, tight-fitting dress and in doing so set a precedent for every single *chanteuse-réaliste* who followed her. During her spot in the revue the backdrop was also black, and she sang 'La Veuve', which suffice to say was the nickname of the guillotine.

Yvonne George, who, had she lived, would almost certainly have eclipsed them all, was on the other hand one of the saddest, most pitiful and most neurotic entertainers ever to face an audience. When she appeared in *En Douce*, singing 'Nous Irons à Valparaiso' and

'Pars', she was twenty three years of age and already suffering from consumption. She too was managed by Paul Franck, who had insisted that she appear in the revue alongside Damia as part of a package deal. Tall and thin, with dyed red hair and a purple gash of a mouth, she disappeared between tableaux to inject herself with cocaine, and always made a point of swallowing an emetic before going on stage to counteract the effects of alcoholism. Had Mistinguett known of this she would have objected. She herself had never taken drugs or drunk more than a glass of wine with a meal, and she had complained to the management about Damia's 'nauseating' habit of chain-smoking.

Real competition, however, came in the form of another great 'lady' of feathers whose name was Barbette.

Mistinguett adored Barbette, who had been born Van der Clyde in Round Rock, Texas, in 1904. As the curtain opened on his tableau, the audience saw a pale blue backdrop, across which had been stretched a tightrope. At first, the beautiful young woman in the blonde wig and enormous ball gown, onto which were attached some fifty pounds of ostrich feathers, was mistaken for the star of the show . . . after all, Mistinguett had performed acrobatics before, and with remarkable skill. Barbette crossed the wire several times, sometimes balancing on one leg, and the act concluded with her unique *chute-d'ange*, wherein she plummeted to a white carpet whilst Edmond Mahieux's orchestra played the lilting theme from *Scheherazade*. Finally, instead of taking the usual bow, Barbette snatched off her wig to reveal a bony, balding head, and the audience was so stupefied on the night of 'her' première that it took them a moment to get their breath back before they burst into applause. Later in his career, Barbette would go one step further by undressing on a couch, and the effect at the end of his act was always the same. Tasteful and elegant, he became one of the highest paid performers in Paris during the twenties and early thirties. Cocteau was so taken by him that he signed him up to play a woman in his surrealist film of 1930, *Le Sang d'un Poète*.

The finale of *En Douce* was really spectacular. During her trip to the United States Mistinguett had discovered a brand of luminous paint especially manufactured to colour flesh, and the tableau opened with a series of naked ebony, onyx, marble and jade 'statues' on a revolve. Suddenly, these moved aside and a glass tank containing twenty thousand gallons of water rose from below the stage, by means of a lift, into which the entire company plunged . . . including Mistinguett!

During the run of the revue, Mistinguett entered into what would be the first of several lucrative business ventures – she opened a cake shop near the Galeries Lafayette, not far from her apartment on Boulevard des Capucines! Her brother Marcel, not at all interested in show-business, had recently begun working for the Bourse, apparently against her better judgement. Stock brokers, she declared, invariably ended up having heart attacks, and rarely lived long enough to retire. When Marcel was asked to hand in his notice by his sister he did so, apparently without creating too much fuss, and Mistinguett installed him as manager of her shop, which she had decided to call Le Père la Galette. The building was a converted stable, and the business was very successful, no doubt because she herself always made a point of stopping off there after the show. Besides Marcel she employed one of the best chefs in Paris, an assistant chef and half a dozen sales-girls. She devised an elaborate gâteau which she named after herself, and did not mind working behind the counter from time to time, where she invariably short-changed the customers, with no questions asked. Le Père la Galette stayed open until 1953.

En Douce closed on 25 May 1923. Two days later, Mistinguett and her company took the train to Lisbon, from whence they set sail for South America. Jacques Charles had left three weeks earlier with the actress-singer Florelle. Mistinguett had not minded this, for the young woman born Odette Rousseau in 1901 was no real threat. During her teens she had appeared in minor sketches at the Cigale, and had recently scored a great success at the Moulin-Rouge. She had also made a number of films with Maurice Chevalier, to which Mistinguett had turned a blind eye because she had it on good authority that her former lover was now having an affair with the singer and dancer Jane Myro, one of the Casino's house-artistes. Had Mistinguett been aware of Jacques Charles' devious plan, however, it is doubtful if she would have left France in the first place.

Jacques Charles had secured engagements for Florelle in the same cities as the ones to be visited by Mistinguett, but not in the same theatres. He had also taken with him most of Mistinguett's songs and sketches. South American audiences, not knowing the difference between an impersonator and the real thing, flocked to see the latest

sensation from Paris. The first port of call was the Cervantes Theatre
in Buenos Aires, where Florelle sang amongst others 'Mon Homme'
and 'J'en ai Marre'. Subsequently, when Mistinguett arrived in the
city she learned to her horror that most of the people who had bought
tickets for her revue had asked for their money back. For the first time
in twenty years she found herself performing in a theatre which was
less than half full, and Earl Leslie was so angry that he threatened to
boycott the tour and return to London. Mistinguett prevented him
from doing this by going to see Madame Rasimi. Instead of giving her
a piece of her mind – and in all honesty, Madame Rasimi could not
be blamed for what had happened, for she too had been duped, and
two years later would be declared bankrupt and forced to close the
Ba-ta-clan – she persuaded her to amend Leslie's contract so that he
got paid at the end of the tour, instead of after each performance. She
then nominated her co-star as her champion, tracked down Jacques
Charles, accused him of treason and organized a duel. Thankfully,
this never took place!

In Montevideo the company fared slightly better, and in Rio de
Janeiro Mistinguett considered herself extremely fortunate because
the audience demanded an encore! She had decided, however, to
end the tour before it became too embarrassing. The contracts were
torn up and returned to Madame Rasimi, who not surprisingly made
herself scarce. Mistinguett then telephoned Florenz Ziegfeld in New
York, against Leslie's advice, and told him point-blank that within a
few weeks she would be paying him a visit and would naturally expect
the lead part in his next Follies! Ziegfeld, never an easy man to get
on with, made it perfectly clear that this was not the American way
of doing things. However, Mistinguett reminded him that his star,
Fanny Brice, had poached her best song and that the least Ziegfeld
could do was offer some sort of compensation. Rather than hang up
on her, the great showman forwarded a contract to her hotel in Rio
de Janeiro!

Before leaving Brazil, Mistinguett decided to broaden her experience of the world by accepting an offer from an Indian tribal chief
to spend a few days in his village. Leaving the fickle Earl Leslie in her
hotel room, she hired a guide to escort her and a few dancers into the
heart of the Amazonian jungle:

The river was three kilometres wide in places, and the natives ran around naked, chasing things with their bows and arrows. I rode on the back of a mule to their settlement. It was midnight, and they held a ceremony in my honour . . . we sat around the fire in the candlelight whilst one of them roasted a child on a spit. It made me feel ill, and I told myself that perhaps I should have gone to see Chinatown instead. A few days later we sailed for New York . . . with the queerest bunch of characters I had ever seen.

The steamer was overloaded with passengers, then, as now, not uncommon in that part of the world. Mistinguett and Leslie were forced to share a cabin with a large family of Chinese and a Hindu cook. She did not mind the Chinese, but the stench from the curry pot, bubbling night and day, nauseated her and after a few days she moved out and camped on the middle deck with the immigrants. Mistinguett was never prejudiced against anyone unless they were snobs, and the lithe young negro ship hands, especially the ones wearing loincloths, made a tedious journey seem worthwhile. In next to no time she had formed an attachment with a young stoker called Casimir. He told her he had been born in France, and of course the inevitable happened and she spent the night in his cabin. When he offered her money 'for services rendered' she was offended, not because he had mistaken her for a prostitute, but because he had failed to recognize her as Mistinguett! She told him to keep his hard-earned cash and added, 'Buy me a monkey instead. That way I'll always have something to remember you by!'

Casimir kept her company throughout the rest of the voyage, and he was good to his word. A few days later he presented her with a marmoset which she immediately baptised Dédé. Two days later the captain himself gave her a chimpanzee, which she named Mon Homme. It was not a gift but an act of revenge on the captain's part because Mistinguett had poached his boy-friend, and it was not until she reached New York that she discovered, more to her amusement than disgust, that it had been taught to masturbate in public. All the same, it formed an integral part of her entourage for some time.

Earl Leslie was not impressed by Mistinguett's behaviour, and when the steamer stopped off at Trinidad for a few days he not surprisingly refused to share a hotel room with her, her lover and her monkeys. The next morning, Casimir took her down to the harbour to watch the pearl-fishers diving into the sea to retrieve the silver coins tossed in by the wealthy American tourists. Mistinguett, always 'one of the boys' and an indefatigable trooper, announced that she herself wanted to have a go. Casimir advised her that this was dangerous, especially in a calf-length dress, and even she would not have stripped off in front of a crowd of strangers. Nevertheless, the first few dives were successful . . . she was a strong swimmer, extremely fit for a woman of almost fifty, and able to compete with the best of them. Then, things went drastically wrong when her dress rose up and wrapped around her face whilst she was on her way back up to the surface. The next thing she knew she was lying on the beach, receiving mouth-to-mouth resuscitation from Casimir. Though subjected to a terrible fright, she soon recovered and returned to the boat to continue her journey as though nothing had happened, and it was only when she reached Cuba that she realized that all was not well. She allowed Earl Leslie to take her to a hospital, suspecting that she had perforated an ear-drum during her diving adventure. The surgeon diagnosed a small growth inside her ear and advised immediate surgery. This meant, of course, that she would have to stay in Havana and catch the next boat to New York, thus missing out on the Ziegfeld revue. Mistinguett decided, as always, that the public must come first. She telephoned New York and arranged to spend several days in a clinic before meeting Ziegfeld. Within hours of setting sail, the pain intensified, and she allowed a poorly-qualified Spanish doctor to operate on her below deck. There was no anaesthetic.

A team of American reporters were waiting to interview her in New York harbour. Most of them had already seen Florelle, and had been greatly impressed by her cool beauty and adorable charm. They took one look at this grumpy woman, sitting on her trunk with her head wrapped in a scarf and with one monkey on her shoulder and another on her knee, and gave her up as a bad job. Earl Leslie booked her into a hotel, and the next morning they went to see Ziegfeld. This great entrepreneur, who had been so excited about meeting the legendary creator of 'My Man', refused to have anything to do with her. His secretary informed her that the revue had not been cancelled . . . there had never been a revue in the first place. Mistinguett is reported to have been 'over the moon' when, six years later, he lost everything after the Wall Street Crash. As a last resort he then asked her to help him out, and deserved her curt refusal. Three years later he died, one million dollars in debt.

For the first time in her life, Mistinguett found herself in a tight corner. Never one to give up a challenge, she realized that this time she would have to submit to defeat, and without seeing any of the sights of New York she booked herself a berth on the next ship to France. As she had very little money, Earl Leslie and most of her company were left to fend for themselves. This was not an act of callousness . . . it was her only choice. She actually got as far as the harbour before being approached by Ziegfeld's rival, a man called Schubert.

Ziegfeld, it appears, was at loggerheads with everyone – this extended as far as his personal relationships not only with the women in his life, but with his friends. He would not pay royalties to his writers and composers, and had a terrible reputation for owing money. Many of the men involved with his revues had received the sharp end of his tongue. Some, like Schubert and Oscar Hammerstein, had been so badly treated in the past that they had vowed never to work with him again. The former, it would seem, only signed up Mistinguett because he wanted to settle a score with his arch-enemy. She did not mind this, though she was sensible enough when signing the contract to demand a down-payment, which she got. This enabled her to make the return trip to Paris to organize the making of her costumes by Erté and Poiret. She would not even consider using any of the American costumiers because at some time or other they had all worked for Ziegfeld. Schubert gave her the script for his revue, *Innocent Eyes*. He had had it especially translated into French. Mistinguett asked for the original, and Schubert hired her an English teacher to accompany her on the voyage. Upon her return to New York, several weeks hence, she would have learned both the script and the language.

One distinguished biographer has somewhat unfairly dismissed Paul Poiret as an updated successor to Boni de Castellane. Though it is true to say that he was very much of a playboy, it must be remembered that, like Mistinguett, he had become rich and very successful only after a great deal of hard work and self-sacrifice, and he certainly was never possessed of any of de Castellane's less savoury habits. The product of a well-placed bourgeois Catholic family, he had rebelled against his parents by leaving home at the age of fourteen to establish an umbrella stall in a department store, after which he had served an apprenticeship with Worth and Doucet. He was fascinated by the East: once he declared, quite seriously, that in a previous incarnation he had been an eastern prince. His costumes were therefore more colourful than those of his contemporaries, with an abundance of gold and scarlet, gilt and beads. The man himself was not at all attractive to look at. He was very fat, and at his countless parties would always appear as a sultan, wearing a cloth-of-gold robe and turban, and sitting on a throne. In spite of their close professional relationship, Mistinguett always refused to go to these, probably because Poiret was a friend of Liane de Pougy, who reminded her too much of her decadent past. As an artist and designer, however, she considered him the greatest innovator of all time. Before working for her he had dressed Mata Hari and Isadora Duncan: for the latter he had gone one step further by designing a windowless room at her mansion. He had also written several one-act plays, and he regularly held exhibitions of his art deco paintings on his barge-restaurant which floated constantly up and down the Seine. Perhaps his most important 'contact' besides Mistinguett was Colette: in 1926 he acted opposite her in the film *La Vagabonde*, which was based on one of her own novels.

Erté, no less flamboyant a character, was a promiscuous homosexual who had been born Romain de Tirtoff in Saint Petersburg in 1892. Speaking of him once, Mistinguett said waspishly, 'He was so camp, next to him even Cocteau looked tough!' The pair had first met around 1916, when Erté, already a leading name in Paris fashion, had been designing costumes for Damia, Fréhel and Gaby Deslys, and she had decided there and then to engage him for herself. This was a simple matter of paying a little more for a product which she claimed was wasted on "otherwise inconsequential nobodies", especially when one of these, she meant Damia, belonged to the race which was inflicting so much misery on her boys in the trenches. His first creation for her had borne the label 'L'Orient Merveilleux', which she had worn during her revue at the Femina. It comprised an ultramarine velvet cloak, with green appliqué motifs and a gold lining and ermine collar. The head-dress had been equally stunning, with fanned-out blue and green egret feathers and no less than two pounds of pearls! In Mistinguett's later revues, Erté really went over the top by designing G-strings (including one for Harry Pilcer) covered in diamonds. Another Erté customer, Ida Rubenstein, was so impressed by seeing Pilcer in all his glory that she commissioned him to design her underwear . . . at the height of the economic depression after the First World War she was reported to be spending no less than thirty thousand francs each month on underwear alone! There is no wonder then, that by the time he began working regularly for Mistinguett, Erté was already one of the richest young men in France. Mistinguett did say in an interview once that of all her designers, barring Gesmar, of course, Erté had remained her favourite because of his exemplary way of life. What she failed to add was that, before handing her his creations, he liked to try them on himself, often in public.

Both Erté and Poiret published their memoirs in later years. Erté, when he was eighty two and still working a twelve-hour day; Poiret, close to death in his filthy attic room, friendless and poverty stricken. Even so, he was able to recapture the glorious years of the twenties:

> Swooning mauves and lilacs, hydrangea blue, honey and corn and straw . . . anything pale, washed-out or insipid had been all the rage for years! All I did was set the wolves loose amongst the lambs . . . reds and purples, and royal blues which taught the world how to sing!

Gesmar, still having problems with his love-life, found himself drafted in to assist the Erté–Poiret team. For five days they worked around the clock, with Mistinguett supervising. It was then that she dropped the bombshell . . . they would have to wait until she returned from New York before getting paid.

Innocent Eyes opened at New York's Winter Garden on 20 May 1924. Two days prior to this she gave a press conference, though she made a point of barring those reporters who had snubbed her earlier. The only problem with her English was that she spoke it with a heavy French accent . . . like Chevalier's it was probably exaggerated because she believed it added to her appeal. Her pronunciation of the name of the revue raised a good many eyebrows and a few laughs as well. *Innocent Eyes* came out as *Innocent Arse*, and the revue found itself involuntarily re-christened! In later years, whenever she thought she recognized an American she would say, 'I remember you. Didn't you come to see my innocent arse?'

Mistinguett made the most stunning entrance the Americans had ever seen, gliding slowly down a silver staircase and wearing a pink gown trailed by a twelve-foot train of ostrich plumes. She sang 'My Man' so convincingly in English that she was applauded and whistled for ten minutes. This of course she misinterpreted as the supreme insult . . . French audiences never whistle unless they are sorely displeased with whoever is on stage. In France it would happen to them all, even to Piaf and Damia, but Mistinguett was having none of it. She flung back a tirade of Parisian argot which might have made a legionnaire blush, and left the stage in a rage. Schubert, waiting in the wings, explained why the audience had whistled: when she returned to the stage, the audience begged her to sing the song again!

> Oh my man, I love him so!
> He'll never know!
> All my life is just despair,
> But I don't care!
> What's the difference if I say
> I'll go away,
> When I know I'll come back
> On my knees some day?
> For whatever my man is,
> I am his for evermore!

Mistinguett, used to having her own way in France, had asked Schubert's permission to stage manage the finale of the revue. This had been denied her. American actresses, she was told – even famous ones – were two-a-penny. Either they did as they were told, or they were replaced. She decided to let this go for the time being. Her partner in the revue was the young American dancer Cecil Lean, formerly a 'friend' of Harry Pilcer. Mistinguett found him arrogant and condescending. She herself had been assigned the dressing room which Pilcer and Gaby Deslys had shared several years before . . . their pictures were still on the wall, and this tiny corner of Paris helped to prevent her spirit from weakening, especially when Lean confidently informed her that the finale which he had helped to devise would go down in history as one of the great moments of American vaudeville. Mistinguett's twenty-five years firsthand experience told her otherwise.

Mistinguett added zest to the role she had played a number of times in the past, and the role which Gaby Deslys had 'borrowed' when making her own American début . . . that of a pitiful little waif who has been sold by her father to the sadistic leader of a gang of thugs, played by Lean. Schubert's idea was that, after dancing the *chaloupée*, Lean should fling her into the river, from which she should emerge dripping wet before singing 'J'en ai Marre' – in English the song was given an almost word-for-word translation and became 'I am Fed Up'. The musicians in the orchestra pit objected to this, and a compromise was reached. For the première, a large sheet of glass was erected centre-stage and the audience, by way of song, were informed that this was the river. Mistinguett was thrown behind it and landed onto a mattress, whilst someone from the property department paddled in a tub of water, making splashing noises. Mistinguett then changed quickly into a replica of the dress which she had worn for the *chaloupée* . . . this had beads sown onto it, supposed to be water! The critics – then as now the Americans had enough weight to close a production after a single performance – absolutely hammered her, and the next day she found herself on the mat in Schubert's office.

Mistinguett did not give in gracefully. Ebullient Americans smoking fat cigars neither impressed nor frightened her, and when Schubert told her that the show would close at the end of the week, she hit the roof! She informed him that she had been engaged for a full season and that she would settle for nothing less. She then went on to demand that Cecil Lean be replaced by Earl Leslie, who was in any case a better dancer. As the latter was appearing in another revue, this was not possible. It was at this stage that Mistinguett threatened to hit the director with her handbag – during the latter half of her career this would be her most formidable weapon barring her fingernails – and he called the security men to have her evicted from his office. Even then, she refused to yield. She told him that unless the revue went ahead, on her terms and no one else's, she would divulge 'certain aspects' of his private life to the press. It is not known for certain what she meant by this, though Schubert must have had something to hide. Anyway, not only did he give her a free hand in the revue, he increased her salary!

The revised finale was a tremendous success. Instead of the mattress, a bathtub of warm water was placed behind the sheet of glass, and though everyone on stage ended up soaked, the effect was decidedly realistic. Mistinguett saved the revue from closure and earned Schubert a lot of money into the bargain with increased ticket-sales. The same critics who had accused her of being a fake now bombarded her dressing room with flowers, and fought amongst themselves to decide which of them would escort her on a sight-seeing tour of the city!

The Americans worshipped Mistinguett, and her personal appearances there were every bit as successful as the ones on stage. Though fashion-conscious, she was never a snob like her predecessor Gaby Deslys . . . indeed, many Americans wondered why they had made such a fuss over this artiste in the first place. Gaby's role of prima donna extended as far as the street, and she had refused to visit the poorer districts of the city which, in retrospect, seems odd, considering the arrangements she had made for the distribution of her fortune after her death. Mistinguett, her marmoset sitting on her head and her masturbating monkey crouched at her heels, was never happier than when munching hamburgers in some downtown drugstore. She flatly refused to patronize the expensive restaurants lining Fifth Avenue.

When Mistinguett said, some years later, that the Americans had nominated her as their new national monument, she was not exaggerating. Even so, when *Innocent Eyes* closed, she turned down a long tour of the United States and Canada because, she said, she was insufferably homesick. The best she managed was a lightning visit to Chicago, no doubt because she had heard so much about the place from Harry Pilcer, and the Americans were forced to wait another eleven years before having the pleasure of her company again.

Staircases, Cat Fights
and an Abundance
of Feathers

When Mistinguett arrived at Le Havre in July 1924, she was mobbed by an enthusiastic crowd who had decorated her waiting roadster with flowers. This put paid to her worries that her French admirers might have forgotten her, and she broke down and wept. Moments later she flew into a rage. Léon Volterra, part of her 'official' welcoming party, was sitting in the back of the car with Jacques Charles. They were told to get out and make their own way back to Paris. Though Mistinguett continued working with them for many years, she would never forgive them for conspiring with Florelle and Madame Rasimi.

Jacques Charles, it would appear, was deeply sorry for what had happened and soon repented. Léon Volterra proceeded to rub salt into her wounds. Prior to her American tour he had set his sights on a magnificent twenty-roomed château at Bougival, fifteen kilometres outside Paris. This had been the last residence of Madame du Barry, the ill-fated mistress of Louis XV who, according to Mistinguett, had gone to the guillotine in 1793 only because she had been stupid enough to trust an underling, something Mistinguett herself would never have done. Early in 1923, Volterra had asked her to drive him to Bougival in the roadster with the excuse that he had wanted to examine the château on behalf of a friend. Initially, she had been taken in by the deception . . . Volterra, in spite of his assets and diverse interests in the music-hall, complained incessantly of being hard up. This was the reason he had given for being unable to finance her trip to America. However, she had since learned from one of her 'spies' that during her absence, the director had put in an offer for Bougival. Mistinguett's ultimate decision to outbid him was two-fold:

> I had already decided to exact my revenge on Volterra, but did not know how to go about this until I happened to see the initials J B over the entrance of the house. Madame du Barry had formerly been known as Jeanne Bécu, but these were the initials of another Jeanne . . . Jeanne Bourgeois! I looked upon Bougival as the great love of my life, somewhere where the children would be secure, happy, and unafraid of the future. For many years the chateau was my own private music-hall. Writers, actors, dancers and directors, singers and designers . . . they all camped out in the lounge. We even put on our own revues. Later on, I turned it into a zoo. . .

Though there would be a child, that of her brother Marcel, the children which Mistinguett referred to in her statement were, in fact, her animals. Like Joséphine Baker, who she was probably trying to outrival, she built up quite a collection, though none of them could have been described as dangerous, and a good many of them would be better treated than some of her entourage!

Though she would later buy a villa near Antibes, Bougival would remain Mistinguett's home for the rest of her life, even though she herself once admitted that she had never settled in there. It also effected a remarkable transformation in both her public and personal life, and earned her an erroneously disreputable reputation. Over the next thirty years, friends and acquaintances would accuse her of intense parsimony, petty theft and just about every eccentricity in the book. Most of it was of course very true, but quite a lot of it was no more than impish fun . . . the girl from Enghien simply could not stop herself from reverting to her roots from time to time!

The parsimony she blamed on those acquaintances to whom she referred as 'spongers': like Edith Piaf she was naturally loquacious and kind-hearted, and like Edith Piaf she was often capable of misinterpreting people and of being fooled into believing that some of her friends were acting on behalf of her interests. Mistinguett tended to look upon life through a rosy haze. Her vision was blinkered. She loved reverently, or hated unreservedly . . . there was never any compromise. Chevalier had taught her an invaluable lesson in ingratitude. Pilcer had let her down. Earl Leslie, some years later, would behave in such an unforgivable way that she would never trust another man again. Much has been written about Mistinguett's character, almost always with the intention of maligning her; yet little has been said as to why she was like she was, or why within months of moving into Bougival she seemingly set about exacting a revenge on the world. The answer is relatively simple. She was a desirable woman, with the innocent, trusting heart of a child, and everyone she had loved or trusted so far in her life had treated her badly. At Bougival she began living for herself, and must never be criticized for this, though of course as in everything else she did, she took it to the point of extremity.

The parties and receptions at Bougival were legion, though one did not necessarily dine chez Mistinguett on caviar and champagne, or in her expensively furnished dining room. Like her bedroom and most of the other rooms in her house, this was only a show-piece meant to impress reporters. A typical Mistinguett luncheon amounted to a few tins of Spam or soup, washed down with mineral water if she was in an entertaining frame of mind, otherwise it was tap water, drunk out of cheap mugs which she had bought from Monoprix! Vegetables were an optional extra, on a bring-your-own basis! Alcohol was wholly out of the question unless for strictly medicinal purposes, and smoking was only allowed outside. Meals were eaten in the damp, unfurnished kitchen, and everyone had to help with the washing-up. If guests were fortunate enough to be invited to stay the night, they were asked to bring their own blankets, and if they were not family or really close friends, there was often a fee.

Dress was almost always formal, even though most of the time Madame entertained in an old bath robe. There were also hard and fast rules regarding transport. Mistinguett's quintet of gleaming motor cars – besides the roadster, she would acquire a Lincoln, a Delage, a Graham-Paige and a white Chrysler – were always kept locked in the garage and used only in the event of a tour or emergency. Only the current lover, providing he behaved himself, was allowed the privilege of riding in one . . . invariably this meant that he had to pay for the petrol. Most of the time Mistinguett got around on a bicycle.

The villagers of Bougival still have fond memories of her cycling to the local store to pick up her groceries . . . and she kept this up until she was well into her seventies.

Undoubtedly, the 'show piece' at Bougival was Mistinguett's bedroom. Designed by the artist Jean-Gabriel Domerge, who had already executed her portrait and who would later paint Suzy Solidor, Manouche and Liane de Pougy, its walls were hung with pale pink satin. The carpet, featuring a scene from one of her revues, was by Gesmar. The fittings and furniture were, to say the least, bizarre. Wherever possible, everything was in glass or mirrors – radiators, dressing tables, the ceiling, and the massive swan-shaped bed; and Mistinguett herself said that this was to enable her to gaze upon her reflection every morning when she awakened. In fact, she is reputed to have slept in this room only once, during a one night stand with Harry Pilcer in 1929. The rest of the time she slept on a camp-bed in the lounge, or in a dusty attic room in a cot which she had bought second-hand from the flea market at Clignancourt. The chairs in her bedroom had come from the same sale, as had the dresser . . . the latter, however, was a valuable lacquered piece dating back to the eighteenth century Ch'ing Dynasty, and which housed her enormous collection of shoes and gloves.

Any visitor to Bougival might have observed the silver gilt cradle standing next to the Chinese dresser. Mistinguett commissioned this during the late forties, not for her niece, but for her monkey, Toto . . . she had named him after the cyclist Louis 'Toto' Gerardin, who had left her for Edith Piaf. Toto, whose personal habits were even more nauseating than those of the monkey she had been given in South America, refused to have anything to do with the cradle and always slept at the foot of her bed in a cardboard box. The current lover, once the tedious but necessary session of love-making had been endured, usually on the carpet in the box room, was always despatched downstairs to sleep with the guests.

Another room at Bougival which was strictly *interdit* was Mistinguett's private bathroom, though until the fittings for this were purchased from the Dolly Sisters in 1935, she was perfectly content to bathe in the kitchen, using an old tin tub which somone had to drag in from one of the out-buildings, and fill from the copper boiler. This must have been quite an ordeal. Even when she was not working, Mistinguett always rose at six for her work-out and bathed at seven, and the procedure would be repeated before retiring. Cleanliness, she declared, was next to godliness and was not an eccentricity. Liane de Pougy and Sarah Bernhardt disliked bathing – the latter hardly ever changed her underwear and slept in a coffin. De Pougy had the revolting habit of going to bed unwashed, with emerald rings on the toes of her left foot. Her lover, male or female, would be given the task of removing these, à la bouche, and placing them on the other foot. 'I was brought up in the country,' Mistinguett said. 'We didn't have revolting habits back in Enghien!' Even so, this did not prevent her from having her new bath installed on a pedestal in front of the window, so that she could look down on the road to Paris!

It was at Bougival, in September 1924, that Mistinguett began rehearsing for *Bonjour Paris*, her new revue at the Casino which had been written by Jacques Charles by way of an apology. Earl Leslie had been signed up as her co-star, and the couple seemed to be getting on better than they had in America. Mistinguett had also met the Duff-Coopers; these were invited to Bougival to watch her putting everyone through their paces, and were apparently treated like royalty.

Mistinguett always had tremendous admiration for the actress Diana Cooper. She had been born Lady Diana Manners, and since 1919 had been married to the English diplomat, Sir Alfred Duff-Cooper. In 1923, the great tragedienne Elconora Duse had been appearing in Paris in what would be her last role ... she died the following year. Mistinguett had been to see her with Jacques Charles and had not been impressed. Her next public outing had been to see Lady Diana interpreting the role of the Virgin Mary, and she had been moved to tears. After the performance she had been asked back to the dressing room, cementing a friendship which would last for more than thirty years. Mistinguett, not one to dole out compliments lightly – especially towards another woman, called Lady Diana the most beautiful creature of the century, and whenever the couple came to Paris they always made a point of stopping off at Bougival.

It was whilst the Duff-Coopers were staying with her that she met the latest addition to her increasing family of pets. Strolling through Paris one night with Earl Leslie, she saw a dog whimpering outside the door of a bistro and was so angry that she entered the building and gave the proprietor a piece of her mind. The man retorted that if she was so interested in the animal's welfare, she could have it and stated a price. Mistinguett paid up and left. Back at Bougival, the little dog jumped up onto Sir Alfred Duff-Cooper's knee and promptly gave him a face-wash. The dog was baptized Alfred, and Mistinguett told Jacques Charles that she wanted him in her new revue and that he and Earl Leslie should have equal billing! The writer was so afraid of offending her that he complied with the request . . . Earl Leslie was not even consulted!

Bonjour Paris opened on 8 November 1924, and as soon as she walked onto the stage Mistinguett received a standing ovation. Her emotion was so great that the orchestra had to play her in several times before she could sing. When the second tableau was announced, Alfred trotted in and raised his leg against the curtain. She then sat down beside him on the stage and serenaded him with 'Ils N'Ont pas Ca' and 'Mon Homme'!

Later on in the revue, Mistinguett appeared in her celebrated bird of paradise costume. Erté's most outrageous creation, at least in those days, it barely covered her thighs at the front, and had a ten foot golden train; the plumed head-dress was almost as tall as she was. It was so successful that she wore it regularly until 1951, when she played for the last time in New York. The song which accompanied it, however, was not one of her best. It was called 'La Parisienne'.

> On l'adore dès qu'on la voit,
> V'la tout simplement c'que c'est
> Une petite Parisienne
> Qui vient faire ses fredaines,
> Au Far West. . .
>
> (They adore her as soon as they see her,
> Quite simply, that's her,
> The little Parisienne,
> Who has just played her pranks,
> In the States. . .)

As she ended the song, Mistinguett glanced towards the wings where Earl Leslie was waiting to come on. At first she was very amused to see him executing the Indian scalp dance – Leslie, it has to be said, was not always the merriest of souls. With her customary 'Vas y mon gars!' she invited him onto the stage, and was even more surprised when he continued his dance! All she could do was improvise, and the audience thought it was part of their act and applauded wildly. It was only after the finale that she realized that Leslie was drunk. His excuses – that one of the stagehands had spiked his wine – were not taken into account. Leslie was told that if such a thing happened again he would be out on his ear. The dance, on the other hand, stayed in the revue.

Mistinguett's eccentricity first became public knowledge on the night of 4 December 1924 when she was invited to the opera. As she had never been before (she confessed on the night that the performance had been dreadful) she was not sure what to wear, so she put on her bird of paradise costume. This resulted in one of the attendants being told to lock her in her box. She was so incensed that she asked for her money back and never went to the opera again.

Bonjour Paris closed in January 1925. Jacques Charles had already begun working on the next revue, and Léon Volterra had aspirations that this one would rival the Pilcer-Deslys revue of 1917 . . . he was already negotiating contracts with the Dolly Sisters, Henri Garat, Viviane Romance and Cécile Sorel. This changed when Jacques Charles took Mistinguett to the première of *New York–Montmartre* at the Moulin-Rouge. Charles, temporarily breaking away from Volterra and the Casino, had written the script for the revue, which was ostensibly a vehicle for the talents of the Hoffman Girls, a group of American dancer-acrobats who had recently scored a triumph working for Cochran in London. The music for the revue had been written mostly by Mistinguett's old friends, Maurice Yvain and Vincent Scotto, but some of the more exciting tableaux had music by José Padilla, who had written songs for Raquel Meller before falling in love with her. Mistinguett was so taken with the production that after the show she went to see the director of the Moulin-Rouge, Pierre Foucret. This was, of course, the supreme accolade so far as he was concerned. Mistinguett then really surprised him by asking him back to Bougival, and here the deal was clinched. She told Foucret that she had no intention of returning to the Casino, and that Jacques Charles' next revue would have to be put on at the Moulin-Rouge or cancelled. The writer was reluctant to end his partnership with Volterra, though when it came to the crunch he had no say in the matter. Foucret then asked her what she was going to do about the other artistes already being considered by Volterra. Mistinguett agreed that all but Cécile Sorel should still be included. Several days later, Foucret returned to Bougival having worked out his finances and spoken to the other stars. The Dolly Sisters had only agreed to work with Mistinguett provided they received equal billing. This infuriated her . . . the Dolly Sisters' spot was scheduled to run for just fifteen minutes, and they had demanded 550,000 francs! Foucret added that once Mistinguett had been paid, there would be little money left to pay anyone else. Jacques Charles threw a fit and threatened to go back to Léon Volterra. Mistinguett settled the argument once and for all. She bought shares in the Moulin-Rouge and nominated herself co-director, with the divine right to hire and fire. Jacques Charles was told that unless he behaved himself he would be replaced by someone else. In fact, Mistinguett did engage José Padilla to write the biggest song in the revue. As for the Dolly Sisters, Mistinguett sent them a message via their agent: if they wanted to continue working in France, then they too would have to toe the line!

La Revue Mistinguett the first to feature her name in the title, took eight months to reach the stage of the Moulin-Rouge. Though finances were no longer a major problem, clashes of personality were. The Dolly Sisters had worked for Ziegfeld in his Follies. They were arrogant and thought themselves way above their European counterparts. The passage of time would prove that they were not. Thinking themselves able to outsmart Mistinguett, which no one was capable of doing, they took their dispute to the Union des Artistes. Though they won their case, it did them little good in the long run; even those artistes who disliked Mistinguett had to reluctantly agree that she was the bigger star, and the affair caused much ill-feeling in the music-hall world. The Dolly Sisters starred in *Show 1928*, at The Ambassadeurs, but there was little else after that.

It is not known precisely why Mistinguett disliked Cécile Sorel. In the relatively cloistered realm of the music-hall, Madame Sorel was something of a one-off. Until the mid-twenties she had never been anything but a talented classical actress, hailed by one critic as the

Lady Hamilton of the Footlights. In 1925, when she was fifty five, she announced that she was going to retire from the prestigious Comédie Française and enter the music-hall. Mistinguett, along with many others, considered this a somewhat ridiculous step to take, particularly as she seemed to be doing so well in her own medium. During the run-up to *La Revue Mistinguett*, Sorel had approached Jacques Charles and asked him to write a sketch especially for her. Charles had consulted the star of the show, who had snarled that such an idea was out of the question. In a fit of rage, Cécile Sorel had set fire to her hair! In fact, the great actress did achieve her ambition several years later, when she was asked to head the cast in Sacha Guitry's *Vive Paris*! at the Casino. Attempting what only amounted to a parody of Mistinguett, she made her entrance down a golden staircase, wearing a diamond-studded gown and a plumed head-dress. The revue was a flop, and precipitated Mistinguett to quip, 'She got where she was with the Comédie Française by lying on her back . . . trying to take the piss out of me, she's ended up flat on her face!'

The other stars of *La Revue Mistinguett*, which opened in the first week of November, did not fare badly. Henri Garat, though he began his career by imitating Chevalier, was twenty three at the time and went on to star in his own revues before beginning a film career in the early thirties. Jean Gabin, of course, became perhaps the greatest French film star of his day. But before the night of the première, Mistinguett went to see the young American woman whom many had already predicted capable of surpassing her, albeit she was only two weeks into her first Parisian revue. . .

Joséphine Baker had been born in downtown St Louis, Missouri, in 1906 to Eddie Moreno, a white Spanish-American dancer, and Carrie Smith Baker, a black woman. As a light-skinned Creole, she was not accepted by the black or white communities, and from an early age sang and danced on street corners because, she said, this was the only way of keeping warm. Her first break had come when she had been accepted for the chorus line of the all-black revue *Shuffle Along*, when the star of the show had been Paul Robeson. Later she had appeared in *Chocolate Dandies* in New York, and this had led to a momentous meeting with Caroline Dudley, who had engaged her for *La Revue Nègre*, which opened in Paris on 26 September 1926. Mistinguett had been invited to attend the première, but had refused because the first half of the evening had included a Damia recital. By the second week, however, the great *chanteuse* had moved on, and Mistinguett went to see what all the fuss was about.

The Théâtre des Champs-Elysées had recently been converted into a variety music-hall by André Daven and Rolph de Maré although it was but a short-lived concept. The setting was familiar to Joséphine, but somewhat disturbing to Parisian audiences: cargo ships against a backdrop illuminated by the moon, men in shabby checked shirts and breeches, women in turbans and flowered skirts. The cast was entirely black. . .all, that is, save for Joséphine. Already painfully aware that the colour of her skin might ostracize her far from home, she had attempted to make herself white by scrubbing herself with lemon-juice. She made her entrance on all fours . . . head down, bottom sticking up in the air, dressed in tattered shorts and an old shirt, dancing and writhing wildly to the strains of 'Yes Sir, That's My Baby'. Later in the revue she came on stage wearing nothing but a plumed collar and a single feather which she had tucked between her thighs. Her partner, Joe Alex, was naked, and the pair danced rhythmically and very suggestively to the pounding of the tomtoms.

'Vulgar!' Mistinguett remarked.

Henri Garat acted as Master of Ceremonies for Mistinguett's new revue, which adapted as its theme the year 1885, and which in part recounted the story of La Goulue. This extraordinary artiste, born Louise Weber in 1865, had worked as a washerwoman and an artists' model before being recruited as a dancer by the Elysée-Montmartre. She was partly responsible for introducing the cancan, and as such was painted by Lautrec and used as a base for Jean Renoir's famous film, *French Cancan*, which told somewhat glossily of the birth of the Moulin-Rouge. It seems very unlikely that La Goulue would have attended the première of *La Revue Mistinguett*, as has often been stated. Extremely coarse and foul-mouthed, her hey day had only lasted a decade: by 1900 she was working in a circus, and performed in and around Paris in a lion's cage. In the winter of 1925, whilst her character was being fêted at the Moulin-Rouge – young, exciting and pretty – she could be found on the outskirts of Paris, old and immensely fat, filming a documentary about rag-pickers. Her death, four years later, passed virtually unnoticed.

Mistinguett's most memorable tableau in the revue (some say

In *Bonjour Paris*, 1924, at the Casino de Paris. (*Popperfoto*)

On Madame du Barry's *chaise-longue* at Bougival with her pet marmoset, Dédé, circa 1925. (*Popperfoto*)

Relaxing at the Côte d'Azure
with friends, 1931.
(*Popperfoto*)

In *Paris qui Brille*, 1931-2.
(*Popperfoto*)

the best of her entire career) was Jacques Charles' '*La Forêt En Flammes*.' She played a character called Maimaine who is set upon by bandits whilst she is out collecting firewood in the forest. All of a sudden, the stage erupts into the most astonishing furore of noise and excitment – fifty cowboys and indians, mounted cavalry and a Wild West locomotive! And as if this is not enough, the electrically-wired trees suddenly burst into flame and change shape! Paris had never seen anything quite so dramatic, yet when it was all over, Mistinguett sat down on a burned-out tree stump and sang one of her saddes songs.

> Les plus sales boulots qui cass' le dos,
> Jamais une caresse,
> Qui m'ferait chaud dans le coeur,
> Des nippes en lambeaux,
> Des trous dans mes bas, j'ai qu'ca!
>
> (The dirtiest, back-breaking jobs,
> Not so much as a caress to warm my heart,
> Clothes in tatters, holes in my stockings,
> That's all that I have!)

Though 'J'ai Qu'ça' would remain Mistinguett's favourite song of all time, the revue contained two other songs which would soon become immortal. 'Ca C'est Paris' would be used as the title for a future revue. 'Valencia', with lyrics by Jacques Charles and music by José Padilla, would give her her first international record success, and she would sing it in both French and English.

Padilla, an extremely difficult man, had begun his career composing for Raquel Meller, the Spanish singer-dancer famous for tossing bunches of violets into her audience. When he had offered her 'El Relicario', she had wanted to adapt it to suit her somewhat weak voice, and Padilla had remonstrated that she should sing the song as he had written it or not at all. They had been in the middle of a passionate relationship at the time. Angry at not being able to have everything her own way, Meller had kicked him out of her apartment, thus forfeiting any hope of singing Padilla's latest composition, 'Valencia', which he had promptly offered to Mistinguett. The original lyrics had been written by Lucien Boyer, but as he was one of Damia's clan of song writers, Mistinguett refused to have anything to do with him and brought in Jacques Charles at the last minute. Padilla knew that here was a star who could not be argued with, and gave in gracefully!

> Valencia!
> Voulez-vous la fleur d'orange?
> C'est gentil, frais et léger!
> Valencia!
> Ces bouquets sont les vôtres,
> Messieurs, prenez-les!
> Seulement, j'en ai un autre
> Qu'vous n'aurez jamais!
> On peut m'offrir une fortune,
> Mais un soir au clair de lune,
> Je l'donnerai pour rien!
>
> (Valencia!
> Would you like an orange blossom?
> It's pretty, fresh and light!
> Valencia!
> These bouquets are yours,
> Gentlemen, take them!
> Only, I have another you'll never have!
> You can offer me a fortune,
> But one evening in the moonlight,
> I'll offer it for nothing!)

Mistinguett liked Jacques Charles' *double entendre* lyrics so much that she actually took out a writ preventing anyone else from singing them. The cover versions, and the later recording by Marcel Amont all feature the original words.

In spite of the success of *La Revue Mistinguett,* its first month was not without incident. Mistinguett was particularly saddened by the death of her friend, the silent film actor Max Linder:

During the Great War, I received word that Max had been killed in the fighting. Imagine, then, my great surprise when I bumped into him in the street, quite by chance! He told me that he wished he could have been killed . . . I thought he was joking. In 1925, he was at the height of his career, and he had just got married. The couple were found in their room at the Hotel Baltimore. After slashing their wrists, they had stuffed the wounds with aconite. Show-business isn't always what it seems, once you dig under the surface. . .

There was also another tragedy of sorts, though not within Mistinguett's realm or theatre, which involved the American dancer, Loïe Fuller. Though she was never really a serious rival, she had taken a leaf out of Jacques Charles' book in introducing special effects in her revues, which primarily were three dimensional. Her first performances at the Moulin-Rouge were almost as sensational as those by Harry Pilcer and Gaby Deslys at the Casino – in her seven veils she had appeared as a human flame, wreathed in luminous gases. In 1925, one of her experiments backfired and she was partially blinded. Mistinguett had had nothing to do with Loïe Fuller since she had become involved with Damia, but was now concerned because some of her cast were afraid of being injured during the exploding trees sequence of *La Revue Mistinguett*. Ultimately she paid to have the routine checked by an expert, but one of her dancers – Viviane Romance, still objected to the sequence and threatened to boycott the revue by walking out. Ordinarily, Mistinguett would have ignored her and let her go. However, it had come to her attention that the dancer had been having a secret affair with Earl Leslie and the crux of the matter was that if Viviane Romance left the revue, so would her co-star.

The ensuing argument, in public, was reported by some of the French newspapers, and is worth including in full because it was one of the rare occasions when anyone actually found the courage to stand up to the Queen of the Music-Hall. Viviane Romance, after receiving a sound ticking-off in her dressing room for disrupting the show, had been fined by Mistinguett . . . this had been in order. She was, after all, the boss!

Romance: Miss, may I have a word with you?
Miss: Get stuffed!

Romance: I just wanted to ask why you'd fined me.
Miss: I've nothing to say to you. . .
Romance: You've nothing to say to me? Well, I've got plenty to say to you! Queen of the Halls. . . you should be called Queen of Shits!
Miss: I'm warning you. . .
Romance: You're nothing but a frightened, swindling old windbag . . . a camel's grandmother! I'm still young and pretty. When you finally conk out, it'll be me who'll be dancing on your grave!
Miss: Fine! I'll make sure I'm buried at sea!

Mistinguett pretended not to be offended by these cutting remarks, though deep inside she felt hurt and betrayed by the young man who had sworn to love her for ever. Chevalier and Pilcer had both left her for younger women, and though she was still only fifty she began worrying about what life would be like once the wrinkles came. These anxieties would remain with her for the rest of her life. As for Viviane Romance, she had practically waved goodbye to what could have been the start of an enterprising career in the music-hall, and it was only some years later that she picked up the threads and enjoyed several successes in the legitimate theatre.

Earl Leslie, not the most intelligent of individuals, should have seen sense and learned reason. Mistinguett, in spite of her often ferocious temper, was never malevolent towards her lovers. Leslie told her that his association with the dancer had never progressed beyond innocent flirtation, and she saw no reason not to believe him. Publicly, he was perhaps the most introverted of all her *chevalier-servants*. When they were alone he was an avid practical joker and she apparently cared enough for him to ask him to address her as Jeanne: for twenty five years, only her brother Marcel had been granted that honour. For some reason, Leslie refused and throughout their relationship he called her Micky. This annoyed her, but she put up with it because she genuinely believed that Leslie had eyes for her alone. What she did not know was that he was cheating on her all the time with a succession of actresses and dancers. His greatest secret – that he had a young wife living in America . . . did not come out into the open until several years later, and as was only to be expected, Leslie was shown no mercy then.

The next revue was *Le Coquelicot*, of which little is known, other than the fact that it had been written by Jacques Charles during the run of *La Revue Mistinguett*. The two were still not on speaking terms after the South American débâcle. In spite of the success at the Moulin-Rouge, any liaison between Charles and Mistinguett had been conducted via an intermediary and the writer had been asked to stay away from the première! There was, of course a solid enough reason why Mistinguett kept him in her employ . . . he was the best in the business. Therefore, when she sent him a message saying that she wanted him to write her a revue centred around the song 'Ca C'est Paris', Charles was only too willing to oblige, and as usual he excelled himself.

Ca C'est Paris opened at the Moulin-Rouge on 21 December 1926, and the opening tableau saw her in her usual working-class guise. This time she was poor Jeannette, a young girl sent out by her father to fish for mussels, only to be set upon by a bunch of thugs who, after attempting to strangle her, lock her inside a barrel and toss her out to sea. Fate, inevitably, comes to her rescue when a tempest washes her up on the Italian coast and she is befriended by a take-off of Mussolini, who persuades her to sing!

> Paris, reine du monde,
> Paris, c'est une blonde!
> Le nez retroussé, l'air moqueur,
> Des yeux toujours rieurs!
> Tous ceux qui te connaissent,
> Grisés de tes caresses,
> S'en vont mais reviennent toujours,
> Paris, à tes amours!
>
> (Paris, queen of the world,
> Paris, she's a blonde!
> Turned-up nose, mocking air,
> Eyes always laughing!

All those who know you,
Carried away by your caresses,
Go away but always come back,
Paris, to your loves!)

The scene involving Mussolini caused some controversy. Only a few years before, the dictator had been elected to power and the wave of fascism swept across Italy. Mistinguett had included the sketch because public performances were often the only way of getting back at some of the people who had rubbed her up the wrong way, and of course she had been treated abysmally by the Italians during her tour there. She was asked to remove the offending tableau, but refused. Someone had told her that during manoeuvres, Mussolini liked to mingle with his soldiers and sing to them. She declared, 'If Mussolini wants to put on a revue and dress up like me, who cares?' Needless to say the sketch stayed in the revue.

'Ca C'est Paris', with its roisterous introduction and catchy refrain, was the first Mistinguett recording to sell a million copies in France, and was also popular in Britain though she did decline an offer to have it translated into English. The song was also responsible for patching up her quarrel with Jacques Charles.

> I was singing the song when I recognized someone in the third row. Suddenly, I cried out, for the monster had had the nerve to come and see me. Indignation and anger got the better of me, and I fainted. When I came to in the dressing room, he was touching my cheek and telling me how worried he had been. Leslie saw that I was crying, and wanted to sock him one. The silly man didn't realize that they were tears of joy!

That night, there was a back stage celebration at the Moulin-Rouge. Mistinguett did not touch a drop of alcohol, as usual. The rest of the cast, including Earl Leslie, got unashamedly drunk. For the first time in more than two years there was an uneasy peace on the home front.

Roundabouts and Swings

La Revue Mistinguett closed in August 1927 and Mistinguett retreated to Bougival with Jacques Charles and Earl Léslie to begin work on the next revue, scheduled to open at the Moulin-Rouge in March 1928. She was more settled in her personal life than she had been for some time: she had made sure of this by ostensibly placing Earl Leslie under 'house arrest', for she had no intention of a repeat performance of the Viviane Romance affair. Leslie seems to have accepted the arrangement willingly. Mistinguett, who had ways and means of finding out everything about everyone, had not yet 'investigated' her lover and Leslie wanted to make sure that she never did.

The new revue was to be called *Paris Qui Tourne*, and now that she had proved her abilities as co-director as well as star, Mistinguett wanted this one to be her best ever. Gesmar had been signed up to make the costumes and design the posters, she herself had written the script with Jacques Charles, and she had engaged the talents of Saint-Granier and the British artiste Little Tich, who was then fifty nine and ailing. And in spite of her earlier altercation with Léon Volterra, she had asked him to help finance the production. In December 1927, her entire company was transferred from Bougival to Volterra's recently-acquired château outside Paris; this included the latest addition to her chorus line, a young man called Jean Gabin.

Away from Bougival, Mistinguett was on her best behaviour, though she still managed to keep everyone on their toes. When Earl Leslie was diagnosed as suffering from nervous debility, he was banished from her bedroom, and the inevitable happened . . . Jean Gabin kept his side of the bed warm, always making sure that he was back in his own room before Mistinguett served Earl Leslie with his morning coffee. The deception was not discovered until several weeks later, by which time it was too late for Leslie to opt out of the revue ... the contract had been signed. Even so, Leslie could have left her. The fact that they were working together did not necessarily mean that they had to live under the same roof. However, the events of February 1928 brought Mistinguett to her senses and had everyone rallying around her, offering what support they could. Two of her closest friends – Gesmar and Little Tich – died suddenly, not simply leaving her in the lurch as far as the revue was concerned, but heart-broken and grieving.

Little Tich had been born Harry Relph in 1868, and had made his Parisian début some twenty years later. He had acquired his name because of his resemblance to the claimant in the so-called Tichborne scandal, in which an imposter had attempted to inherit a large fortune. Standing little more than four feet tall, his act had been as sensational as it had been ridiculous ... with a deadpan expression and a pair of enormous boots longer than he tall, he had presented monologues and vulgar asides. One of his greatest triumphs in Britain had been at the London Hippodrome in 1900 when he had been billed as Petrolio Pakporck Vanderstor, the Absent-Minded Millionaire, in *Giddy Ostend*. He had gone on to become a founder member of the Grand Order of Water Rats and in 1906 had been appointed King Rat. His true artistry, however, had been more appreciated by the French, and in 1910 he had been accepted into the Académie Française. French audiences, even those who could not understand English, simply adored his 'Since Poor Father Joined the Territorials', which he probably would have included in Mistinguett's revue.

> He puts poor Ma in the trashcan,
> To stand on sentry guard!
> And me and Brother Bert,
> In his little flannel shirt,
> He keeps drilling in the old back yard!

Though they had never appeared together in a major revue, Mistinguett and Little Tich got on so well socially that it was rumoured that they had once had an affair. This was untrue, of course: though their common link was the music-hall, they were from totally different worlds.

> Little Tich was so tiny and ugly that in order to keep up his millionaire's image, he had to apply mind over matter, and in reality he was a sad man. We first met after my show at the Casino. He asked me to dance with him, and I give you my word, I never noticed his smallness. When he complimented me on my performance, I was utterly gob-struck . . . such kind words, coming from one so great!

Gesmar's death was, of course, a deeply personal loss, and one from which Mistinguett never really recovered because it happened so quickly and was not expected . . . he was, after all, only twenty eight. Neither was the cause of the young man's death professionally established. According to the obituary notices, he fell ill with a simple chill and died in his sleep two days later. There was no post-mortem. For more than a decade this strange, highly-strung individual had tagged along behind his idol like a little lost dog, making friends and enemies alike amongst her entourage. That she loved him like a son, and that he was a genius many years ahead of his time, practically goes without saying.

> He was so delicate and feminine that one angry word would have broken him in two. He was so good, poking fun at the 'real men' of the music-hall . . . the virile types who had everything down below, but nothing at all up top. He worked his fingers to the bone, and he earned a fortune which he frittered away. He never paid a taxi-driver with anything less than a hundred-franc bill, and he never asked for the change! When he died his parents asked me what had happened to all his money. I didn't know what to say because I feared they would blame me for his extravagance. . .

Gesmar's funeral, in February 1928, was a gay affair in every sense. Besides the family, Mistinguett, Harry Pilcer and Earl Leslie, his lovers past and present turned out in colourful profusion . . . many of them in drag. As the coffin was lowered into the ground, one of these stepped forward and sprinkled confetti into the void. Others threw streamers into the crowd and sang a chorus from 'Mon Homme'.

Writing of Gesmar's death from her Bougival home in July 1954 caused Mistinguett to think of her own death; only a few weeks before she herself had been diagnosed terminally ill. It was the first time she had confessed her true feelings about her own particular brand of religion, and though many admirers were surprised by her comments she was not being irreverent.

> I will die when my time comes, when I get to be sick of living. As long as there isn't any pain, I won't be afraid. God is inside me. I never take people too seriously when they pray to the Virgin Mary because I don't believe in intermediaries. Cut out the middle man, if you know what I mean, and go straight to the Boss. After all, He's the one who made us!

Harry Pilcer too had lost a very dear friend, a young man who had nursed him through his second nervous breakdown, and he was invited to spend a few days at Bougival. Like Chevalier, there was no hope of any reconciliation, though it is believed that he and Earl Leslie did not get on. Mistinguett did not care about this . . . all her friends were with her, and what they had to say about each other was immaterial. She was also probably sleeping openly with Jean Gabin, which cannot have made the atmosphere at Bougival very convivial.

The première of *Paris Qui Tourne* was moved forward to 18 April 1928, two weeks after Mistinguett's fifty third birthday. Once more Earl Leslie danced the Legomania, and Saint-Granier sang 'Ramona', which he had introduced at the time of the Great War. Jean Gabin, acting as Master of Ceremonies like his father before him, also sang a duet with Mistinguett:

> Marie-Marie,
> C'est une gosse de Paris!
> Dis veux-tu qu'on s'marie?
> Celui là, il m'a compris!
>
> (Marie-Marie,
> She's a kid from Paris!

Can you say when we'll be married?
As for him, he'll understand!)

Morton, the illusionist and 'decapitator' who had appeared with
Mistinguett many years before at the Scala, also had a spot in
the revue, which probably explains why she decided to include
the Madame du Barry sequence . . . this and the fact that she was
living in the famous courtesan's house. Like the skit on Mussolini
from the previous revue, this caused a great deal of trouble. For
the first time ever, a real guillotine was seen on a French stage in
a comedy routine. English visitors to the Moulin-Rouge thought the
scene hilarious . . . not so the *préfecture de police*, who banned it after
just three days.

Madame du Barry, of course, à la Mistinguett, could not lose her
head without going through a lamentable grilling in her condemned
cell at Louveciennes and without offering a final song, in this case 'Les
Boulevards d'Aujourd'hui'!

Sur les boulevards aujourd'hui,
Quand un monsieur vous poursuit,
On s'dit d'abord: 'De quel pat'lin est-il?'
Moi j'ai un truc, j'ai appris
Quelque mots d'tous les pays.
I love you . . . Ich liebe dich!

(When a man follows you on the boulevard today,
One begins by asking, 'Which village is he from?'
I have the knack,
I learned a few words from each country.
I love you . . . Ich liebe dich!)

When Mistinguett cooed 'Ich liebe dich!' she was not simply
offering words of endearment . . . the accent was decidedly on the
word 'dich', which she pronounced 'dick'. Madame du Barry had
been fond of this part of the male anatomy, she declared, and so was
she. When Earl Leslie accused her of being too vulgar, she merely
retorted that in this respect he himself 'had been standing at the end
of the queue' and that he was jealous of his predecessors because 'all

of them, even Chevalier, had been suitably well-endowed'. And to hammer home the point that she was gradually getting fed up with him, she made sure of leaving the theatre every night on Jean Gabin's arm.

One of the sensations of *Paris Qui Tourne*, from a back-stage point of view, was a handsome young Italian dancer called Lino Carenzio. Mistinguett had met him in December 1927 at a party thrown by Emilienne d'Alençon, which may probably explain a lot. Madame d'Alençon, a contemporary of the horrendous Liane de Pougy, had been renowned for keeping a string of mean and moody lovers – mostly of indeterminate sex – since the turn of the century, and Carenzio was no exception. Mistinguett engaged him for the revue not because of his looks but because he was an inordinately good dancer. Any interest in him, sexually, had quickly diminished when he had begun an affair with a young male *chanteur* who would soon become one of the greatest in all France. Normally, this would not have deterred her. Earl Leslie and Harry Pilcer, and probably Maurice Chevalier, had all been successfully wooed away from male suitors. This one, however, was different. Not only did Carenzio despise women, he was also reputed to be violent towards them. For the time being, Mistinguett pushed him to the back of her mind and even turned a blind eye when, after ending his relationship with the *chanteur*, he began working his way indiscriminately through her chorus.

'Too arrogant,' she quipped. 'And he's an eye-tie!'

What she did not know at the time was that, inadvertently, Lino Carenzio would spark off a series of events which would dramatically transform both her public and personal life.

The first of these occurred half-way through the run of the revue at the Moulin-Rouge. Lino Carenzio, using his affair with the *chanteur* as a means of power, began dictating to the staff and management of the theatre, most of whom knew exactly how to deal with him. Fradet, Mistinguett's secretary at the time, did not. Unknown to the star of the show, there was a clash of fists in the street outside the theatre, and this resulted in her being left in the lurch, with no right-hand man to manage her affairs. A friend, the actress and dancer Gina Palerme, came to her rescue. One of the richest women in Paris, she had recently been photographed by Marcelin

Desboutin, who in his hey-day took famous pictures of everyone, it seemed, except Mistinguett. Whilst sitting in Desboutin's studio, Gina Palerme had begun chatting to his fifteen year old daughter, Marcelle, a Mistinguett 'groupie' who had waited, unsuccessfully, outside the stage door of the Moulin-Rouge for two weeks just to catch a glimpse of her idol. Mistinguett, of course, had ignored her, though not purposely . . . unless admirers were handsome and male, they rarely received so much as a fleeting glance. A few days later Gina Palerme had told Mistinguett about the girl, and an 'interview' had been arranged, ironically on the very day that Fradet had called in at the theatre to pick up his severance pay and give his ex-boss a piece of his mind regarding the kind of company she was keeping!

Mistinguett remembered the occasion with sincere amusement:

> The dog entered first . . . a little fox-terrier which took a fancy to my dressing room. I've always had a fondness for animals. They're more faithful than men and don't answer back. Then the girl ran in, red-faced, pretty, wide-eyed and breathless. She told me her name was Marcelle, and that she had just passed her fifteenth birthday. She reminded me of myself, as a girl in Enghien. Every night after the show she came to see me. Sometimes the Rocky Twins were there, with Henri Varna. Between us, we decided to baptise her Fraisette. She became my companion and personal secretary, and four years later we became sisters!

Henri Varna belonged to the same school of directors as Léon Volterra and Oscar Dufrenne, who believed it was essential to spend money to reap more than adequate rewards. Unlike some of their contemporaries they were not specifically interested in drawing the working-class Parisian public for which Mistinguett had an unashamed fondness; their targets were the wealthier and tourist classes who preferred to forget about their troubles and be entertained with a blaze of colour and noise. Though Damia, Fréhel and Yvonne George continued to play to packed houses all over France, even they did not attract the masses the way some of the lesser-known, less-talented artistes did at big halls such as the Casino and the Moulin-Rouge. Varna and Dufrenne had been connected, at some time or in some way, with every major hall in Paris and were fêted as the gods of their trade. Varna had just signed up the Rocky Twins, a pair of Norwegian transvestites who were very successful offering an engaging but sometimes crude impersonation of the ill-fated Dolly Sisters; something bound to please Mistinguett. A few months before he had signed an advertising contract with Mistinguett. The company had been Cherry Rocher, for which Varna had come up with the slogan, 'Le cherry de mon chéri est mon cheri!' Mistinguett was not new to advertising. Way back in 1912 she had been paid to have the caption under one of her publicity photographs, 'I have never used a soap which procured the same sensation as Cadum. Not only is it essential for my skin, it keeps my complexion just right!'

When Varna was introduced to Marcelle, he was as impressed by her cool beauty as he was frightened of her snarling, angry dog. He offered her a part in his forthcoming revue at the Casino, hoping that by doing so he would be able to persuade Mistinguett into working with him and Dufrenne at the Casino, now that the hated Volterra had been bought out. Mistinguett did not take much tempting, though she was sufficiently worried for her new protégé – Marcelle's health was delicate – not to subject her to the rigours of the music-hall. Varna found this amusing. Pointing to the girl, and remembering the slogan he had thought up for Cherry Rocher, he said, 'Tu es fraîche, tu es fraise! La fraisette de ma fraisette est ma fraisette!'

> The baptismal ceremony took place in the corridors of the Moulin-Rouge. Earl Leslie was god-father . . . the Rockies were godmothers, and Varna himself gave her the blessing!

In fact, when *Paris-Miss* opened at the Casino on 14 November 1929, Fraisette was included in the chorus line. Though nothing is recorded of her subsequent performances, they cannot have been too memorable for Mistinguett herself claimed that her 'sister' made a better secretary than music-hall star.

Prior to this, during the summer of 1929, Mistinguett and her young companion were invited to stay with Charles Cochran at his London home, in the company of the Duff-Coopers and the Chilean millionaire, Arturo Lopez. Earl Leslie was left to stew in his juices at Bougival . . . Mistinguett was afraid that if he came to London he would never return to Paris, and she was probably not wrong. Needless to say, her visit to England was not without adventure. To begin with, Lino Carenzio had travelled on the same boat from Calais. Keeping cautiously out of sight, he had revealed himself to her on the train between Dover and London and had received such short shrift that he had got off again at a railway station in Kent!

News that the Queen of the French Music-Hall was about to hit London reached the city one hour before she did and when she stepped onto the platform at Victoria Station she was met by a delegation of female activists. This is not as ridiculous as it seems, for they had heard of the banned guillotine sketch in the revue with Morton and wanted to ask her to participate in their campaign to abolish the death penalty! Mistinguett, who always regarded herself as a-political, would not comment, though her speech on sex equality created the misconception that she was a feminist: had the Pankhurst brigade known more of her amorous activities in France, they would probably have given her a wide berth!

> They used their umbrellas like bayonets to attack the bobbies who tried to prevent them from marching up to the House of Commons. They had my sympathy. Any woman deserves the vote, so long as she votes for what the politician has between his ears, and not between his legs. In my opinion, women could govern just as well as men because they're impartial. Men may be said to wear the trousers, but they often forget that it's we girls who wear the knickers!

The Rocky Twins were certainly wearing such apparel, not just on stage at London's Kit-Kat Club, but out in the street, when they were arrested for public indecency during Mistinguett's visit! Though she hurried to their rescue and even gave the judge a ticking off for accusing them of immorality, she turned down Cochran's offer of a revue. The English would have to wait almost twenty years for that honour. 'This visit is for purely personal reasons,' she told the reporters who had gathered outside her hotel. 'Leave me alone!'

Charles Cochran became one of Mistinguett's closest friends. Through him she met all the British stars of the day, including

Noel Coward and Tilly Losch, who always made a point of inviting her to their opening nights whenever she could afford the time to make the trip. Cochran also taught her to speak English with a cockney accent . . . she loved the East End of London and its quaint, down-to-earth pubs, though she never drank anything stronger than ginger beer. She also loved taking a charabanc to Brighton, providing it was driven by a woman, and it was here, whilst they were picnicking on the beach, that Cochran promised to have his latest London revue, *Evergreen*, translated into French for her to star in at the Casino. It is a great pity that this never happened, for Mistinguett would have excelled.

Though Mistinguett did not play a professional engagement in London until 1947, when she was over seventy, she did attend a number of private functions. Though the press were barred, many of Cochran's friends and acquaintances were interested in meeting the woman who had allegedly seduced Edward VII, and Mistinguett was cautious to give nothing away one way or the other. And, of course, she was always asked to sing 'Mon Homme' and 'Valencia'. She also devised, with Cochran, her brief but celebrated *Dictionary of Theatrical Terms*, which was for some years fêted by the British 'camp' set, and which resulted in her being noticed by Jean Cocteau.

Actor/Actress:	The one who is congratulated if the revue is a success.
Author:	The one who is blamed if it is a flop!
Successful Author:	The one whose name appears in the programme in letter the same size as the man leasing the theatre to the director.
Unsuccessful Author:	See drama critics!
Public:	A body of optimists wanting to have fun whilst hoping all will turn out well in the end.
First-Night Audience:	A body of optimists wanting to have fun whilst hoping all will turn out bad in the end!
Cochran:	Noel Coward's idea of the greatest force in the theatre today.

Noel Coward:	Cochran's idea of the greatest force in the theatre today!
Impresario:	One who borrows from the rich to give to the poor.
Make-up:	A disguise which an actress puts on when she is about to leave the theatre.
Pearls:	Something an actress loses.
Publicity:	See pearls!
Rehearsals:	A method of wasting a producer's time where actresses learn a script which they could have learned at home.
Dress-rehearsal:	Another method of wasting time wherein an actress forgets everything she has learned so far.

'Writing about Cocteau,' Mistinguett said, 'only makes me want to hide my pen in what Maurice Verne called my garden of plumes and feathers!'

Though by no means a work of literary genius in the Cocteau school, Mistinguett's memoirs – a triumph of mind over matter, penned during her twilight years when she was far from well – are of an immensely readable quality and unlike some of Cocteau's tomes, do get straight to the point. They were also written to be enjoyed by the general public, and never set out to impress intellectuals, which was how Cocteau defined Mistinguett.

> The orchestra strikes up 'La Matchiche'. Mistinguett makes her entrance under a shower of flowers, fist on hip, battling with her sombrero and draped in a Spanish shawl. She sings the song, then leaves with another floral salute. Then we draw straws to see which one of us will meet her after the show, this brave woman who embraces patriotism, who sparkles in her eagerness to please men and who enflames the lights of the town.

It is not known exactly when these two great *monstre-sacrés* met for the first time, though it may have been at that most celebrated of society meeting-places, Le Boeuf-sur-le-Toit in 1925.

Le Boeuf, as it was affectionately known, had opened on the rue Boissy d'Anglas in 1922, and had been immediately baptised 'the cradle of current Parisian society'. Amongst its earliest patrons were Mistinguett and Chevalier . . . though never together; the painters Picasso and Marie Laurençin, and contemporary poets and musicians such as Aragon, Pierre Larrieu, Auric and Poulenc. Here, in 1925, Yvonne George had had a triumphant season, accompanied at the piano by Philippe-Gérard, who would later pen a number of Edith Piaf's biggest hits. Le Boeuf was not, however, just another artistes' paradise. When Mistinguett first began going there it was a picking-up place for wealthy society ladies such as Liane de Pougy and Emilienne d'Alençon, for gigolos such as Lino Carenzio and for highly-promiscuous homosexuals, of whom Cocteau himself was a supreme example. One incident in particular was much-publicized, and was recounted by Manouche in her memoirs, ghosted by Roger Peyrefitte and written throughout in the third person.

> Cocteau loved to shock. He was tense, irritable, thin as a pencil, with the eternally twitching mouth and quivering nostrils of an overbred greyhound. Manouche was there one night. The poet-self-styled-genius was drinking Scotch, and the bar was crowded three deep. There was this businessman, sitting with a lady who was evidently not his wife. Cocteau thrust his face between them and bawled at the bartender, 'A shot of freshly-ejaculated semen, my good man!' Not only the couple, but several others walked out as well.

Cocteau was at this time courting the young film director, Marc Allégret, whom he had poached from the writer André Gide, more than thirty years Allégret's senior. The feud between the two great men lasted on and off for forty years, and was never more potent than at Le Boeuf in the mid-twenties, with Mistinguett taking sides, depending on her mood. It was with Cocteau, Allégret, Harry Pilcer and Fraisette that she went to see her friend Yvonne George at the Empire during the late summer of 1929. It was a memorable concert, if only for the fact that a brawl erupted in the street amongst a group of sailors and homosexuals, and a man was stabbed to death. After this harrowing episode, Yvonne announced her retirement. She was only thirty two, but what many of her admirers did not know was that she was chronically ill with tuberculosis and that her doctors had given her but a few months to live.

Between them Mistinguett and Cocteau hatched a plot to aid the dying *chanteuse*. Funds were raised and Paul Franck, the director of the Paris Olympia took Yvonne to a sanitorium in Switzerland, from where the instruction was given to place her obituary notice in a Paris newspaper. The object of so drastic an exercise was ostensibly to prove to Yvonne that the people of Paris cared enough about her to mourn her death, which is, of course, exactly what happened. Then Paul Franck placed a second announcement in the same newspaper, stating that a mistake had been made, and Cocteau set about organizing the singer's comeback by stage-managing her final recital early in 1930, at the Grand-Ecart in Montmartre. Mistinguett and Pilcer were present, and all admitted some years later that their efforts had only hastened Yvonne's end. George-Henri Rivière, one of Cocteau's song writer friends, provided her with a handful of new songs, though the old ones were the best received, including 'Pars', a very dramatic song which had once been sung by Mistinguett.

> Mon désespoir reste mon secret,
> Nous n'sommes qu'deux étrangers.
> Pars, sans un mot d'amour,
> Pars, laisse-moi souffrir. . .
>
> (My despair remains my secret,
> We're but two strangers.
> Go, with no word of love,
> Go, let me suffer. . .)

Many people, including Mistinguett, found the spectacle of Yvonne George coughing up blood on stage whilst clutching the curtains for support too much to bear. The public suffered with her, partly out of admiration of her worn, cracked voice, and partly because she herself had prophesied that she would die on the stage. This did not happen. She returned to the Swiss sanitorium, and a few weeks later escaped her blouses-blanches and caught the train to Genoa. Here she booked into a sleazy dockside hotel, and after spending a last night in a sailor's arms, committed suicide. Though it had been expected, Mistinguett was devastated by the news of her death and was one of the mourners at her funeral.

Yvonne George's illness temporarily brought Mistinguett and Pilcer together again, though he only spent one weekend with her at Bougival, probably because of Earl Leslie. Much of their reunion was spent at the apartment on the Boulevard des Capucines, which she had kept on 'in case of an emergency'. It is a great pity that the pair did not become amorously engaged again, for Mistinguett was going through what she called one of her blue periods, something which only a Pilcer or a Maurice Chevalier could have rectified.

Pilcer was starring in *Paris qui Charme* at the Casino. It had opened on 28 May 1929, and was the very last revue put on there by Léon Volterra. Pilcer's co-star was yet another old friend going through a bad patch. Marie Dubas, though one of the greatest chanteuses-réalistes of her day, was not really suited to working in a revue, and she was also in the middle of a somewhat messy entanglement with the writer Pierre Benoit, which inevitably ended badly. Pilcer himself does not appear to have been romantically linked with anyone, and was still *maladive*, suffering from bad nerves and mourning the death of Gaby Deslys. Like Mistinguett he was worried about growing old, even though he was only thirty nine and still dashing and very handsome. According to Erté, who confessed to having a crush on him, he kept the wrinkles at bay by applying an astringent lotion to his face each morning, which kept his skin tightly stretched until the evening performance. Whatever he did, it worked well . . . when he performed for the last time in Cannes when he was over seventy, he looked much younger. During the latter half of his career, Pilcer also borrowed Mistinguett's staircase routine for his finales, playing the role of a polite, elegantly-dressed drunk whilst the orchestra played his most famous song, 'I'm Just Wild About Harry'.

Pilcer stayed in Paris long enough to attend the première of *Paris-Miss*, where he had the misfortune to be invited to a back stage party which included Earl Leslie and Max Dearly. The latter had just opened at the Théâtre Marigny in *Bouvard et ses Filles*, and his presence at Mistinguett's opening night was not to wish her luck, but to rub salt into her wounds. The Marigny had just been taken over by Léon Volterra, and the revue itself had been written by

Mistinguett's former lover, Louis Verneuil. Pilcer returned to his villa, and Mistinguett would not see him again for another seven years.

It was probably Max Dearly who pinned the name Missolini over the sign on Mistinguett's dressing room door ... an act intended to infuriate her, but which only succeeded in delighting her! She declared, 'If I'm a dictator, it's only because I happen to be a perfectionist!'

The designs for *Paris-Miss* were by Paul Colin, inspired by Gesmar and Poiret, and now coming into his own. Previously, he had designed the posters for Joséphine Baker's first Parisian revue, and had been criticized for describing the star of the show – this had not been Joséphine, but a large black actress called Maud de Forest – as 'looking like an oriental carpet-seller', and the revue itself as 'a shock of shaking bottoms, wigs and tits'. Joséphine herself had been dismissed as 'a boxing kangaroo, a rubber woman, and Tarzan's mate'. This only delighted Mistinguett, who would later re-baptise her rival with the somewhat inglorious title Banana Tits! The reason for this, of course, was that in her next revue Joséphine appeared on stage wearing nothing but a belt of bananas. Colin's designs for Mistinguett were much the same as they had been for Damia – a larger than life portrait, painted or sewn onto the backdrop, which was very effective. The first tableau depicted a Dickensian Regent Street, which in turn became rue de Lappe, and the Champs-Elysées. Mistinguett wore a crinoline gown and bonnet, and played the proprietress of Hortense, a fashionable flower shop frequented by a string of handsome men, each of whom had come to buy flowers for their sweethearts, but who ended up dancing and singing with the owner. The song they sang, aptly-titled, was 'On Me Suit':

> J'peux pas faire un pas
> Quand je sors d'chez moi.
> On me suit, j'sais pas pourquoi,
> J'entends des tas d'propos gallants!
>
> (I can't take a step
> When I go out.
> I don't know why they follow me,
> I hear all kinds of gallant remarks!)

The Rocky Twins, appearing on stage for the first time since being 'rescued' by Mistinguett in London, were an unexpected sensation. The speciality was a game of hide-and-seek which took place behind a tree. One would go behind the tree trunk dressed as a gallant young man, and the other would emerge from behind it in drag, to the astonishment of the audience who at first believed there was some kind of magic involved, or that they were witnessing a quick-change Barbette. Their off-stage behaviour, however, no longer impressed Mistinguett.

> They were so ravishing, and knew it, to the extent that each night after the show they would allow themselves to be kidnapped by beauty-enthusiasts of both sexes. I suppose it was to be expected because they were Norwegian, but I disapproved.

Jean Sablon also made his singing debut in *Paris-Miss*; previously he had danced in Rip's *Au Temps de Gastounet*, at the Bouffes-Parisiens in 1927. Within a few years, this young man would be dubbed Le Chanteur de Charme, though it is doubtful that he would have made any impression at all had it not been for Mistinguett's generosity in allowing him to stay in the revue once she suspected him of having an affair with Jacques Charles. In fact, Mistinguett later realized that she had made a mistake, though she would never have admitted this . . . Sablon liaised with Jacques Charles only because he had taken a shine to Fraisette, which in time would cause another explosion.

The finale saw Mistinguett in a fabulous silk bridal gown, designed by Poiret, which featured a hat with a vast, turned-up transparent brim, and a single plume. 'The only time you'll ever see me in a wedding frock,' she cooed, before breaking into a chorus from one of her sauciest songs:

> Il m'a vue nue-e,
> Toute nue-e!
> Sans cach-trucs ni soutien-machins,
> J'ai rougi jusqu'aux vaccins!

(He saw me naked,
Totally naked!
With neither G-string nor thingamy,
I blushed right up to my lymphs!)

The lyrics to 'Il M'a Vue Nue' had been written by Rip for the earlier revue, *Ca C'est Paris*, but had been disapproved of by the prudish Earl Leslie. It is interesting to observe that the music was by Pierre Chagnon, an apparently fearless individual who, not content with arranging most of Mistinguett's songs, was also working as Damia's musical director! One night, however, Mistinguett was asked to drop the song because the French president was sitting in the audience. She refused to do this, and when she came off stage after the finale she found him waiting in her dressing room with Henri Varna. When Doumergue told her that he had found the song offensive, she shrugged her shoulders and said, 'Tough shit!'

Paris-Miss closed in the summer of 1930, when much of Europe had a relatively new name to conjure with. . .

He was a new celebrity of the music-hall, but one who refused to tread the boards . . . otherwise he might have had an enterprising career. For the time being, no one took him seriously. His name was Adolf Hitler.

Mistinguett's struggles were much closer to home than they were to Germany. Her relationship with Earl Leslie, never the calmest of affairs, had now deteriorated to such a point that she could not stand to have him near her, and his threats to return to the United States were not only taken seriously but wished for. Mistinguett was so keen to get him from under her feet that she even offered to pay for his passage. Before this happened there would be one final, agonizing battle.

'Those Damned Americans!'

Joséphine Baker and *La Revue Nègre* had been dismissed by Mistinguett as vulgar. When someone had mentioned, casually, that here was a woman capable of dethroning her, her remarks had been typically cutting: 'Before you know it, she'll be on her way back to the jungle. I've nothing to worry about!'

The so-called 'jungle' image had quickly been replaced by one of great sophistication. In 1926 Joséphine had appeared on stage at the Folies-Bergère in a silver gown covered in hundreds of tiny white feathers. Half-way through the second song the dress had collapsed about her feet to reveal a belt of sixteen banana-shaped crescents and nothing else. News of this reached Mistinguett, and she went to see her. She told reporters, 'I never had to show my breasts on stage to get myself noticed,' which was of course true. The rivalry between the two would last another thirty years, and it has to be said that none of it was Mistinguett's fault. Joséphine's origins may have been humble and her success unprecedented, but during her early days she was reckless, egotistical and lacking in diplomacy. Later, of course, she would change for the better and earn much respect from her peers for doing so. For the time being Mistinguett considered her a pain in the neck, and she was probably not wrong.

Joséphine had arrived in France with two marriages behind her ... the first had been when she was just thirteen. In 1927 she issued a statement that she had married again, this time to a mysterious Italian count called Pepito Abatino. In order to show that there were no ill-feelings, which of course there were, Mistinguett had invited the couple to her apartment on Boulevard des Capucines. This had turned out to be as much a publicity gimmick as the marriage itself. There had been no wedding, and the Italian 'count' was, in fact, a stone mason called John Wells, who became her business manager and mentor, and organized her first European tour.

Joséphine was asked to 'clean up' her act, which Mistinguett advised her not to do. Prior to her appearance in Vienna, priests denounced her from pulpits, and anti-rascists handed out leaflets urging people to stay away from her show. The Ebony Venus, as the French called her, acquired the title of the Black Devil. For her première, however, she proved herself all sweetness and light. She wore her long gown buttoned up to her chin, and opened her act with a wistful rendition of 'Pretty Little Baby'.

The real problems occurred when Joséphine returned to Paris in the summer of 1930. Mistinguett, too, was organizing a tour, which would be followed by a new revue at the Casino. For the first time since visiting the United States, she was preparing a tableau in which two of the songs, 'You're Driving Me Crazy' and 'Mon Homme', would be sung in English. Though Joséphine would never have dared sing Mistinguett's signature tune, she did steal the other song, and the consequences were dire to say the least. Mistinguett organized a meeting of her boys; she stationed these outside the theatre where Joséphine had been booked to appear, and they picketed the spectators! Joséphine carried on regardless, and the song and show were a great success.

Soon afterwards in September 1930 Joséphine exacted her revenge. When *Paris Qui Remue* opened at the Casino, she did not steal one of her rival's songs . . . she stole Earl Leslie! For Mistinguett, this really was the last straw. Leslie was evicted from Bougival and his clothes thrown out of his bedroom window. Two days after the revue opened, Mistinguett was at the Casino begging him to return, and when he refused to do so she threatened to tell the press that for the last five years he had been living a lie. Surprised and shocked that she had found out about his marriage and afraid of losing his popularity should such a scandal be splattered over the front pages of the tabloids, he returned to the fold and for a while all seemed well.

Paris Qui Remue was one of the most successful revues ever staged at the Casino and ran for more than a year. Though an excellent dancer, Earl Leslie had never purported to be a singer and he was replaced by Adrian Lamy, one of the most bizarre enigmas of the French music-hall. Like Harry Pilcer he had started out as a male prostitute, but unlike Pilcer he never changed his ways. He duetted with Joséphine in the two big songs from the revue, '*J'ai Deux Amours*' and the suggestive 'Voulez-Vous de la Canne A Sucre'? These were massive successes commercially, and earned the pair a lot of money. A few years later, Lamy made a number of records with Damia, who attempted to get him to see the error of his ways. He never did. In 1940, when he was only thirty five, he was butchered to death by the young man he had refused to pay for services rendered after he had picked him up in an Orléans dive.

In October 1930 Mistinguett began auditioning for the troupe which would accompany her on her tour. The female turnover was relatively small . . . many of her boys, on the other hand, left after a season, though there was never any shortage of fresh recruits. The auditions themselves, and especially the interviews which followed, were tough. Each young man was told to dance with one of the chorus girls. If he seemed all right, he was asked to dance with Mistinguett. Once he had got through this stage, he was asked to remove his clothes . . . this always took place in front of the entire company, and if he was lucky he was allowed to keep on his underpants. Mistinguett, of course, was not looking for cheap sexual thrills: any scar or bodily imperfection, and the man was sent away. Usually, she would audition fifty and engage less than a dozen. For the tour she wanted sixty, and by the time the full troupe had been engaged, Earl Leslie's patience had been stretched to the point of no return. He had also been replaced in Mistinguett's affections by Lad, a young American dancer who hated him from the moment he set eyes on him. To add to the complication, Lino Carenzio was also signed up for the tour!

Almost nothing is known about Lad. Tall and undeniably good-looking, he often appeared on stage dressed in black and with a five o'clock shadow which succeeded in making him look like a convict. He had a Jekyll and Hyde character which saw him in the darkest of moods one moment, then playing absurd practical jokes the next. He could not speak a word of French – not that he ever said much that was not offensive or vulgar – and was not helped by Mistinguett, who refused to speak to him in anything but French unless it was to teach him yet more filth!

The company left Paris immediately after the Christmas of 1930 for Algiers, and whilst the others were unpacking their trunks

Mistinguett, Lad and Fraisette went on a shopping expedition to the local souk, where in a rare act of extravagance she bought a sultan's outfit for herself and Fraisette, and traditional costumes for the rest of the company. Needless to say, this took some time, and every stall-holder within the market offered the customary glass of mint tea. This did not affect Mistinguett, who had the constitution of an ox, Fraisette and Lad were laid up the next day with what she called the 'Arab trots', and for a short time Earl Leslie was allowed to accompany her on a sightseeing tour before all had to settle down to the serious business of work.

On the eve of the dress rehearsal – Mistinguett had decided to wear her sultan costume for the première – she visited Lad on his sick bed and showed him the beautiful clothes she had bought for herself. He informed her, quite seriously, that she would not be allowed on any Algerian stage unless wearing the customary *moucharabieh*. Frantically, she began rushing around the souks in search of this hitherto unheard of item of apparel, only to be told by the forewarned stall-holders that no respectable lady would ever dream of asking for such a thing. Mistinguett hurried back to Lad and told him that the first night of the revue would have to be cancelled. The expression on his face revealed that she had been the victim of one of his practical jokes. A *moucharabieh*, he informed her, was one of the intricate grills which the sultans nailed to their windows so that their women could see what was happening in the street without being seen themselves!

'I'll get my own back,' she declared.

Eventually she would, but for the moment Lad caught her out again when she and her company were invited to a couscous supper at the house of an impressario. He had a quiet word with the host, accepting full responsibility for what was about to take place. Mistinguett, as guest of honour, was invited to sit at the head of the table. A whole sheep was brought out on a big silver platter, and everyone given a more than ample portion . . . except Mistinguett, who was told by the host that as the supper was being held in her honour, she would have to honour the ancient custom of eating one of the sheep's eyes. . .

With a nimble gesture, he stuck his fork into the head and plucked out an eye. It was a case of doing as the host asked, or running the risk of offending him. I closed my eyes and took

a deep breath. My teeth began clacking like castanets. I was going
to faint! It did not take much getting down but even now, after
twenty five years, I can still feel it coming back up.

The supper ended, of course, with a display of belly-dancing, which
rather than impress Mistinguett, only irritated her. She told her host
that his girls were dancing too slowly. To make a point, she herself
got up on the table and showed him how it should be done. This
was, ostensibly, a greater insult than it would have been not to
swallow the sheep's eye, but the host took her advice in good stead.
Needless to say, when her revue opened, there were belly dancers,
à-la-Mistinguett, in almost every tableau!

From Algiers, the company moved to Oran, where they put
on Mistinguett's adaptation of *The Tempest*. It was not an easy
production – there were difficulties transporting the twenty or so
tons of props and costumes overland, and the spectators had already
begun arriving at the theatre before the stage-hands began working
on the sets.

Mistinguett's costume for the finale of *The Tempest* was very
similar to the one worn by Elisabeth Welch in the film of the
play, directed many years later by Derek Jarman. Lad, very much
the exhibitionist, appeared on stage wearing a loin-cloth. He had
disobeyed the edict of the day by not shaving his chest, and when
the loin-cloth came off to reveal a diamond-studded G-string similar
to the one which had been worn by Harry Pilcer at the Casino,
Mistinguett was bombarded by complaints from the town dignitaries.
She simply shrugged her shoulders and quipped, 'If you've got it,
flaunt it!'

Lad had, of course, taken too many liberties, and it was whilst
the company were playing in Oran that Mistinguett got her own
back for the tricks he had played in Algiers. The handsome young
American was one of the few associated with Mistinguett who was
not interested in bedding members of his own sex, and though women
in this part of the world did not go to the theatre as much as they
did in Paris, Lad managed to fall in love with one of the locals. His
major problem – his inability to communicate – was soon sorted
out by Mistinguett, who agreed to write everything down for him.
Obviously, he had forgotten the events of the recent past!

Speaking of the occasion a few years later, Lad was unable to resist a smile:

> *Lad*: Miss, how do you say, 'I am unattached.'
> *Miss*:'I am well-hung!'
> *Lad*: How do you say, 'I think you're very beautiful.'
> *Miss*:'You've got lovely tits!'
> *Lad*: And, 'Would you like to go for a walk after the show tonight?'
> *Miss*:'How's about a nice fuck up against a sand dune?'

Normally, she would have been against her current man even looking at another woman, though in this instance she was sure that Lad would return to their room red-faced. In fact, she did not see him until lunch-time the following day . . . in her own words, 'He was so knackered, he could hardly walk!' The Algerian girl had read his endearments, and instead of reporting him to her family, had indeed spent the night with him on the dunes! Mistinguett was angry, but she knew that she only had herself to blame, and by the time the company left Oran, Lad had once again become her 'exclusive' property, much to the annoyance of Lino Carenzio, who had hoped the episode might enable him to take Lad's place. Earl Leslie, on the other hand, was not bothered . . . he had fallen in love with one of the girls from the chorus.

The company sailed for Spain, and here there was almost a repeat performance of her disastrous tour of Italy during the First World War. The director of the theatre in Barcelona told them that their revue would have to be cancelled because the stage-hands, decidedly anti-homosexual, had gone on strike. Lad, with his flair for diplomacy, informed them that he was more than willing to display that he was as normal as anyone, and to a certain extent they relented. On the night of the première, however, they walked out because they claimed that they had seen something horrendous taking place in one of the dressing rooms. Lad was ordered to put his muscles into action and fix the sets, and Mistinguett herself, when she was not on stage, worked the curtains. Earl Leslie was given the unwelcome task of sweeping the stage before the performance. The revue was well received, and the following night the stage-hands turned up for work as usual, full of apologies. Mistinguett's boys – gay or not, they were all big, strapping fellows – prevented them from entering the theatre.

During her stay in Barcelona, Mistinguett was invited to the bullfight. No one had told her that the matador killed the bull . . . it was assumed that she already knew. She did not, and caused such a rumpus that she had to be escorted from the stadium in tears. Later she wrote to her friend Alfonso XIII, asking him to ban the sport. It was a nice gesture, which of course could never have been taken seriously.

The company moved over the border to Perpignan. Here, one of Mistinguett's girls was taken ill, and replaced by Fraisette.

> I had changed my mind about her going into the music-hall. The girl needed a chance to express herself. She was a total flop! She almost fell down the staircase, and by the time she started singing, all the others had finished. She was a good secretary, but a lousy entertainer!

Fraisette accepted Mistinguett's criticism, ostensibly because she was closer to the star than anyone else. Earl Leslie did not. He accused her of being too harsh, and there was a nasty exchange of home truths *en route* for Brussels, the next leg of the tour. When Leslie threatened to return to Paris, he found himself on the receiving end of Lad's fist. This incurred the boss's wrath. She loved to watch her men fighting, so long as they were fighting over her. Earl Leslie was told to behave himself: Lad was told that their affair was over.

Belgium was, of course, Mistinguett's favourite country apart from France. She herself was half-Belgian, and her first major straight play had been staged in Brussels. There had even been a time, upon her coming of age in 1896, when she had thought of assuming Belgian nationality; she had only decided to keep her French citizenship, she later said, because she had been born in France.

Once the bags had been unpacked Lad, hoping that he might be given a second chance, offered to take her out to lunch and was surprised when she accepted. They ate at a little café in the Grande Place, and afterwards went to see the Mannekenpiss, which was as usual dressed in a colourful costume. Mistinguett wanted to know 'what it looked like' and Lad obliged by stepping into the pool and removing the statue's trousers. By this time a small crowd of onlookers had gathered about the couple. Not surprisingly one of these was a press photographer. Lad told him that the Mannekenpiss ought to be reconstructed so that it ressembled something worth looking at, and offered his services as the new model. Exposing himself, he urinated into the pool. Twenty years before, Mistinguett might have been amused. Apologizing to the crowd, she walked away in disgust.

Her problems with Lad, however, did not end there. By some strange twist of fate, Damia was appearing in Brussels. When Mistinguett was formally introduced to King Léopold and Queen Astrid after her show, she was horrified to find that the great *chanteuse* had spent the evening sitting with them in their box at the Cirque Royale. But this was not all! Damia had booked into the same hotel as Mistinguett, and since the episode at the Mannekenpiss had been escorted around the city by Lad, who told her that he had been celebrating his twentieth birthday, which may or may not have been true . . . he certainly cannot have been much older, and Damia had one thing in common with her rival, the fact that she was not one to turn her nose up at what would today be regarded as a toy boy.

Though Lad was still seducing his audiences with his loincloth routine, he had been condemned by Mistinguett to share a room in a cheap hotel with two other male dancers, whose nocturnal habits nauseated him so much that he moved out after the first night. Whether he was actually sleeping with Damia is not known, and he must have been suitably close at hand because Mistinguett had appointed him as her chauffeur, not a very rewarding position for a young man who liked to live life to the full, for this invariably meant that he had to get up at six every morning and drive her to some rendezvous or other. Two days after opening in the Brussels revue Mistinguett was informed that her 'chauffeur' had been seen in her Chrysler driving Damia to an engagement, and that he had agreed to drop her off at the railway station that very morning. The ensuing showdown would have been worthy of one of Damia's more dramatic songs! Mistinguett waited in the hotel foyer until Damia's luggage had been placed in the back of the car. Damia was standing on the pavement when Mistinguett revealed herself, and Lad, thinking himself about to be murdered, ran off. Mistinguett jumped into the car, drove off to the railway station, and emptied the contents of Damia's suitcases onto the tarmac. She found Lad some time later, drowning his sorrows in the hotel bar and promptly clouted him with her handbag!

The last country on Mistinguett's agenda was Holland, which she apparently did not like because she was criticized by the *Commissaire de Police*, in Volendam, for turning up at a reception in trousers. When she was not organizing the evening performances, she spent much of her time fishing with Lad. Astonishingly, she had forgiven him for the Damia affair, and because she felt very much alone in a country which she thought had rejected her, she had dismissed him as chauffeur and taken him back as her lover.

The Mistinguett-Lad reunion was in effect short-lived. The tour ended at Rotterdam in August 1931, and only hours after taking her final curtain call Mistinguett returned to Paris – she herself was behind the wheel of the Chrysler, with Fraisette sitting beside her. The rest of the company had been left in Rotterdam to 'mop up' after the show and make their own way home.

Reading through the mail and the manuscripts which had piled up at Bougival, Mistinguett was disappointed to discover that she had not been missed. After eleven months, Joséphine Baker was still packing them in at the Casino, and according to the press reports *Paris Qui Remue* looked as though it would play indefinitely. Janet Flanner, who as 'Genet' was French correspondent for *The New Yorker* between 1925 and 1939, and whose memoirs and reviews were published collectively in 1972 under the title *Paris Was Yesterday*, wrote,

> Miss Baker's revue is as full of staircases as a Freudian dream, with excellent British imported dancing choruses of both sexes, a complete Russian ballet, trained pigeons, a live cheetah, roller-skaters, the prettiest Venetian set of the century, a marvellous first-act finale, acres of fine costumes, the four best cancan dancers in captivity, a thriller in which Miss Baker is rescued from a typhoon by a gorilla, and an aerial ballet of heavy Italian ladies caroming about on wires.

Appearing in *The Tempest*, Algeria, 1931. (*Popperfoto*)

In the Chinese room at the Boulevard des Capucines, early 1930s. (*Popperfoto*)

With Lad in the sketch *Dans les Bouges la Nuit*, Brussels, 1931.
(Popperfoto)

Mistinguett may not have seen Janet Flanner's review. Nor was she impressed that Joséphine Baker's eccentricities were well on their way to rivalling her own. She herself only kept monkeys, cats and dogs, whereas Joséphine could now be seen strolling along the Champs-Elysées with a leopard on a chain (this may have been the 'live cheetah' from *Paris Qui Remue*) which was attached to a diamond-studded collar valued at a million francs. She still believed that Joséphine was a mere flash in the pan . . . she was after all only twenty five and a foreigner. What Mistinguett did read was Janet Flanner's somewhat condemning article of 1930 in which the future of the French music-hall was more or less committed to the obituary column. Immediately she set out to prove the American wrong by putting on a revue which she believed would upstage them all.

Setting up her temporary court at the Boulevard des Capucines apartment, she summoned Henri Varna, Oscar Dufrenne and that old stalwart, Jacques Charles, and told them that the new revue would be called *Paris Qui Brille*. The word spread like proverbial wildfire, and within four days she had auditioned more than a hundred boys, but had come up with only ten she thought suitable for what she considered the crowning point of her career. Present at the auditions, and no doubt enjoying every moment, was the controversial artist Marie Laurençin, who found time to paint Mistinguett's portrait. Marie had designed the sets for Diaghilev's ballet, *Les Biches*, and was delighted that Mistinguett had chosen her forty sixth birthday (30 October 1931) for the première of *Paris Qui Brille*. This was of course pure coincidence. Mistinguett did not like her very much because she had just painted Joséphine Baker, but she was good publicity and therefore invaluable. Although she painted many of the top stars of the day and had been the great love of the poet Guillaume Apollinaire, she is remembered today for her portraits of young girls, many of whom she is reputed to have seduced, including Janet Flanner, and of whom she said, 'Why should I paint dead fish, onions and beer glasses? Girls are so much prettier!' With her at Boulevard des Capucines was her maid, Suzanne Morand, whom she hoped might be given a part in Mistinguett's revue. She was not. Several years later Marie legally adopted her, and Suzanne eventually inherited her vast estate.

Amongst those whom Mistinguett did engage were a quartet of young men, all in their twenties, but not of the regular homosexual persuasion. These were two pairs of duettists . . . Destrey and Dawson, and Pills and Tabet. Though little is known of the former two – Dawson disappeared after the revue and Destrey was found dead on a park bench – Pills and Tabet became very famous, both in France and America.

Jacques Pills had been born René Ducos, in Tulle in 1910. Shortly before the Second World War he would marry Lucienne Boyer, and in 1952 he would become the first husband of Edith Piaf. What appealed to Mistinguett in 1931 was that Pills was said to be having an affair with Joséphine Baker . . . indeed, it would soon be rumoured that they had married, though there has never been any substantial proof. Georges Tabet was taken on, ostensibly, as part of the deal. He was not a dancer or singer, but a kind of jazz pianist who accompanied Pills with his interpretations of the songs of Mireille and Jean Nohain, then the rage in some of the more sophisticated clubs of Paris. Tabet was in fact described by Mistinguett as 'looking like an ugly rhinoceros' when she first auditioned him. One of his front teeth was very prominent, and though it was late at night before she got around to seeing him, she told him that she expected the tooth to be gone when he turned up for rehearsals at nine the next morning. Tabet did not let her down . . . he pulled the tooth out himself. Mistinguett then told her quartet that henceforth they would be billed as The Double Two, and told them to learn 'Le Temps de Cerises', which she wanted them to sing barbershop-fashion in the revue.

Mireille Hartuch was probably the most original artiste to appear in Paris during the late twenties and early thirties. In 1928, when she had been just twenty two, she had met the writer Jean Nohain, and had dropped her surname after they had written their opera, *Fouchtra*. Nohain was the lyricist, and Mireille's music, simple yet ironic, had an instant appeal not only to intellectuals, but to the working classes. The opera had never been staged but one of its songs, 'Couchés dans le Foin', was a massive success when Mireille performed it in a Broadway revue. When she returned to France, she gave the song to Pills and Tabet, and they performed it in *Paris Qui Brille*. In 1931 it won them the Grand Prix du Disque, and they later recorded it in English, at the same time as the Andrews Sisters, whose version was known as 'Lazing in the Hay'.

As with the previous revue, the scenario and publicity bills for *Paris Qui Brille* were by Paul Colin, who added the slogan, 'Featuring Ben Hur's chariot, a snowstorm, and a roman orgy'! Varna and Dufrenne had themselves engaged 'The Original Sixteen Jackson Girls and the Ten Jackson Boys' and a peculiar pair who performed under the name of Charpini and Brancato, then at the height of their success. Charpini would stand in the foyer, greeting the spectators with rhetorical remarks and would later be accompanied at the piano by his partner, improvising duets from *La Belle Hélène* with lyrics which made no sense whatsoever. Marie Dubas, whose own revue – also directed by Varna and Dufrenne – opened at the Empire two weeks before that of Mistinguett, was so impressed by the Charpini-Brancato routine that she secured them and Pills and Tabet for her showcase *Sex-Appeal 1932*, which opened at the Casino the following spring, and which included not only her celebrated 'La Charlotte Prie Notre Dame' sequence, but the only impersonation of Mistinguett which the great star approved of and encouraged.

Paris Qui Brille was the perfect vehicle for Mistinguett . . . not only was she *meneuse de revue* and stage manager, she also collaborated on most of the songs, an important aspect of her career which many of her critics and biographers have always chosen to ignore. This may well be an accidental oversight – the lyrics were signed in the name of her son, Léopold de Lima, who was apparently still living in South America, desperately short of money but too proud to enlist his mother's help. This situation was rectified as soon as Léopold received his first 'royalties' cheque, for he sailed for Paris at once for what must have been an exceedingly tearful reunion. It has also been suggested, but not proved, that Léopold's sudden incursion into the world of song writing coincided with the death of his father. The subject must have been discussed with her son, but Mistinguett never mentioned it in her memoirs or to any of her friends. As far as she was concerned, Monsieur de Lima had died the moment he had taken her son away from her. Neither was there any question of the young man returning to Brazil . . . Since leaving school he had attended university and had become a doctor. Mistinguett put him in touch with all the right people in Paris – there were few people from any walk of life with

whom she was not familiar, either personally or by way of contact
– and he was offered a position with a hospital. When he was not
working, she never let him out of her sight.

Until now, most of Mistinguett's revues had been renowned for
their spectacle and colour, and not for the quality of the songs –
Ca C'est Paris and *La Revue Mistinguett* were exceptions. *Paris Qui
Brille*, besides the Pills and Tabet number, contained seven Varna-de-
Lima songs which Mistinguett recorded between October 1931 and
March 1932. Not all were commercial hits. 'Le Tambour Major' was
overlooked by the French, and 'Oh! Que J'aime Paris' was released in
Britain on a compilation album in 1989, where the English title was
given as 'Back to Gay Paris', which is how Mistinguett announced it
when she sang it during her last visit to the United States in 1951.

'J'ai des Touches', sung as a duet with Lino Carenzio, was one
of the wittiest songs in the Mistinguett repertoire. Carenzio played
a corporal, and during the sketch the stage was filled with horses
trained by Houcke, one of the best circus trainers of his day. This
was another slap in the face for Joséphine Baker, whose animals in
Paris Qui Remue had all been made out of papier mâché. According
to Mistinguett's record company, the studio version of the song was
made with Lad or Earl Leslie, which is not possible, the former could
not speak French and the latter had a noticeable accent, besides which
at the time of her visit to the studio both were out of favour, and in her
eyes not worthy of committing a song to posterity. This leaves Lino
Carenzio . . . and Harry Pilcer, who had apparently turned up for yet
another attempted reunion.

The other numbers from the revue became minor classics of the
chanson. All subsequently sold more than a million copies, though
not in Mistinguett's lifetime. One song which could only have been
written by her, far different from 'Garde-Moi', Sous les Ponts' and
'Nuit de Paris' was 'A Travers les Barreaux d'l'Escalier'. It reminds us
of the circus as it used to be, and begins with an inimitable town-crier
repartee which is as vulgar as it is innovative:

> Méfie-toi bien du Grand Ferdinand,
> Je sais que c'est un enjôleur!
> Il la guettait à son passage sur le palier,
> Elle dut subir ses outrages jusqu'au dernier.

Il lui fit perdre son courage,
A travers les barreaux d'l'escalier!

(Watch out for Big Ferdinand,
I know he's a wheedler!
He blocked her passage on the landing,
She gave in to his insults until the last.
He made her lose her courage,
Across the rails of the staircase!)

Two weeks into the revue, Fraisette became ill with pleurisy. Mistinguett was so concerned that she even thought about taking time off to look after her. Jacques Charles stepped in and at the end of November, after Fraisette had spent some weeks in a clinic, offered to drive her to his villa in Antibes. Mistinguett appointed her brother Marcel as the girl's bodyguard. She also told Fraisette to be on the look-out, once she was feeling well again, for a villa for herself.

'Somewhere for me to retire to,' she added.

The Villa Mistinguett and
the European Tour

Shortly before dispatching her secretary-cum-house-buyer to Antibes, Mistinguett organized a meeting of her entourage backstage at the Casino . . . but only after she had ensured that Fraisette, Marcel and Léopold would not be there. She then announced that, for the benefit of her delicate health, Fraisette would have to be found a husband and that there were two contenders for her hand . . . Mistinguett's son or her brother! Between them, they decided that Léopold would be the best man for the job. Léopold, when consulted, refused to have anything to do with the idea. He informed his mother that he was not interested in women, only his career. Mistinguett misinterpreted this and accused him of being homosexual, which of course he was not. She then sought out her brother. Marcel told her that Fraisette was a very dear friend, but as he was not in love with her he could not possibly marry her. He also informed Mistinguett that Fraisette was having an affair with the singer Jean Sablon. Mistinguett refused to believe this, but one night when she caught her secretary playing the singer's records in her bedroom, she thought it might not be a rumour after all. The whole of the next day was spent visiting her friends and collecting Sablon's records, which she burned in the back garden at Bougival.

Paris Qui Brille closed in March 1932, and that same night Mistinguett received a telephone call from her brother. The sojourn in Antibes had succeeded in killing two birds with one stone. Fraisette, fully recovered from her illness, had found a villa, and Marcel had asked her to marry him. Back-stage at the Casino Mistinguett threw a celebration party, though everyone was allowed only one drink – the company had to be up early next morning to travel to Berlin.

Mistinguett hated Germany. The tour had been organized by her part-time manager, Mitty Goldin. Born Mitty Goldenburg, he had begun his career as a tenor in the church near his native Budapest. In Paris, he was renowned for his sheer professionalism, but loathed by some artistes because of his tendency to offer stingy fees. Though he was not yet as important to the music-hall as he soon would be, working for Goldin offered any artiste a certain amount of prestige. He was ultimately responsible for launching Edith Piaf and Charles Trenet as *vedettes* – prior to this they had been supporting artistes. Few of his 'discoveries' actually confessed to liking him, and though Mistinguett calls him a friend in her memoirs, they detested each other. The brief tour of Germany was a financial disaster. Some of the theatre directors, who had entered into an agreement so that she might have a percentage of the box-office takings, sold most of the seats at less than half price. Worse still, they gave many away as concessionary tickets to government workers and their families. When she returned to Paris in April, Mistinguett told the press she did not wish to talk about the tour because it had been the bitterest disappointment of her career: she only mentioned it briefly in her memoirs. She then went to see Mitty Goldin and warned him that unless he compensated her with a tour which would be a guaranteed success she would personally escort him back to Hungary. This was not just an idle threat . . . Mistinguett's power in music-hall circles at this time was such that anyone who failed to please her could easily have been forced into involuntary retirement. Also, she still had financial interests in some of the theatres upon whom Goldin relied for his income.

Stopping off at Bougival only long enough to give instructions to her entourage for what would be their longest tour, and to telephone her closest friends – these included Fréhel, Dranem and the actress Gaby Morlay – she left for the south of France.

The villa which Fraisette had chosen for her was exactly what she would have chosen for herself. It was a sizeable white building set in several acres of landscaped gardens and fronted by palms and olive trees. She was not impressed, however, by its name – Champ Tercier – and asked her friends to come up with a more suitable alternative. They did, and it was re-baptised Villa Mistinguett! And of course, the 'unveiling' ceremony had to be the talk of the town. Practically every musician in Juan-les-Pins was invited to join in with the fun and make as much noise as possible. This got the new owner into trouble with the local dignitaries, particularly the Mayor of Antibes, Aimé Bourreau – the name amused Mistinguett because it is the French word for executioner! Bourreau served her with a summons for disturbing the peace, and was promptly told what to do with it.

Several days later, Fraisette took her sister-in-law to a club in Juan-les-Pins which she had taken a shine to during her convalescence. Mistinguett was so impressed that she offered to buy the place. She said, 'If I buy my own establishment, nobody will be able to stop me letting my hair down every now and then!' The price was right, and one month later the club was hers . . . though she had to buy it as a partnership deal with a local entrepreneur called Michel Georges-Michel.

The glass door, during the day-light hours when the club was closed to the public, was protected by a sheet of wire-mesh and Mistinguett quipped that the place reminded her of her father's fatal chicken-run back in Enghien. The name stuck. La Cage aux Poules opened in July 1932 and almost immediately incurred the wrath of Aimé Bourreau, who tried to impose a ban on the club staying open until the early hours of the morning. Mistinguett retaliated by turning up outside his house in the middle of the night armed with several jazz bands which only stopped making a din when Bourreau promised to relent. He was then invited to the re-opening ceremony of La Cage aux Poules (the interior had been designed by Mistinguett's friend, Zig) and when he left at six the next morning, he and the star were the best of friends!

Two aspiring members of the music-hall were present at the inauguration ceremony. One would achieve fame as the greatest *chanteur-poète* of all time. Aged just nineteen, his name was Charles Trenet. The other would achieve notoriety for nothing in particular, other than that she became Mistinguett's confidante and, some years later, the most celebrated gangster's moll in all France. Her name was Manouche.

The same age as Trenet, she had been born Germaine Germain into a wealthy family, and had entered Mistinguett's 'service' in much the same way as Fraisette Desboutin. According to her memoirs, she had been introduced to her idol by Mistinguett's dentist, Raymond Daumal. Mistinguett herself said that she had taken her under her wing when she was seventeen because her parents had disowned her after she had been expelled from her English finishing school for selling condoms in her spare time. Apparently, Mistinguett had been less alarmed by this than she had with the rumour that an otherwise respectable catholic girl had been consorting with the likes of Daumal, a Jewish homosexual who had decided 'to turn the other way' once he got Germaine in the dentist's chair . . .

> The great star shot a puzzled look at Daumal. 'What are you doing with young girls? You know I've always loved the polite boys you bring me!' Germaine refused to be pitied. 'It's true,' she said. 'At the convent school in England we were taught to convert the Jews. Raymond saw something in me, as it were. Whilst I did the converting, he did the drilling!' Mistinguett stared at the girl. She said, 'You must be out of your mind, Raymond, sacrificing your pretty boys for a stuck-up little goose like her. Why not send her back to the barnyard where she belongs?' Germaine was already aware of her quick wit . . . she was never short of an answer. She retorted, 'I may be a barnyard goose, madame, but at least I don't have to earn my living by performing in front of a bunch of drooling idiots. Anyone can shove a feather up their arse and say they're Mistinguett!' It was this exchange, between the young girl and the great star of the music-hall, which cemented a friendship which existed for life. It continued as it began, for it was untainted by illusion. Those two understood each other's faults and virtues, without their love for each other diminishing in the slightest way.

Unofficially, Mistinguett became Germaine's godmother and there was a second baptismal ceremony back stage at a music-hall. The name she selected for her protegée was Manouche, which on the face of it sounded no more ridiculous than her own pseudonym. For the rest of her life Manouche would never be known as anything else.

Towards the end of August, Mistinguett returned to Bougival. With her were Manouche, Earl Leslie and most of her company. Fraisette and Marcel stayed on in Antibes. Lino Carenzio and the rest of the troupe agreed to be in Algiers for 1 October and what would ostensibly be the first engagement in a very long, fraught schedule.

For several weeks, Mistinguett busied herself in preparation for the tour. She had not ordered new costumes, but many of the old ones needed adapting or altering. Manouche had decided not to accompany her on the tour, prefering instead to stay with her mother who lived alone at a big house in Vincennes, and was still mourning the death of her husband, who had succumbed to a heart attack shortly after his daughter's return from England. Mistinguett understood, but she was disappointed that she would not have the company of another woman during the tour. Having a confidante close at hand would have helped her to cope with the growing depression caused by the fact that there was no man in her life.

Mistinguett's evenings were a riotous affair; they were now more exciting than they had been for some time. In spite of her youth and upbringing, Manouche was remarkably worldly, and unashamed that she was still having an affair with Raymond Daumal. Though Mistinguett did not drink, there were parties every night at two of Paris's less-respectable cabarets. Jean-et-Bobs, which was in the heart of Montmartre, was hardly the sort of place where one would expect two women to dine alone. It was run by the drag-queen Odette, and attracted a very rough crowd indeed. La Vie Parisienne was slightly more up-market. It had been opened by the singer, Suzy Solidor, and was a forerunner to the establishments opened after the Second World War by Léo Marjane and Lucienne Boyer.

Suzanne Rocher had been born in Brittany in 1901, and her advent into the music-hall had been purely accidental. When she had arrived in Paris it had been to open an antique shop. This had folded after only a few months and a friend – the painter Van Dongen, noted for his music-hall canvasses – had told her: 'If you want to save your furniture, sing, and make sure you sing from the very depths of your belly!' Suzy had taken the man's advice, and her shop had been converted into a night-club, where she appeared every night dressed as a sailor, with her long blonde hair flowing over her shoulders. Like Mistinguett she had an unusual voice, in her case a very deep baritone, and on stage she looked both beautiful and foreboding. Her stance, on the other hand, was ungainly, which is why she introduced a number of props . . . a fringed orange shawl draped over the piano upon which stood a lamp, the only light in the establishment which was kept on during her performance, enabling the audience to see only her angular features. Her first recordings, cut around the time she first met Mistinguett, were the appropriately titled 'Tout Comme un Homme', and the song which Mistinguett borrowed from her repertoire but never recorded, 'Du Soleil dans Mon Coeur':

> Ta gaieté met du soleil dans mon coeur,
> Et ta douceur séche mes pleurs,
> Ton regard m'ouvre un merveilleux séjour,
> Et ton amour fleurit mes jours!

> (Your gaiety puts sunshine into my heart,
> And your gentleness dries my tears,
> Your glance opens within me a wonderful abode,
> And your love blossoms my days!)

Although Mistinguett and Suzy Solidor never really got on, they would have a certain amount of respect for each other which would last until the German occupation, when the activities of the latter were highly suspect. The singer was also notoriously lesbian, which found her few favours with a woman who never tired of telling friends and acquaintances that she had never been anything but 'man-mad' . . . though as has been seen, this had not always been the case. Even so, once the explosion came in 1944, when alleged collaborators were forced to face up to their misdemeanours, Manouche found herself capable of retaining the friendship of both women without creating much fuss or opposition from either. During Mistinguett's European tour she spent much of her time at La Vie Parisienne.

Mistinguett and Earl Leslie left Bougival during the first week of October 1932. After spending the night in Marseilles, they sailed for North Africa to begin the first in a series of seven engagements. The revue, a *mélange* of fifteen years' experience in the music-hall, was so successful that this leg of the tour lasted until the middle of December. Christmas was spent in Tunis and might have been a miserable affair with so much dissention amongst the leaders of the troupe, had it not been for Fraisette, who joined them on Christmas Eve. Marcel had apparently decided to stay in Antibes, not just to keep an eye on the villa but because he was having second thoughts about getting married. Mistinguett was upset in any case, for no one had remembered to pack a Christmas tree . . . Fraisette made one, using the feathers from one of Mistinguett's head-dresses!

Once the festive season had been dealt with the company – all eighty of them – sailed back to Marseilles, then took the train to Geneva. Mistinguett was not too pleased about appearing there; the place reminded her of Chevalier, and was a hive of unhappy memories. As if aware of her resentment, the audiences there gave her a luke-warm reception, and when she began her tour of the other Swiss cities she cut some of the sketches from the revue, which only resulted in her being paid short by some of the theatre directors. She swore never to perform in Switzerland again.

> The Swiss weren't interested in me . . . only in their silly cuckoo-clocks and wristwatches. Leslie bought hundreds of the things and sent them to his American friends. He always had his name etched on the dial, so that he wouldn't be forgotten. Somebody gave me a typewriter! Mind you, I deserved it after spending all morning walking around the factory! As for the directors and impressarios, they were all thieves!

From Lausanne, the company travelled to Rome, yet another city which rekindled unwelcome memories. She refused to work in the theatre whose director had impounded her costumes, all those years before. In Milan, during a radio broadcast, she launched an attack on Italian food, claiming that only the French knew how to cook spaghetti! Incognito, she entered a cookery contest . . . her speciality was pasta asciutta, and surprised even herself by winning first prize!

It was whilst she was working in Milan that she was asked to make a diversion and play the Admiral Platz in Berlin. What she told the director, over the telephone, is unprintable, and the Germans never even thought of asking her to perform for them again. One city she did like was Vienna, and the Viennese felt exactly the same way about her. Every night she found herself showered with flowers and wooed by admirers . . . even if she was almost sixty, she did not look it.

She rented a suite at the Imperial Hotel. The entire floor above her had been taken over by her company, whose expenses almost totalled as much as they were earning. Because she was happy, Mistinguett was in a rare benevolent mood, and did not mind picking up the tab at the end of the stay. She was also delighted when the manager of the hotel informed her that she was sleeping in the bed which had been used by the Austrian Crown Prince, though not so amused when he added that it had also been slept in by Hitler, who was on the front page of every newspaper in Europe after recently becoming chancellor of the German Third Reich. She bought carbolic soap, scrubbed herself from head to toe, and told Fraisette to burn her night-dress.

Throughout the tour, the wily Lino Carenzio had attempted and failed to get into Mistinguett's bed, no doubt because most of those who did usually ended up a few rungs further up the music-hall ladder of success. One young man who bettered himself in this way was the Austrian dancer, Frédéric Rey.

Aged just seventeen when he fell in love with Mistinguett, Frédé, as she affectionately called him, had made his début at the Théâtre Ronach. He had not caused much of a sensation, though he had been engaged for another review which had been shelved to make way for Mistinguett's extended run. Every night, prior to her performance, she had seen him loafing around in the wings, helping the stage hands, and her curiosity had got the better of her. She confided in Fraisette that he was the most beautiful man she had seen since Pilcer, and the ever-faithful little secretary was asked to make a few 'discreet' enquiries. As Fraisette could not speak German, she enlisted the help of the dancer Ben Tyber who, for want of something better to do, was consoling Lino Carenzio until the opportunity arose for him to seduce the boss. Tyber brought Mistinguett the happiest news she had received for some time . . . the young man's name was Fritz, and he wanted to know her better!

A meeting was arranged with Ben Tyber acting as interpreter in Mistinguett's bedroom. Fritz explained that he was bored with the Austrian music-hall, which was not a patch on the French one, and that he would like to audition for a part in one of her revues. Ben Tyber was sent away, pleased that for the time being Lino Carenzio would not be taken away from him. The next morning he made a point of sending the Italian into Mistinguett's room with her breakfast, and of course Fritz was still there. That same evening, just before curtain-up, he was auditioned. Mistinguett informed her company that she had seen enough of his body during the night, and that if he could walk down a staircase the way Pilcer had done, the job would be his. He could, and it was. Within a few years, as Frédéric Rey, he would become one of the Moulin-Rouge's most important acquisitions.

When Mistinguett's revue closed at the Théâtre Ronach, she decided to spend an extra week in the city. Originally she had planned to return to Paris for a few days before resuming the tour. Instead, she attended several receptions and went to see Frédé's parents, who were delighted their son had achieved his heart-felt desire to enter the French music-hall, but no doubt unaware that he was having an affair with a woman who, though undeniably attractive, was forty years his senior.

She then set about getting him out of the country. Although his parents had given him their blessing, he did not have the necessary papers, and Mistinguett of course was unwilling to wait for what she dismissed as red tape. He accompanied her on the tour, with his papers always arriving in a country one day after he had left it, and when he eventually made his entry into Paris it was in the bottom of a wicker-basket, under a heap of feathers and underwear.

Prague, Mistinguett confessed, was something of a let-down after Vienna. The only thing she remembered about the city was being asked to leave her hotel room after she and Frédé had been caught cooking spaghetti on a portable stove, one of the many possessions she could not manage without if she was not in France.

Stockholm was slightly more exciting because on the night of her première an admirer gave her a white dove, which she baptised Chérie, and with which she was photographed everywhere she went. The dove was even included in her revue, which gave the cluster of press reporters waiting to interview her enough reason to believe she was an eccentric. Mistinguett told them that the dove was the least of her eccentricities, and that if she ever visited Sweden again she would show them her famous monkey. It is perhaps as well for them that she never did. Even so, her visit was not without the usual controversy. When Earl Leslie took her into a jewellers' shop – in spite of Frédéric Rey, like Lino Carenzio he had no intention giving up on her, no doubt because funds were running low – and when the man behind the counter made some 'lewd' suggestion, she pocketed a charm bracelet and walked out.

As in Vienna, the company had taken over a whole floor of their hotel, and though she was not amorously interested in Carenzio or Leslie, this did not prevent her from watching them like a hawk. One night she was sitting on her balcony, taking a breath of fresh air before going to bed, when she saw them leaving the hotel with their shoes in their hands. Dressing quickly, she and Frédé followed them. They had been invited to a nude bathing party at which several press photographers were present by a group of Swedish prostitutes. Striking a blow against immorality, she banged the offenders' heads together and made them return to their hotel minus their clothes, which had been disposed of by Frédé!

The designer Zig was present at the Stockholm première. He had recently been in trouble with the French authorities for refusing to do military service and had been imprisoned. As with Chevalier, Mistinguett had campaigned for his release, but in this instance her plea had fallen on deaf ears and Zig had been compelled to serve his sentence. After she had finished her performance in Stockholm, Mistinguett was a little surprised to see Zig walking onto the stage to present her with a bouquet of flowers; usually someone was 'planted' within the audience, ready to step forward at the appropriate moment. The bouquet, she observed, was unusually heavy. Zig had concealed a large number of spoons amongst the blooms and as Mistinguett raised the bouquet to her nose, they clattered to the stage. The audience applauded wildly, thinking it was all part of the act. Mistinguett was not amused. Excusing herself, she left the stage and the offending bouquet found itself wrapped around Zig's neck. Had she not been wearing one of his elaborate creations at the time – a short pink gown with a feathered train, and an almost idiotic-looking cocked hat with a cluster of plumes one foot taller than she was – it is doubtful that he would have worked for her again. Indeed, it was only after Frédéric Rey's intervention that she decided to speak to him again.

Mistinguett's tour of Norway was ostensibly the end of the road for Earl Leslie, who had been taking too much for granted and for far too long. Not quite by chance, he managed to get himself introduced to the father of the Rocky Twins. When they had been launched in Paris by Mistinguett a few years before they had been under-age, and their father, already furious upon discovering that his sons were not only homosexual but transvestites as well, had threatened to sue her, though he had soon changed his mind when the Twins sent him a portion of their salary, which was considerable. When Mistinguett came off the stage one night, Leslie contrived to have the Twins' father, wearing his officer's uniform, waiting in her dressing room. Leslie must have been disappointed to watch his plan back-fire . . . rather than give Mistinguett the sharp end of his tongue, her antagonist had turned up only to ask her out to dinner!

The tour continued and Mistinguett increased her menagerie. She had arrived in Oslo with the dove perched on her shoulder: she left, dragged along the station platform by a pair of adult great danes. One elderly admirer, a fishing enthusiast, had never been more serious when, after a show, he asked her on an expedition because he was confident of catching her a live whale! 'Buy me some flowers,' she said. 'I don't have much room in the fish tank at Bougival. And why do I want a whale when I'm surrounded by so many sharks?'

The company moved on to Warsaw. This was another city which met with Mistinguett's disapproval because the theatre director had insisted on using some of his own girls in the revue, the lightest of whom weighed in at eleven stone. She told him, 'I don't perform with elephants!' The director had allowed her to have her own way, but docked her fee for the revue which resulted in her walking out of the theatre. There were then further problems at the railway station when the guard refused to allow her onto the train with her dogs. Leslie's suggestion that she leave the dogs behind ultimately cost him her friendship. She turned on him in front of the press photographers in the station forecourt. When he called her Micky and worse still attempted to kiss her, she hit him with her handbag.

By the time the company returned to Paris in July 1933 there was little left to say. Leslie took up with a German dancer called Pia and soon afterwards asked her to become his wife. He was still under contract to Mistinguett, which meant that he had to ask her permission to leave the troupe and pay the usual forfeit. Mistinguett told him that she was so keen to see the back of him that no forfeit was necessary. When Pia telephoned Bougival to thank her for her benevolence she was told 'accidentally' that Earl Leslie already had a young wife in America. The dancer, one of the first striptease artistes in France, immediately returned to her native Hamburg. Earl Leslie attempted to solve his problems by turning to drink, and for several weeks pestered Mistinguett wherever she went. There was a vicious confrontation at a society party where home truths were flung around from both sides. The hapless Leslie, threatened by Mistinguett's heavies and probably with another bashing from her famous handbag, fled for his life and the pair never met again. For a while he formed his own dance company, based in Monte Carlo, and once he had obtained his divorce married a dancer whose stage name was Carmen. Soon afterwards he returned to the United States.

Mistinguett, worn out physically and emotionally, telephoned her brother in Antibes to check up on his wedding plans. At the end of July, instead of returning to her villa, she took Fraisette to London where they spent a week with Noël Coward and Sir Charles Cochran. Again the possibility of a British tour was discussed: again it was turned down. 'The British would neither accept nor understand me,' she said. Some twenty five years later, Edith Piaf would issue the same statement. In London, Noël Coward escorted her to a performance of *Helen*, then playing to packed audiences at the Pavillion. After the show, he is reputed to have told her that *Evergreen* had been written with her in mind. What is certain is that Mistinguett did make enquiries about having the revue translated and staged at the Casino de Paris, providing she could have Coward as her leading man. The actor may have considered such a suggestion horrendous. Away from her patch, Mistinguett was always on her very best behaviour, but Coward could hardly forget his first visit to Paris in 1909 when he had met Max Dearly back stage at the Moulin-Rouge. Expecting a convivial tête-à-tête in the stars' dressing room, he had been witness to the most violent quarrel in the history of the music-hall!

Early in August, Charles Cochran drove his guests to Croydon airport, from whence they flew to Paris. A further week was spent at Bougival, where Mistinguett's costume for her brother's wedding had been delivered during her absence. She then drove down to Antibes to what ostensibly would be an extension of one of her revues.

The wedding took place on 21 August 1933 and the reception was held at the Hôtel Martinez in Cannes, some eleven kilometres from Antibes. Mistinguett herself had written out the invitation cards, stressing that as the bride would be wearing white, so would everyone else. Frédéric Rey was meant to have been her escort for the weekend, in spite of the fact that many people in Paris had accused him of being her gigolo. As with Pilcer, Mistinguett had made the mistake of neglecting him by going to London. Léon Volterra had engaged him for a revue, in which he had danced virtually naked, and by a remarkable coincidence the Mexican-American film star Ramon Novarro had been invited to the première. His latest film, *Mata Hari*, which he had made with Greta Garbo, was showing in Paris and one of his plum lines – 'What's the matter, Mata?' – had become a comic byword amongst the English-speaking section of the music-hall. Frédé had been worshipping Novarro for a long time; he had seen *The Pagan* in Vienna, and the actor's splendid physique, which had incurred the censor's wrath, had given him the idea for his new routine at the Casino. When the pair met in Frédéric's dressing room, it had been love at first sight. Novarro's maxim was, 'If you've got it, flaunt it!' As soon as Mistinguett found out that her handsome young lover had dropped her for another man, she telephoned Volterra and ordered him to drop Frédéric from the revue. The director refused. Nude dancers were good box-office, nude male dancers even more so.

The Rey-Novarro affair, coupled with the fact that Leslie was no longer around to cause trouble, offered Lino Carenzio a heaven-sent opportunity to muscle in on Mistinguett's affections. When her son Léopold telephoned to say that he would be unable to attend Fraisette and Marcel's wedding on account of pressure of work, she used the Italian as a last resort to keep up her important public image. Ultimately, she allowed herself to fall in love with him.

The Bourgeois wedding was the society event of the year, and as usual Mistinguett, and not the bride, occupied the central position on the stage. At midnight, the entire party left the hotel and descended to the beach, where most of the guests stripped off their white outfits and donned swimming costumes. Mistinguett declined to take a dip, and instead took a promenade along the beach with Carenzio. She observed a lithe-bodied young man, standing away from the crowd, with his arms around a pretty girl. Someone had told her that the girl's name had not figured on the guest list, and she went to investigate. When the young man turned around she recognized her son, Léopold, and he informed her that the girl who had 'gate-crashed' the party was his wife. The pair had decided to marry secretly, no doubt to avoid being upstaged by the groom's mother. Mistinguett was disappointed, though far from angry. The most important thing in her world at that moment was not her son's happiness, but the fact that he had proved himself 'normal'.

Rigolboche!

By the time Mistinguett arrived with her troupe at Bougival in the September of 1933 she had already thought out most of the ideas for her next revue at the Casino. In fact, she was in for something of a shock . . . the ageing siren, Cécile Sorel, was still there, proving that a lot of money can be made through having little talent. Mistinguett had attended the première – her acid comments have already been observed, though she had been unusually polite when the star had asked her to dine in her dressing-room. Now she was annoyed that the public could have been so gullible. Cécile's revue, *Vive Paris*!, in which the major sketch was entitled 'Maîtresse de Rois', had already run for several months and looked like running for several more, and Mistinguett had no intention of waiting until the star stepped down . . . or, as she put it, dropped down. This time there was no heated exchange between Varna and Dufrenne, which might have delighted Madame Sorel. Mistinguett quietly went to see Paul Derval, the director of the Folies-Bergère, and asked him if she could stage the revue there.

Derval, who had been born Alexis Pitron d'Obigny de Ferrières, was something of an innovator in French music-hall in that his fascination for the naked female form had resulted in his being partly responsible for what is generally regarded as the world's first striptease. This had taken place in broad daylight in the street outside the Moulin-Rouge, as a wager between himself and a drunken entrepreneur at the students' Bal des Quatz' Arts. Extremely good-looking, muscular and tall – qualities which were not shared with many of his contemporaries – Derval had been attracted to Mistinguett for some time, though she soon made it clear that their relationship would never be anything but a professional one. It also has to be said that, albeit inadvertently, Paul

Derval paved the way for the demise of the musical revue, for after Mistinguett, with few exceptions the major stars of almost all the Parisian revues were not the big names following in her footsteps, but the breasts of the dancers, one unsavoury characteristic which applies to the present Moulin-Rouge and Lido. Mistinguett foresaw this as early as 1933 when she said, 'One day, sex will take over.'

Folies en Folies opened towards the end of 1933, and was more of a recital than an actual revue, although the costumes were as lavish as in her earlier productions, and the songs were, as usual, ahead of their time. Only a star of Mistinguett's calibre could have got away with anything quite as vulgar as 'Tout ça n'Arrive qu'a Moi'!

> Le jour de ma première extase,
> Comme y avait une fuite de gaz,
> Et une grande explosion!
> J'ai tout perdu,
> Excepté ma vertu. . .
> Mais quelle sensation,
> De voir le ciel. . .
> Par le trou du plafond!
>
> (The day of my first ecstasy,
> There was a gas leak,
> And a big explosion!
> I lost everything but my virtue,
> But what a sensation to see the sky
> Through the hole in the ceiling!)

This song only got worse towards the end. The biggest success from the show, however, was Albert Willemetz's 'C'Est Vrai', and considering Mistinguett had not supplied the lyrics herself, the *parolier* must have taken an enormous risk in presenting her with a song which was a public declaration of the real Mistinguett, warts and all. 'C'Est Vrai' became her secondary theme tune and along with 'Mon Homme' stayed firmly in her repertoire for another twenty years. Even today when one sees an artiste imitating her (more often than not a female impersonator) the song is usually this one:

On dit quand je fais des emplettes,
Que j'paye pas c'que j'achète,
C'est vrai!
On dit que j'ai la voix qui traîne
En chantant mes rengaines,
C'est vrai!
Mais j's'rais pas Mistinguett
Si j'étais pas comme ça!

(They say that when I go shopping,
I don't pay for what I buy,
It's true!
They say I have a voice which drags
Whilst I'm singing my refrains,
It's true!
But I wouldn't be Mistinguett
If I wasn't like that!)

Mistinguett recorded the song in September 1935 with Pierre Chagnon and his orchestra, and it remains one of her greatest commercial successes. It brought her unexpected praise from the novelist Colette, not one of her favourite people.

Mistinguett is now national property. Her entrance is made with the greatest simplicity. She wears a diamond-studded hat and advances so close to the public that one can smell her delicious fragrance. Neither has she allowed herself to become big-headed. During the long storm of applause one witnesses the change in her pale blue eyes whilst they fill with tears. I would like to include a sonnet, written in honour of this spiritual diva who possesses the most beautiful legs in Paris, and the most gracious smile in the whole world. . .

The sonnet, penned by an essayist who signed himself only as Lacombe, was so condescending that even Mistinguett thought it pure kitsch. It ended:

Her character is honest, pure her eloquence,
Her benevolences discreet gestures.
Hearts such as hers set Paris aglow!

Lino Carenzio was now firmly ensconced as Mistinguett's beau, and
when the Folies revue closed she made a point of showing him off as
much as possible. Maurice Chevalier had returned from Hollywood
for a brief respite from a successful series of film musicals – *The
Merry Widow*, which he had just made with Jeanette MacDonald, was
awaiting release. Chevalier was also experiencing marital problems.
Before leaving for the United States some years before, he had married
Yvonne Vallée, and the couple were now living apart, waiting for their
divorce papers to come through. Naturally, Chevalier was invited to
spend a few days at Bougival. Frédéric Rey, who for the time being
had mended his ways by ending his affair with Ramon Novarro, had
been forgiven and even given his own room, though needless to say
Mistinguett charged him board, and everyone, including Chevalier,
was politely reminded to bring a box of groceries. Mistinguett's excuse
for her parsimony was invariably the same . . . whenever a guest was
expected at Bougival, the store in the village had either closed early or
gone on strike! Fraisette, still employed as secretary whenever she was
in Paris, which was not often during the first years of her marriage, was
put in charge of checking-in these provisions as they arrived.

It is not clear whether Mistinguett was deliberately taking advantage
of Chevalier's imminent divorce in order to ensnare him for herself,
though the photographs taken in her garden at the time show them
looking relaxed and happy. Neither does Chevalier appear to have
minded the presence of Lino Carenzio and Frédéric Rey. It may well
be that Maurice Chevalier's attitude towards Mistinguett was the same
as hers had been at the height of their love affair: a recognition that
though it had been almost impossible to stay apart for more than a few
days without pining for each other, being together only resulted in an
even tenser situation on account of their stature within the music-hall
community. As for Carenzio and Rey, they took advantage of the
trauma caused by Chevalier's presence to become attached to each
other. Jean Gabin, one of the other guests at Bougival, decided not to
become involved with anyone: he spent most of his sojourn looking
after Mistinguett's animals.

Although Jacques Charles had already written Mistinguett's next revue, she told him that for a few months at least it would have to be put on ice. The reason for this was nothing to do with Chevalier: she had injured her knee during a fall on stage at the Folies-Bergère, though she had managed to hide the fact from her public. The torn ligament would dog her for the rest of her career. Like Edith Piaf, who during the last years of her life sang with all the odds stacked against her, Mistinguett refused to give in to illness and injury, though she was deeply upset when her doctor warned her against driving her car, for this, she declared, impeded her independence.

In fact, there was little work until the summer of 1935, when she accepted a tour of Belgium with an adaptation of the Folies revue. She and Carenzio shared a suite at the Grand Hotel in Brussels, which was used as their base for the tour. All began well . . . the pair were invited to dine with Léopold III and Queen Astrid at the royal palace, and their recitals at the Palais d'Eté were nothing short of triumphant, especially the sketch entitled 'Dans les Bouges la Nuit', which she had played with Lad during the previous European tour.

It was in Brussels that Mistinguett met the man whom she often referred to as 'my demon spirit' or 'the cheesy bastard'. His name was Léo Kok.

Virtually nothing is known about this young man, other than that he had been born in Holland, and that for a number of years he had directed a club in Berlin called Jonny's, after the Marlène Dietrich song. It is doubtful that he had met Mistinguett during her visit to Berlin . . . she had refused to see anyone, and had since sworn never to speak to a German again. Kok turned up in her dressing room one night after the show. As soon as he mentioned that he had travelled all the way from Berlin to meet his idol, Mistinguett ordered her chauffeur, Charles, to throw him out into the gutter where he belonged. The episode should have ended there, but it did not. The next night, when Mistinguett stepped up to the footlights, she saw that of the first two rows of the stalls only two seats had been occupied, even though she had been informed before going on that the revue had sold out. In order to make his point, Kok had purchased fifty seats!

Kok's reasons for his recklessness were made obvious after the show when an intrigued Mistinguett asked him back to her dressing room, ostensibly to question him before throwing him out again. Watched by her entire entourage, he fell to his knees and declared that he had been madly in love with her since watching her descend from her train in Berlin! She only found this laughable. Pointing to his beer gut, she asked him when his baby was due, but even this was taken as a compliment. Finally, as he would not take no for an answer, she hit him with her handbag, and he left!

The tour progressed, and Mistinguett experienced what she described as one of the saddest tragedies of her life. A few nights after coming to see her show for a second time, the Belgian king and his Swedish-born queen had left for their villa at Halisorn, in Switzerland. On 29 August 1935 they were involved in a car crash. Astrid, who had just celebrated her thirtieth birthday, was killed outright. Mistinguett took the news badly when it was broken to her one hour before she was due on stage, and that night she came very close to cancelling a show for the first time in her career. Walking onto the stage a few minutes before curtain-up, she told the audience that any applause would only be in memory of the dead queen. Many of her more comical numbers were left out of the performance, and she wore a black dress for 'Au Fond de Tes Yeux', the song which had been written to proclaim her love for Harry Pilcer. The Belgians were deeply moved and bombarded her with flowers, which she sent to Queen Astrid's funeral.

Throughout the rest of the tour, Lino Carenzio's behaviour was rather strange. Much of the time when they were not working or rehearsing he declined to accompany Mistinguett on her excursions into the Belgian countryside. She does seem to have been aware of his relationship, if it could be thus termed, with Frédéric Rey, and appears to have been willing to turn a blind eye. After all, she was holding the purse strings and she knew that he would come running back to her once he ran short of money, and she also knew that, contract or no contract, anyone who displeased her could be dropped from her productions without so much as a word of argument. When she received word, however, from a reliable authority, that Carenzio had been consorting with Léo Kok behind her back, she was furious. Because she did not wish to tarnish her reputation amongst the Belgians, who after her respect towards Queen Astrid regarded her as a divine being, she decided not to spoil things by giving her difficult Italian partner the sack. This, she declared, would have to wait until they returned to Paris. Instead she placed him under 'house-arrest' and forbade him to leave his hotel room. By the time the company reached Paris in November, however, she had forgiven him and he was offered a supporting role in her new revue, the appropriately-titled *Un Coup de Veine*, a retrospective revue which opened at the Théâtre Porte Saint-Martin. It was a show which she not only loathed, she closed it half-way through the run.

Though Carenzio had been given more than his share of verbal warnings, publicly and otherwise, he continued seeing Léo Kok in Paris, and it soon became obvious that the Dutchman's original fascination had not been for Mistinguett, but for her partner. Carenzio was summoned to Bougival and asked to make his choice. He chose Léo Kok. When Mistinguett told an American reporter, 'Watch out for the Eye-Tie . . . he's going to end up having Kok trouble!' she was not joking.

> I decided to set him up. He was absolutely loaded, so I worked out a way of ruining him. The next time he invited Lino out to dinner, I decided to go with him . . . I took the entire troupe to the Boeuf, and we ordered the most expensive dishes on the menu!

The plan back-fired. Someone in the troupe warned the pair what was about to happen, and they left a note with a waiter to say that they would be delayed but did not mind paying for the meal. When the bill came there was a note attached saying that the couple had left for the Côte d'Azure. Mistinguett did not argue. Paying the bill she left the club, collected Fraisette, and in spite of her wrenched knee drove overnight to her villa in Antibes. Here she found the offending pair 'canoodling like a couple of love-sick adolescents'.

Her methods of dealing with the Carenzio-Kok affair were some-what bizarre. Rather than send the Dutchman packing – she actually blamed Carenzio for leading him astray – she pretended to befriend him by engaging him as her partner for her forthcoming Paris revue, scheduled to open at the Alhambra in the spring of 1936. Carenzio was dropped. He was made to leave the villa there and then, and as he had no money, he had to seek shelter in a refuge for waifs and strays. Kok, however, was not billed under his real name. That, Mistinguett declared, would have been giving him too much credit for what he had done. The billboards advertising the revue hailed him as La Petite Tête de Fromage (Little Cheese Head). He was called this not because of his pasty complexion or the fact that he had been born in Holland, but because Mistinguett had been told that during his 'private' moments with Carenzio he had nurtured a fondness for dressing up as a milk maid.

Without a doubt, the Christmas of 1935 was the happiest in Mistinguett's life. It was spent at Bougival. Chevalier, now divorced from his wife, was guest of honour, but if Mistinguett was hoping to effect another reconciliation she was in for a shock . . . Chevalier announced that he had fallen in love with the song writer Nita Raya who, at twenty, was twenty seven years his junior. Mistinguett told him that he should be ashamed of himself, for one newspaper had already called him a 'dirty old man'. She then summoned Frédéric Rey, who was forty years *her* junior! As for Lino Carenzio, the moment Mistinguett left Antibes, he emerged from hiding and moved into her villa with Léo Kok.

Fraisette and Marcel arrived at Bougival on Christmas Eve. Mistinguett had gone into Paris to do some last minute shopping – not that anyone ever received much in the way of gifts – and when she returned was told to keep out of the salon because a surprise had been laid on for her. This made her suspicious, but Chevalier, who was in on the act, promised her that it would be a most agreeable surprise.

A few hours later Léopold arrived with his wife. It would seem that for some reason Mistinguett disliked her daughter-in-law, probably because she had been told that the young woman, and not Léopold, had engineered the secret wedding. Suffice to say she is hardly mentioned in Mistinguett's memoirs, and Mistinguett would often pretend to forget her name. During the evening there was a telephone call from Harry Pilcer, who had been invited to join in the festivities and who now announced that he was staying in Cannes. Had Pilcer turned up with Chevalier almost ruling the roost at Bougival, Mistinguett's proposed party would have been tantamount to a boxing match.

At midnight, the guests filed into the salon. In front of the enormous spruce tree a nativity scene had been set up, but when Mistinguett approached the crib to examine the baby Jesus, the child moved.

Marcel proudly announced: 'That is Jeanne Bourgeois. . .the new one!'

Delighted as she was, and a little amazed that Fraisette had managed to conceal her pregnancy from her, Mistinguett told her brother that as far as the world was concerned there would only ever be one Jeanne Bourgeois, and several people in the room no doubt mused that at times even this was one too many.

> I baptised her with salty tears. My niece . . . my Micky! She looked so much like me, and I felt proud to be sharing such a moment with Maurice Chevalier, until he turned to me and whispered: 'Why couldn't it have been us?' I thought to myself: 'What a load of shit!'

Fleurs de Paris, at the Alhambra, was a great success and more than made up for the losses incurred by the previous revue. Fortunately for Mistinguett and the other performers, Léo Kok never made it as far as the première . . . he succumbed to an attack of smallpox. Attempting to return to Holland he was stopped at the border by customs officials, who refused to allow him to leave France whilst suffering from a notifiable disease. Rushing back to Mistinguett, he begged her to help him. She sold him a pot of her famous yellow skin lotion. This was the substance that she had brought back from America and which she used to colour the torsos of her male nudes for her statue tableaux. This time Kok was allowed to cross the border since he also had a 'doctor's' statement to the effect that he was suffering from jaundice. Several days later Mistinguett received a telephone call from an Amsterdam hospital to say that her demon spirit had died. In many ways she was relieved.

Lino Carenzio was summoned to Paris at the eleventh hour to learn Kok's part. All, it seemed, was forgiven. During the run of the revue the couple were approached by the young director Christian Jacques and presented with the script for what would become Mistinguett's best loved and most famous film, the semi-autobiographical *Rigolboche*.

Shooting began during the summer of 1936 and took only a few weeks on account of the limited budget. Mistinguett, though sixty one, managed to play a twenty five year old unmarried mother with comparative ease, and it is interesting to note that one of the children in the film was played by Henriette Rageon, looking much younger than her eighteen years. Later she would become famous in France as the great *chanteuse*, Patachou, and infamous in Britain as the cabaret entertainer who, during her London appearances, would often step down from the stage and snip off the neck ties of various antagonistic gentlemen in the audience. Patachou, though never a dancer, was in some ways one of Mistinguett's most hated rivals. Some years later she would be 'discovered' and launched by Maurice Chevalier. Mistinguett said: 'When I saw him kissing that woman in the middle of the street, I felt sick to the stomach and wanted to throttle the pair of them!'

The script itself was simple but effective. A young woman is forced to work as a prostitute in a dockland dive in order to support her child and prevent him from being claimed by his drunken father. During her plight she is kidnapped by the father's henchmen and whilst being rowed across the harbour to meet her fate, accidentally stabs one of them. Fleeing to Paris, she finds herself in an agent's office, auditioning for a revue. The agent recognizes her potential and engages her to appear in his club. She changes her name to Rigolboche and is, of course, a tremendous success, descending a staircase whilst crooning 'Pour Etre Heureux, Chantez!' and baring enough of her thighs to have part of the scene cut by the British censors when the film was released here in 1937.

> Dans la vie, malgré tout c'qu'on raconte,
> On peut être heureux de temps en temps.
> Moi qui n'aime pas les gens qui s'démontent,
> Je vous donne un conseil épatant:
> Pour être heureux, chantez!
>
> (In life, in spite of what people tell you,
> You can be happy from time to time.
> I don't like people who pull each other to pieces.
> My startling advice is:
> If you want to be happy, sing!)

Throughout most of the film, Rigolboche was far from happy. The friends of the murdered thug follow her to Paris, and only her motherly instincts and the love of her public keep her from going under. There is a very moving scene when she rocks her child to sleep with a refrain from 'Au Fond de Tes Yeux', (there was an almost identical scene in *Les Amants de Demain*, which starred Edith Piaf, twenty two years later). All ends well, of course, when Rigolboche's mentors receive their come-uppance, and the film closes with the celebrated staircase sequence on stage at the Casino de Paris. Mistinguett, not Rigolboche, slowly descends wearing fifteen pounds of plumes on her head and with an enormous girdle of plumes strapped to her waist. Passing along a line of handsome tuxedoed studs, she is met by Lino Carenzio, who dances with her in a dream-like sequence before relieving her of her wrap and escorting her back to the steps. The sequence was an absolute masterpiece, and for one reason. Christian Jacques had been worried about the ending of his film . . . the fact was, he had run out of cash and could not afford to build the set. Mistinguett was so keen to include the sequence that she offered to loan him the money. Lino Carenzio, in effect, saved her the bother by arguing with her and walking off the set before the film had been completed. So a compromise was reached; a piece of film, shot during a Mistinguett-Carenzio performance at the Casino in 1932, was added on, which explains why the visual and sound quality of *Rigolboche* changes alarmingly for the better towards the end!

Mistinguett returned to her villa in Antibes with Carenzio; incredibly, she was still madly in love with him, and even when he announced that he had been offered a contract with a London theatre, she did not protest too strongly. Chevalier and Pilcer had taught her the problems of trying to hang onto a man by forcing his hand, and when Carenzio left it was apparently with her blessing. *Okay for Sound*, put on by the British impresario George Black, opened at the Palladium in November 1936 and proved so successful that when the Italian telephoned Mistinguett a few weeks later, he informed her that he was considering staying in England for good.

Mistinguett cancelled her next revue. Lonely and unhappy, and realizing for the first time in her life that the years were creeping up on her, she decided to leave France. The great entertainers of the day, in particular Damia and Fréhel, drank themselves senseless or took cocaine whenever they were feeling down. Mistinguett travelled. It is a fact that, had she not suffered from these occasional bouts of depression, England and the United States would never have seen her.

Burning the Candle
At Both Ends

On 3 December 1936 Mistinguett sailed from Le Havre for New York and for what would be the turning point in her career. These really were the great years, and the fact that she had not reached her peak until the age of sixty only increased her massive appeal on both sides of the Atlantic. This time, however, there was no man to keep her company, certainly not in the accepted sense, and none of the usual adventures to occupy her mind during the long, fraught journey, much of which was spent alone in her cabin, muffled against the dreadful cold. Her companion was the dresser she had engaged at the last moment before leaving Bougival – a pretty young transvestite whom she had baptised Guilda and who also acted as a dummy for her dress designers. Guilda, by all accounts, was not very good company and suffered terribly from sea-sickness. He looked so much like a real woman, however, that one American reporter mistook him for Mistinguett's daughter!

The press conference which took place at the Waldorf Astoria in January 1937 was unusual so far as Mistinguett was concerned. She answered the questions which she called her 'regulars', such as what was her favourite colour or her preferred brand of soap. She was then informed by the establishment that if she agreed to hold a second conference the next day, she would be paid one thousand dollars, cash in hand . . . an inordinate sum in those days.

The 'conference' turned out to be one of the largest pre-advertisement campaigns America had involved herself in since the explosion caused by Sarah Bernhardt's arrival some years before. Mistinguett was asked to make a list of her favourite products – soap, underwear, headache tablets, even toilet paper and sanitary towels. She found this amusing, especially when substantial amounts of cash were pushed her way to persuade her to change her mind and endorse some of the lesser-known American products. She was also delighted when a manufacturer of biscuits, who had learned of her brother's shop in Paris, offered her a small fortune to have her picture printed on the lids of cookie tins. The problems began when she was asked to endorse a brand of sewing machine.

'I get headaches from time to time, and we all have to use toilet paper,' she declared. 'As for sewing machines . . . I've never used one, and neither would I wish to. If I can sew up all my dresses by hand, then so can everyone else!'

One product which caused a great deal of consternation was a patent medicine called Liberator. Even though Mistinguett read the jargon printed on the label, she could not work out what the medicine was for.

'That isn't important,' she was told. 'All you have to do is stand in front of the microphone and read what is written on the card.'

The words were, 'I cannot get through my day unless I've had my Liberator before going to bed.' The product was a well-known laxative!

Mistinguett's version, and it went out live on air to millions of astonished Americans, was, 'Even if I did suffer from constipation, I wouldn't broadcast it to half the world. However, if I did find myself bunged up, then I would take a good dose of Liberator!'

During her first week in New York Mistinguett earned more money from advertising than she had in her last three French revues put together. Her last endorsement brought in several thousand dollars and was for a brand of fountain-pen, which she used to print the notice which she pinned to her dressing room door, announcing that from now on she would only be interested in singing, dancing and having fun.

Tickets for her recitals on Broadway had sold out whilst she had been crossing the ocean from France, and she had been offered an open contract and a free hand in the production of her shows. On the night of her première, during the interval, she was interviewed in English by the writer and critic Sinclair Lewis, and again this was broadcast to the nation.

Lewis: Miss, you've become a legend in America. You're almost as famous here as you are in France. Some people even name their pets after you. You are a shining example of everything that is represented by the word Paris.

Miss: I'm astonished by that. . .

Lewis: There have only ever been two truly great French stars . . . yourself and Sarah Bernhardt. When the divine Sarah appeared in public wearing a certain kind of glove, she was copied by women all over America. She used to buy them in bulk, just so that she could leave them behind, wherever she went. Hundreds of theatres all over the country have Sarah's gloves on display . . . you can see them, hanging up in little glass cabinets. Have you ever thought along the same lines?

Miss: Sure. I keep reading in the newspapers that my legs are the loveliest in Paris. I thought of tossing my old stockings into the audience. I'm sure they wouldn't mind if I took them off after the finale. . .

It was whilst she was appearing on Broadway that Mistinguett began descending into the audience. She would single out the handsomest man on the front row and serenade him with 'My Man', though by this time she had been supplied with a new lyric by Reginald Arkell which today sounds so ridiculous that one wonders why she accepted it in the first place, particularly as the adaptation introduced by Fanny Brice, which Mistinguett had already sung, was just as good as the original Willemetz-Charles version which she had sung as far back as 1920.

> If you could see how he dances at a ball,
> You'd go dippy!
> For his toes, goodness knows,
> Never touch the floor at all,
> He's so nippy!
> I guess you'll confess,
> He's a dream in evening dress

Leaving Croydon Airport, October 1938. (*Topham Picture Source*)

A studio portrait taken during the shooting of *Rigolboche*, 1936. (*Popperfoto*)

At the London Casino, December 1947. Still wowing them at 72! (*Popperfoto*)

When you meet him.
When his eyes show surprise,
He's a dimple in disguise,
I could eat him!
He's the very latest out,
There is no doubt,
And when he holds me in his arms
I want to shout!

She had also discovered another song, 'I'm Feeling like a Million', which had been written by Herb Brown for a second-rate American film. The lyrics, it has to be said, were just as appalling as Arkell's.

Though I'm flat, though I'm broke,
Though I'm bent, I'm content!
Though I haven't got a dollar,
A shilling or a sou,
I'm feeling like a million,
And I want to get this over to you!

Mistinguett took to the song in a big way and was incensed when someone informed her that it had been in Joséphine Baker's repertoire for some time, and that the star was thinking about commissioning a French adaptation. She was already familiar with some Herb Brown songs, albeit indirectly. He had written most of the songs for the 1928 film, *Broadway Melody*, and the following year had collaborated with Arthur Freed on 'The Pagan Love Song', which Ramon Novarro had warbled in the film which had inadvertently opened the gates on his passionate affair with Frédéric Rey. Novarro's skimpy costume in the film had been considered extremely immoral by some critics who had later been willing to accept Rey's diamond-studded posing pouch, or even less when he had appeared in his own revue at the Folies-Bergère.

Joséphine had already sung 'I'm Feeling like a Million' on Broadway, and one leading critic had dismissed her performance, with or without the song, as 'pure, unadulterated crap'. On Christmas Eve 1935 she had opened in *The Ziegfeld Folies*, an engagement which had been organized by her fake husband, John Wells, alias Count

Abatino, and which had been closed by the critics. Separating from Wells, Joséphine had returned to France and a few months later had received word that he had died of cancer. Mistinguett had dismissed her rival's reactions as typical: within months of her mentor's death Joséphine had married the French industrialist, Jean Lion. Like her previous trips down the aisle, it had ended in divorce. Though Mistinguett found it impossible to prevent Joséphine from singing her latest hit in English, and this was not through lack of trying, she did stop her from singing it in French by going to see Herb Brown and purchasing the music rights, which she sold to her French composer friend, Marc Cab. She then telephoned her son Léopold and told him to begin writing her a French text – the Americans were already eager to meet the writer of some of Mistinguett's most famous songs, even though at this stage in his 'career' he had not so much as picked up a pen!

From New York, Mistinguett moved to Chicago, where she had performed solely for sentimental reasons thirteen years before. This time she was terrified of going out alone because she feared she might be kidnapped by gangsters though this did not prevent her from dining with one such who has never been named. The phrase, 'Is that a gun in your pocket, or are you pleased to see me?' was not coined by Mae West, but by Mistinguett, who immediately decided to commit the adventure to posterity. She began writing the lyrics to 'Mon Gangster' in a Chicago hotel, and the song would be set to music on her return to Paris by Marc Cab. It became one of the big record successes of 1938, along with 'Je Cherche un Millionaire' and the re-recording of 'Mon Homme'.

After a few recitals in Chicago which she quietly dismissed as forgettable, Mistinguett travelled to Hollywood. She was afraid of flying, so she took the train, and this added four days to her schedule. The queen of the French music-hall, so used to creating a fuss and making a spectacle of herself in Paris, actually hated Hollywood! She had been expected to arrive with a menagerie of monkeys. One reporter was even disappointed when she descended from the train carrying her own suitcase and not wearing her plumes. Others made a fuss of Guilda: incredibly, no one had yet discovered his secret. The company, which numbered around forty, were invited to a reception at the home of the ageing film star, May Robson, who apparently had

taken few lessons in diplomacy because she had also invited Myrna
Loy and Robert Montgomery, who had both worked for Florenz
Ziegfeld. *The Great Ziegfeld*, the bio-pic of the showman's life, had
just been put on general release and Mistinguett was asked for her
opinion on the motion picture which had been MGM's most costly
since Ramon Novarro's *Ben Hur*. She was not impressed. She accused
the director, Robert L Leonard, of copying some of the tableaux from
one of her Casino revues, and there was ill-feeling all round when
Mistinguett watched the staircase sequence with a somewhat over-
made-up Virginia Bruce descending under an immense mushroom of
flowers whilst the chorus sang 'A Pretty Girl is like a Melody'. Worse
still, Fanny Brice had been given a part in the film.

Mistinguett adored Robert Montgomery because of his earthy
charm, though she found Clark Gable condescending and Robert
Taylor 'too much the other way'. Joan Crawford she liked. 'I believe
she has all the prospects of being a good bitch!' she said. As for
Myrna Loy, Fanny Brice and Virginia Bruce: 'They are the pits,' she
declared.

During Mistinguett's Hollywood première, Guilda executed a
brilliant impersonation of Barbette. When he took off his wig at
the end of his act, however, his only gratification was to be booed.
Mistinguett defended him after the show. Shrugging her shoulders,
she told reporters that in France a person's sexuality always took
second place to artistic merit, and added, 'Only you Americans keep
your dirty secrets under cover.' This was almost certainly aimed at
Robert Taylor, whom she had accused of 'trying to get off with one
of my boys'. Her honesty was not appreciated by the Hollywood set,
though she was offered the leading role in a film, which she turned
down. Before leaving Tinsel Town she visited an artist's studio, where
she asked politely if she might 'have a go'. The subsequent canvas,
upon which she did a rough impression of a bunch of arum lilies,
later sold for several thousand dollars!

Disenchanted and unenlightened, Mistinguett returned to New
York. In Harlem she attended a baseball match, and agreed to
autograph the winning team's jock-straps in their locker-room.

Harry Pilcer had told her about some of the exclusively gay
establishments in this part of the world, and she visited one. The
transvestities who earned their living impersonating Greta Garbo

and Marlène Dietrich amused her. One evening she walked in on a young man drenched in pink feathers and singing 'Ca C'Est Paris' in near-perfect French. She declared, 'When you walk into a club and see a man dressed up as yourself, then only then do you realize how famous you are! I'm not ashamed of saying that I cried my eyes out!' The young man was engaged to appear in her show at the Rainbow Room. Neither he nor the wealthy industrialist he introduced to her have ever been named, though the meeting resulted in Mistinguett having an affair with the latter, who seems to have been of sufficient importance to ensure that her season at the Rainbow Room was extended by a month. The couple's excursions, when she was not on stage or rehearsing, included visits to Long Island and an evening in an opium-den. She refused to participate in the activities there, she said, because she had witnessed the withering effects of the drug on Jean Cocteau.

It was in New York in January 1937 that Mistinguett became involved in arguably the most bizarre adventure of her whole life, and again it seems to have begun with an outing arranged by her new lover. She was accompanied by a former dancer from the Moulin-Rouge who had left her company some time before to marry an American businessman. This young woman, again she is not named in Mistinguett's autobiography, informed her of a religious institution which had recently been founded by an eccentric Californian as a means of establishing world peace. The incident was widely reported by most of the American newspapers, but little was revealed because the man, whoever he was, bribed the journalists into keeping his name a secret, ostensibly because he and his family had been threatened by the Ku Klux Klan!

It was the strangest proposition anyone had ever made. 'Mistinguett . . . do you read William James?' There was an embarrassing silence before I replied, 'My dear man, I'm not an intellectual. William James isn't exactly what I would call bedside reading!' Then the man replied, 'William James reaches us by divine hypothesis!' I told him that the Sisters of Providence had never taught us that, and he added, 'Then they were wrong . . . very wrong!' He then told me that he owned a fruit-canning factory valued at five million dollars, and at first I assumed he was going to ask me to sign some kind of contract wherein I would have to eat nothing but bananas for months on end. Instead, he said, 'Mistinguett, I'm a widower. My wife was a very accomplished woman, and I would like you to succeed her.' I was touched, until he told me that he had just founded a new religion which he called 'The Divine Hypothesis', and which he claimed would put all conventional religions to shame. He said, 'Fifty thousand people have already been converted, and it occurred to me that I might enlist your help in spreading God's word. Think what it would do for my cause . . . and for America . , . if I announced that I had converted the great Mistinguett by asking her to become the wife of God's representative on Earth!' I couldn't help myself . . . I just burst out laughing and said, 'Can you imagine what the French would say if I became a female pope?' The poor man walked away, less offended than I would have thought. . .

William James had in fact founded the school of pragmatism, a doctrine which judged philosophical assertions by their practical bearing upon human interests. It endured for many years after his death in 1910, and was one of many which flourished in America during the early thirties, based on the Lutherian system. The subject was brought up at Mistinguett's next press conference, and she told reporters that she had almost accepted the man's offer. 'I thought of Liane de Pougy,' she said. 'After all, if a perverted bitch like her could turn to religion, what's to say I wouldn't have made a fine pope?'

A few weeks later, Mistinguett returned to France. Bougival had stood empty during her absence, and her monkeys had been allowed to run amok. Her cook, Caro, had dropped in from time to time, though Mistinguett had locked most of the rooms and hidden the keys. Most of her friends had been telephoned from Le Havre, but there was no welcoming committee this time. Lino Carenzio was still appearing at the London Palladium. Léopold was in Belgium, and Marcel and Fraisette were at the villa in Antibes. Manouche turned up at the house, but only because she happened to be in Paris at the time. Fortunately, a very delicate situation, and Mistinguett's famous temper, was soothed by the arrival of the Hungarian director Mitty Goldin, though he too had been unhappy with Mistinguett's decision to remain in the United States longer than scheduled. Joséphine

Baker's revue, *La Joie de Paris*, was still playing to packed audiences. In all there would be three hundred and forty six performances. The highlight of the revue was a portentous song called 'Si J'Etais Blanche', which had lyrics by Henri Varna. Mitty Goldin was also worried about the age difference between the two great stars. Mistinguett, at sixty two, was more than thirty years Joséphine's senior, and Goldin knew that a large portion of Mistinguett's popularity was attributable to the fact that she had almost always played the part of the young girl, the Titine of the streets, without appearing ridiculous. He also feared that like Cécile Sorel, she would one day overstep the bounds of good sense and fall flat on her face and make a fool of herself. Mitty Goldin had, of course, made a futile attempt to engage Joséphine during Mistinguett's absence. It was something which had almost cost him his reputation and fortune.

> So far as Mitty was concerned, a celebrity was a suit of armour, and of course he knew where all the dents were. He regarded stars as ordinary people, with lots of luck and little talent. Joséphine Baker was his battle-horse. Unfortunately, the horse had lost the war before the fighting had started. Mitty and Black Pearl had entered into arbitration . . . he had organized a press conference, booked one of the biggest theatres in Paris, and he even had Joséphine insured! Soon afterwards Black Pearl had been taken ill, probably after stuffing herself with money, and Mitty had found himself down the pan . . . broke!

In order to recover his losses after the failed Joséphine Baker affair, Goldin had borrowed money and bought an old, disused cinema called the Plaza on the Boulevard Poissonière. It had been refurbished and reopened as the ABC. As such it quickly became the pinnacle of French entertainment and remained so until the present Olympia reopened under the direction of Bruno Coquatrix in 1954. The first star to top the bill at the ABC was Lys Gauty, an extremely likeable lady popular with Parisian audiences during the thirties with songs such as 'La Chaland qui Passe' and 'Nostalgie'. After a great deal of pestering from her impressario-songwriter Raymond Asso (he was also Marie Dubas' song writer and secretary for a while) Edith Piaf had opened there as *vedette* in March 1937. Mistinguett caught the closing recital on 15 April, and even though she confessed that 'Mon Legionnaire' had made her cry, she always pretended to dislike 'that funny little bugger in black'. Worse still, Piaf was followed by Damia, whom Mistinguett liked even less than Joséphine Baker.

Towards the end of April 1937 Mitty Goldin signed Mistinguett for a recital-revue, *Chansons de Paris*, and the première was set for the end of June. The problems were horrendous, and made even more so by the endless back stage fights between the ebullient director and his equally difficult, short-tempered leading lady. Mistinguett began by demanding Lino Carenzio as her partner. Goldin rang George Black at the London Palladium and was told that *Okay for Sound* was approaching its five hundredth performance, and in any case Carenzio had already stated that he would never work with Mistinguett again for all the money in the world. The great star flew into a rage and threatened to sue the director, who is reputed to have slapped her . . . something no man had ever dared to do without risking a fate worse than death. Subsequently, Mistinguett evicted him from his own theatre, and though they did eventually make up, for the rest of their lives they detested each other.

Mistinguett began searching earnestly for a partner for the new revue, and for a new male chorus. She moved out of Bougival for a while, and spent a week supervising the team of interior designers she had engaged to refurbish her Paris apartment. During her travels she had collected hundreds of Chinese knick-knacks, and her bedroom was transformed into a miniature Shanghai.

The new revue began to take shape by a remarkable twist of fate. One morning the doorbell rang and she herself answered the call. She was astonished to find a pale and trembling Léo Kok standing on her doormat. The Dutchman explained his predicament. He had recovered from his attack of smallpox. The man in the next bed at the Amsterdam hospital had died of the disease, and the doctor who had telephoned Mistinguett had managed to get the names mixed up. Mistinguett was not interested in explanations. Had the circumstances been different, Kok would almost certainly have been given short shrift. Now she was so lonely that she invited him into the apartment and he stayed for six months, though he never became Mistinguett's lover. She had never forgiven him for robbing her of Lino Carenzio.

Mistinguett declared that her new chorus line would have to be exclusively gay. This, she said, would eliminate the risk of her falling in love with one of them and having her heart broken again! She told Kok, 'Buying pretty boys is just like buying lobsters in the market. You always have to barter to get a good price and a nice tender specimen!' Needless to say, the troupe engaged for the ABC in 1937 were physically perfect, though none of them were considered suitable partner material. The search was extended to some of the minor music-halls and clubs, and by the middle of May she had found not one leading man, but two. Léo Kok, who had in any case been placed at the top of her list of reserves, was also signed up.

Georges Lambros Worlou had been born in Alexandria in 1915, and upon joining Jo Bouillon's orchestra as lead guitarist had dropped his surname. A few years later he would achieve world fame as Georges Guétary, and in 1951 he would star in the musical film *An American in Paris* opposite Gene Kelly and Leslie Caron. Mistinguett first saw him at the Alhambra, where she observed that he had a 'better than average' body lurking beneath his gleaming white silk shirt. She said, 'His voice enthralled and seduced me. I knew I would have to have him, so I sent Léo back stage to make the arrangements.'

Whilst Lambros was more than willing to work for the ageing siren – the fact that he was a musician and not a dancer did not bother her, for she had decided to teach him the tricks of her trade – Jo Bouillon was reluctant to let him go, and Mistinguett herself entered the fray. Bouillon became the enemy; even more so ten years later, when he married the Black Pearl herself. What infatuated Mistinguett the most about Lambros, apart from the obvious, was his curious accent. He told her that though he had been born in Egypt, he was in fact Greek. He was worried about the perils of breaking a contract with a man of Bouillon's standing in the music-hall. 'Leave that to me,' she said. That same night, Lambros moved into her apartment, and a few days later Bouillon issued her with a writ. The battle, a nasty one, was fought in the court-room at the Palais de Justice, and Mistinguett won.

I wanted him, and I got him. I was content, and at once baptised him the Hunk. He was a nice man . . . a genuine man who never played practical jokes on me, and who never tried to screw my girls . . . or my boys back stage. I wasn't sure how far he wanted to go in the career he had chosen for himself, though he was more than willing to try. I began by teaching him how to walk on a stage . . . that inimitable glide where the foot no more than brushes against the boards. He was perfect!

Mistinguett's other partner was a boy-friend of Léo Kok: the pair had first met in one of the seedier dives then, as now, commonplace in the back streets of Pigalle. His name was Carlos Machado, and he was a highly-strung Mexican who would cause more than his share of trouble.

A shiver ran down my spine! What a beauty! Imagine a cross between Rudolph Valentino and Clark Gable and you have Machado. He said, 'I want to partner you. I want to sing and dance for you. I want to do everything for you because I am an artiste!' I told him to go ahead. His singing voice was a disaster, but I put that down to lack of training. He was also hard up . . . and you know how benevolent I am when it comes to helping others! I engaged him!

During the weeks leading up to the ABC première Mistinguett was clearly burning the candle at both ends, and in the middle as well. It was almost a repeat of the situation she had found herself in when first coming to live in Paris, when her little band of hoodlums had taken it in turn to sleep with the then up-and-coming young star. This time she was not sleeping with Kok and Lambros, though Machado was allowed this most supreme honour, as were another dancing pair called Kramer and Zibral, whom Kok had picked up in a gay bar. Zibral, it appears, had only been signed up because of his slight resemblance to Maurice Chevalier, something which was even more obvious when the show opened to the public, for Chevalier was invited to the première though, needless to say, Mistinguett made him pay for his ticket.

Zibral's sketch was entitled 'Ma Pomme', after one of Chevalier's most celebrated songs, and the young dancer appeared – horror of horrors – sporting a straw hat. Mistinguett played Marie, an old

woman dressed in rags with down-trodden shoes and a tattered
felt hat decorated with straw and thistles. She walked onto the
stage waving a big umbrella; when this was opened it was full of
holes. Zibral danced around her whilst she recounted the tawdry
events of her long-lost youth. Then she left the stage for a moment,
and returned dragging an enormous harp which she plucked whilst
crooning 'J'En ai Marre'.

This sketch was the biggest success of the revue, but whilst the
public acclaimed the two stars, Chevalier only became more and
more infuriated. Meeting her back stage he told her that unless
she changed the name of the sketch and ordered Zibral to drop
the straw hat routine, he would never have anything to do with
her again. Normally she would have relished the intimidation and
a good dressing room brawl: for Chevalier, however, she would
have done anything. She retitled the sketch 'Titine', and it became
the most famous of her many roles during the last two decades of
her career. 'Miss *was* Titine,' Michel Guyarmathy, the director of
the Folies-Bergère, told me when I interviewed him for this book in
October 1989. 'She belonged to the people, she only sang for the
people . . . the ones up in the gallery. The snobs sitting in the front
row never interested her at all.' After she played the role for the first
time, Chevalier himself walked onto the stage and congratulated her,
and even she was forced to admit that the great man had inadvertently
done her a good turn by his fickle behaviour.

Throughout the run of *Chansons de Paris*, Mitty Goldin only
visited his theatre when Mistinguett was not around, though he
would have been the first to admit that she had worked a miracle
so far as his bank account was concerned. Even so, the revue closed
after just three weeks. Goldin's sure-fire recipe for success was that
the programme at the ABC should change every two or three weeks
to ensure freshness and variation. The concept was later copied by
Bruno Coquatrix and worked exceedingly well.

Mistinguett, who thrived on arguments and self-created problems,
was disappointed at the stalemate situation between herself and the
director, though for the moment she decided to let things go. Mitty
Goldin, without seeing her or even speaking to her on the telephone,
sent her on a tour of France, and there were sell-out performances
in every city and town. Carlos Machado, now that he had passed

through the 'factory' process, almost surpassed Lino Carenzio in popularity: not only was he a good dancer, he also had a fine, strong singing voice. After the tour most of the company disbanded.

Mistinguett and her lover retired to Antibes. They had been there just three days when Mistinguett received an urgent call from Mitty Goldin, who apologized for upsetting her – the first and last time he ever climbed down from his pedestal – and informed her that he had engaged her for another revue. Surprisingly, her fee was not discussed. The Isola brothers had placed the Théâtre Mogador at Goldin's disposal, which in itself was enough to tempt anyone, but when Mistinguett asked for details of the new programme, she was told that the script had yet to be written! Mitty Goldin would play the same trick on Edith Piaf some years later: *La P'tite Lili* would become one of the biggest triumphs of Piaf's career, though she too would always loathe Goldin for his devious dealings and apparent hatred of everyone. Goldin told Mistinguett that she had just two days to return to Paris and clinch the deal. On top of this, she was asked to provide all the songs, and Goldin made a point of stressing that the finale would have to be written by Mistinguett herself! She agreed, but when she asked to sign the contract, Goldin informed her that no such document had been drawn up.

Emile and Vincent Isola were a pair of music-hall entrepreneurs who thought big and ultimately ended up practically inconsequential. Stage carpenters by trade, they had entered show business with a conjuring act at the Folies-Bergère in 1886. By 1901 they had made enough money to lease the Théâtre des Capucines, and two years later had taken charge of the Moulin-Rouge and the Parisiana, where they employed Jacques Charles as their general secretary. When they informed Mistinguett of their ideas for the scenario for the new revue, she accused them of being extravagant and egotistical, and she was not wrong. Their demise came suddenly, a few years later, and they ended their careers as they had begun, working as a second-rate juggling and conjuring act.

Ca C'Est Parisien was an abject disaster from the initial rehearsals onwards. The songs, all of them written as planned by Mistinguett, and mostly to Léo Kok's music, were good, but insufficiently rehearsed. Carlos Machado insisted upon singing two of them himself, against Goldin's and Mistinguett's better judgement. One,

'Bonsoir Chérie', was so bad that he was whistled off the stage. The finale was even more catastrophic. Earlier, Mistinguett had sung and danced in front of a massive three-dimensional cut out of her legs, wearing a flowing white Guyarmathy creation which had attracted gasps of admiration from the audience. She had asked for this to be used for the finale, particularly when Mitty Goldin had announced that the staircase had not been finished. However, Mistinguett had tested this during the afternoon dress rehearsal and though the paint had still been wet, she had given the structure her approval. Whilst making her entrance for the finale, though, her foot became entangled in a trailing wire at the top of the staircase, and whilst trying to right herself against the rails, the entire structure collapsed and she fell twenty feet to the stage below. Fortunately, she was caught by one of the stagehands, and after only a few seconds emerged from behind the backdrop, smiling as though nothing had happened. Many of the audience thought it a part of her act, and applauded. When she tried to walk towards the front of the stage, she found herself unable to move and, in extreme agony, sang the song which she had written only days before:

> Quand il entre au bal musette,
> On dit: Voilà Petite Tête,
> Un malin qui a fait son chemin!'
> Mais il n'a pas l'coeur d'une crapule,
> Il a des scrupules!
> Quand P'tite Tête serre une femme dans ses bras,
> Tout est merveilleux entre ses bras nerveux!
>
> (When he walks into a bal musette,
> They say: 'Here's Little Head,
> A know-all who's done well for himself!'
> But he doesn't have a blackguard's heart,
> He has scruples!
> When Little Head takes a woman in his arms,
> All is wonderful within his nervous arms!)

Mistinguett made no secret of the fact that she had written the song with Léo Kok in mind, and though he had lost all hope of ever becoming her lover, he could count himself one of her close friends, which was infinitely more valuable. Mistinguett usually stuck by her friends through thick and thin, whereas once a lover tired or displeased her, more often than not he was dropped like a hot brick, with as little compassion as possible.

Her anger, once the curtain had fallen on the first night, was uncontrollable. The carpenters responsible for the faulty staircase were summoned to her dressing room. Both were fired on the spot and when one offered her back chat, he found himself on the receiving end of her fist. According to her friend Roger Normand, this was worse than being hit by her handbag. Another team of carpenters were brought in from another Isola establishment. They worked overnight without so much as a break. Sitting in a rocking-chair, Mistinguett supervized the operation and was so pleased with the finished result that she placed them on her permanent pay roll.

Carlos Machado, not the most sensitive of men, then attempted to muscle in on her generosity by demanding an increase in wages. He was earning around ten thousand francs per night, which was probably more than he was worth, and he now demanded that this be tripled. In doing so he brought his otherwise convivial relationship with the star to an abrupt, bitter end. She refused his demands, and he threatened to boycott the revue . . . this was of course only too easy, for none of the stars, including Mistinguett, had signed a contract. This time it was Machado who received a smack under the jaw, and Mistinguett told him that if he left her now, she would make sure that he would never work again. For the moment, the cocky young Mexican relented.

The disaster of the première almost repeated itself only hours before curtain-up on the second night. Whilst checking the scenery, Mistinguett collapsed and had to be carried to her dressing room. A doctor was summoned, but by the time he arrived most of the audience had taken their seats, and the chorus for the opening sketch had assembled behind the curtain. Mistinguett had developed a fever, and the doctor diagnosed pneumonia . . . ostensibly the after-effect of her fall the previous night. Mitty Goldin was all for cancelling the performance, but Mistinguett would not allow this. The tradition that the show must go on, no matter what, coursed strongly through her veins. It would be inherited some years later by Edith Piaf and

Marie Dubas, whose final recitals took a severe toll on their health, but which nevertheless turned out to be the greatest performances of their careers.

Mistinguett was carried onto the stage, and during the first half of the show all went well. Then during the interval she collapsed again and had to be given a morphine injection, very much against her will. Mitty Goldin knew that it would be impossible to try arguing with her, though he did beg her not to attempt her descent of the staircase during the finale. This of course was asking too much, and when that most magical of moments came, Carlos Machado and Léo Kok stood at the bottom of the staircase with bated breath. Though in very great pain, she made it, and they were actually dancing when Machado asked her if she had made up her mind about his increase in salary. She replied that she would pay him whatever he desired, so long as he used the money to finance his passage back to Mexico. Machado decided that it might be best to stay put!

'Fairyland!'

Many people, critics and admirers of Mistinguett alike, agree that Henri Varna's revue, *Féerie de Paris*, which opened at the Casino de Paris in 1938, was her best ever. The songs were sublime, the dancing excellent. Eight years before, in Bordeaux, Mistinguett had worn fifteen pounds of feathers on her head, but this was nothing compared with the staircase sequence at the Casino . . . there were forty pounds of plumes in all, wired to her frail-looking body, and trailing twenty feet behind her. Her head-dress was seven feet tall! After the première, demand for seats was such that tickets were sold on the black market for ten times their value. Most of the songs were written by Marc Cab and Léo Lelièvre. Others were by Pierre Bayle and Mistinguett herself. The greatest success of all, of course, was Herb Brown's 'I'm Feeling like a Million', which had been supplied with French lyrics by Mistinguett's son and given a jazz arrangement by Léo Kok, perhaps his only worthwhile contribution to the *chanson*.

> C'est facile d'être chic
> Quand on a beaucoup d'fric,
> C'est commode d'épater
> Quand on est argenté,
> Et qu'surtout on n'a pas à compter!
> Je cherche un millionnaire. . .
> C'est pour ca que je fais le Boulevard!
>
> (It's easy to be chic
> When you've got lots of dough,
> It's convenient to astonish
> When you're silver-plated

And above all when you don't have to
count!
I'm looking for a millionaire,
That's why I'm 'doing' the Boulevard!)

'Je Cherche un Millionnaire' became a hit virtually overnight, and
was the top-selling French record of 1938. It was also very popular
in Britain and the United States. By the time war was declared
in 1939 it had sold five million copies worldwide and earned its
writers a fortune. Mistinguett sang it on stage with Carlos Machado,
though she was not satisfied with his performance and their original
recording, after a good deal of wrangling, was scrapped. It is Léo Kok
who is heard duetting with her on the 78 disc released towards the
end of 1938.

Like all my songs, as soon as it was performed away from
the revue-stage it lost much of its effect. On stage the public
saw Machado making his entrance . . . flexing his pectorals and
flashing his velvety, almond-shaped eyes. They didn't seem to
notice that he had big, sticking-out ears and too much grease
plastered on his hair. The sketch always ended with a big, man-
eating kiss . . . a kiss which had been often practised in private,
but which had the ill-fortune to become professional.

Another superb song, which Mistinguett dismissed as out-dated
even before she had recorded it, was 'Sous les Becs de Gaz'. Pierre
Bayle wrote the music, and she told Léopold that she wanted a
semi-comical lyric centred around the word 'gas'. It remains one of
the liveliest songs she ever sang, and was so original in its concept
that it could easily have been introduced by that doyenne of 'java'
singers, Fréhel, who attended the première and congratulated her in
her dressing room after the show.

Sous les becs de gaz,
Quand j'suis un peu 'gaz',
Je m'en vais tailler une bavette,
Avec des copains qui n'sont pas rupins,
Ou des fétards en gognette!

(Under the gas-lamps,
When I'm a little winded,
I tuck into a sirloin steak
With my mates.
They're neither gluttons nor revellers!)

The American critics who saw the show, with its largely male chorus, referred to it by its English title, *Fairyland*. This may have been unfair, but not inapt. Mistinguett called it her Egyptian revue because when it opened, the seventeen year old King Farouk was in Paris for the first of many visits. He went to see the show one night, and was of course invited back to the dressing room. Mistinguett was not impressed . . . she even sang a song, privately, in his 'honour' which, had the young man heard it, would have grossly offended him.

King Farouk! King Farouk!
Hang his bollocks from a hook!

Also, there were two Egyptians in the chorus line – George Lambros and Reda Caire. The latter had been born Joseph Gandhour in Cairo in 1908, and had taken his stage name from the city. He was one of the earliest charm-singers in Paris, though he lacked the sincerity and *joie de vivre* of a Trenet or a Sablon, and his annoying habit of standing motionless whilst performing a song caused Mistinguett to label him the Mummy. Several years later she gave him permission to sing the song which she had used to open the revue, though when Reda Caire performed 'Je Vous Ai Reconnu', he robbed it of its original excitement and magic.

Je vous ai reconnue,
Madame à vos jolies fossettes,
À votr' petit nez en trompette!
Vous le monsieur barbu,
Votr' barbe est superflue!
Vous pouvez l'retirer. . .
Je vous ai reconnu!

(I've recognized you,
Madame, with your lovely dimples,
And your nose in the air!
You Monsieur, with the beard,
It isn't necessary!
You can take it off. . .
I've recognized you!)

It was during the run of *Féerie de Paris* that Mistinguett met her greatest enemy, one which she would have in common with Damia, Fréhel, Marie Dubas and many of the great entertainers of the day. The microphone! Damia, who sang in the biggest halls in France until her retirement in 1956 when she was sixty seven, proudly confessed that she had never used one. Marie Dubas had a horror of machinery in general, and though her repertoire contained some four hundred songs, she only recorded sixty. This 'horrible encumbrance' entered Mistinguett's world because of the comparatively weak voices of her 'crooners'. She refused to use one herself, however, and never allowed the trailing wire to come anywhere near her whilst she was performing, fearing another fall. She declared, 'This lump of metal is something I would rather do without. It doesn't even look nice. It's rather like a man's cock with a Christmas pudding stuck on the end. If the people at the back can't hear me, tell them to clean out their ears!'

There was also another enemy, of sorts. Michel Georges-Michel, Mistinguett's business partner and co-director of the night club in Antibes, also worked as a columnist for the magazine *Candida*, and it was he who persuaded her to give a series of interviews with one of France's most respected journalists, Maurice Verne. These so-called confessions were published in tabloid form and stirred the passions and interests of Hubert Griffith, a British journalist then working as a Reuters agent in Paris. Griffith, who considered himself an authority on the *chanson*, was not satisfied with Verne's articles and decided to attempt a better job. He began what must have been the most arduous task of his career, as recorded by an article which subsequently appeared in *The Times*:

London knows Mistinguett merely as a rare, very decorative visitor who may be pointed to excitedly, but is never mobbed even by autograph hunters. To remedy this defect in our theatrical education Mr Griffith decided to translate her confessions, recorded by Maurice Verne for a French newspaper. As more was needed to make the material long enough for a book, an interview was arranged. Mr Griffith went to see her at the ABC . . . and discovered how not to interview a celebrity. Descriptions of his desultory meetings with her are amongst the most amusing passages in an entertaining book that gives vivid glimpses of her against the background of Paris. Mr Griffith deftly exploits his difficulties to show both her and the city all the more clearly. Her adventures among the American manufacturers of patent medicines must have been embarrassing enough, but these were mild compared with the attempts to convert her to a new religion which needed the boost of a 'female pope'. Perhaps this is why Mistinguett, who is in London this week, has not appeared on the stage here. Anything that could happen here could only be an anti-climax!

With extreme reluctance, Mistinguett gave Griffith permission to go ahead with his book, but warned him that if anything untoward was printed, she would sue him for every penny he possessed.

The revue at the Casino closed, and during the summer of 1938 she began making arrangements for a tour of Europe. Meanwhile, the political situation on the continent had begun to worsen. On 29 September Hitler, Mussolini, Neville Chamberlain and Edouard Daladier signed the Munich Agreement, and although the war clouds were temporarily dissipated, everyone knew that the storm would break sooner than later. This momentous date in the history of the world was doubly important for Mistinguett, for it was on this day that the British publishers Hurst and Blackett launched her memoirs! On 12 October she flew to Croydon, and at the airport was greeted by hundreds of fans who had seen her on stage in Paris. The following evening she was guest of honour at a Foyle's literary luncheon at Grosvenor House. The occasion was part of a combined publicity campaign to launch her book and one by Charles Laughton's actress wife, Elsa Lanchester, entitled *Charles Laughton and I*. The other guests included Lupino Lane and the actresses Constance Cummings and Ursula Jeans. Though she was alone and a little out of her depth, Fraisette having been left behind in France, this did not prevent Mistinguett from occupying the centre-stage. When asked to propose the toast, she announced in very good English,

> 'I am not a political woman, but an actress. All the same, I bring the best wishes of the French people to the people of England. I came from Paris because I should like to try and kiss Mr Chamberlain, whom we in Paris call "Good Chamberlain", but I am told that he has gone fishing! He is a good man, so get your glasses raised!'

Mistinguett held a press conference at Croydon airport the next morning and autographed copies of her memoirs, which she seems to have liked, in spite of the fact that she refused to meet Hubert Griffith again. Reporters were told that she had read the book from cover to cover, although, in fact, she had gone no further than the fly leaf. Her admirers accompanied her to her plane; one gave her an enormous bouquet of pink and white carnations, and was rewarded with a rare kiss before she burst into tears. The photograph which appeared on the front pages of a number of British newspapers the following day is, in the opinion of the author, the most beautiful Mistinguett ever had taken. She is seen clutching her flowers and her legendary handbag, whilst waving goodbye to the country which, after France, she loved more than anywhere else in the world.

'I love you all!' she sobbed. 'I'll be back. Please don't forget me!'

The European tour began at once. Mistinguett hoped that it might last several months, in fact it lasted less than a fortnight, and under the circumstances might have been better not taking place at all. Two female members of her troupe were German, and though this had never caused problems before, in spite of Mistinguett's attitude towards Germany, it did now. Several of her dancers were brave enough to advise her to dismiss them, and were themselves dismissed. Others left of their own accord, instead of leaving Paris with a company of sixty, Mistinguett left with less than forty, and even then she was unsure how long they would stay with her the further the tour progressed. Georges Lambros also dropped out at the last moment, and this caused her the biggest headache of all, for neither Kok nor Machado were suitably accomplished to draw much attention from foreign audiences, and Kramer was above everything else a dancer and not a singer.

Mistinguett managed to fumble her way through a number of engagements in Brussels and Switzerland, and during the third week of October the company arrived in Rome, a city she had not forgiven, even after more than twenty years.

Because of her former association with Lino Carenzio she was invited to a private showing of his first film, *El Feroce Saladinno*. Though never one to dwell too much on the past, and in particular that part of her past where she had made mistakes, Mistinguett realized that Carenzio had been her best partner since Harry Pilcer, and therefore decided to get in touch with him. After his London Palladium revue he had played in a season at the New York Casino: this had proved so successful that he had been transferred to the London Casino. The brevity of Mistinguett's visit to London, plus the fact that Carenzio had not been foremost in her thoughts at the time, had meant that she had not been interested in meeting him there. Now, things had changed. From her hotel in Rome, she dispatched a telegram. Carenzio was told that, though Carlos Machado was a more than suitable lover, as a partner he was hopeless and that as a result of this she had decided to abandon her European tour and set off for South America.

The fact that Carenzio should have been contacted at all, whilst Mistinguett was having an affair with someone else, points to the fact that since their split she had not stopped loving him. She realized, of course, that she was clutching at straws, and that her plea would almost certainly fall on deaf ears. It did not. Carenzio arrived in Rome just two days later, admitting that he was still head over heels in love with her and that he had broken his contract just to be with her. Carlos Machado was turfed out of Mistinguett's room – he immediately took up with one of the male dancers, allegedly the same one who had been keeping Léo Kok company, and all was apparently well. The next morning the company headed for Marseilles. Incredibly, its numbers had increased rather than decreased during the tour, and a few days later everyone set sail for Argentina.

Towards the end of December 1938 Mistinguett opened at the Casino in Buenos Aires. There had been fights on board ship between Carenzio and Kok, hardly surprising considering the former had bedded the boss before 'eloping' with the latter. Mistinguett's handbag, however, prevented the problems from getting too much out of hand, though matters did come to a head in Buenos Aires when she gave Kok his marching orders and also forbade him to see Machado. Within days he had secured himself an engagement at the Embassy Theatre, and before the company moved on, Mistinguett was astonished to learn that he had become the seventh husband of a wealthy Argentinian socialite who bore the title Elvira de Prates Mendes Goncalves. Mistinguett sent a message of condolence to the bride, and pressed on with the tour.

Léo Kok was no great loss . . . his only importance, she later said, had been one song and the introduction to Machado. The Mexican, however, had also had enough. Refusing to play second fiddle to Carenzio, he himself left the troupe and soon afterwards married a rich heiress and returned home to Mexico. There was a further incident when two of her male dancers were arrested after they had been caught importuning young boys. They were, of course, dismissed at once and left to fend for themselves. When the authorities approached her and asked if she was interested in bailing them out, Mistinguett retorted that they should be locked up and the key thrown away. Her only distress was that her company had been so drastically reduced that to continue with the tour might be worthless, for several more dancers were suffering from dysentery.

Between shows in Brazil, Mistinguett telephoned Fraisette at Bougival – her major concern when far from home was the welfare of her animals. She also kept in touch with her friends. Many of these, such as Mitty Goldin and Marie Dubas, were Jews, and well aware what would happen should war be declared. In April 1939 Marie Dubas opened at the ABC in *La Revue Déchainée*. Though the first few nights had been sold out weeks in advance, and the revue looked like breaking all the house records, Mistinguett advised her to cancel whilst the going was good and leave the country as soon as possible. She also contacted the singer Marianne Oswald, at that time appearing in her one-woman show in New York's Greenwich Village.

Marianne Oswald remains the most controversial of all the French *réaliste* singers. Jacques Prévert had called her 'a terrifying pleasure to know and dread', and Albert Camus had described her songs – more spoken than actually sung – as being 'heavy with soot and flame'. It is not easy to comprehend why she should have been a friend of Mistinguett. She had been born in Lorraine in 1901, just a few kilometres from the village where Damia had spent much of her childhood, and it is interesting to note that whilst many French people loathed Marianne because of her 'German' birth yet revered Damia who was never considered anything but French, Mistinguett was still hailing her rival as 'that fucking Nazi', whilst Marianne Oswald was condoned for 'her noble French blood and spirit'.

Mistinguett also pitied the singer for her 'simply abhorrent childhood'. When very young she had been physically and sexually abused by her father, who had ended his days in a lunatic asylum. As a result of this, Marianne had run away to Berlin, where she had been launched in the legitimate theatre by the classical German actress, Erika Meingast. Their love-affair had been well-splattered all over the front pages of the German newspapers at the time, and unable to cope with the publicity Marianne had fled to Paris where in 1929, with neither bags nor money, she had been welcomed by Jean Cocteau, who had soon afterwards launched her at Le Boeuf-sur-le-Toit. For some unexplained reason she had become part of the clique surrounding Yvonne George, and when introduced to Mistinguett at the time of Yvonne's final recital, everyone had been surprised to see the two women getting on like a house on fire. Marianne Oswald, with her dyed red hair which was hardly ever brushed, her black dress, and her chalk-white, granite-featured face had always resembled something out of a child's nightmare. Mistinguett, who with the sole exception of Marie Dubas' 'La Prière de la Charlotte' had never liked any of the *réaliste* songs, admired Marianne's repertoire, which was just as bizarre as she was: Cocteau had supplied her with 'Anna la Bonne', but Prévert's 'La Chasse à l'Enfant' had caused riots when first performed at Le Boeuf. 'You've got to be a hard-bitten cow to get on in this business,' Mistinguett once declared. 'Perhaps that's why I've always liked Oswald!'

Marianne's problems had escalated in December 1936 when she had given a recital of Brecht and Weill songs in Paris . . . heckled by some of the spectators, she had begun singing in German. When asked by reporters, after the show, why she had never married, she had retorted, 'Because I'm a lesbian and because I've always been interested in what's between a man's ears, not his legs!' The fact that Marianne was thus inclined was unimportant so far as Jean Cocteau's set was concerned . . . few of his friends could have been dismissed as 'normal' in the accepted sense. That she was a Jew, however, meant that her personal safety might not be ensured if ever war broke out, as Mistinguett had explained to her in the summer of 1937. 'Find yourself a man,' she advised. 'Keep your legs and your mouth shut, and you'll have little to fear!' Several weeks later Marianne Oswald had entered into a marriage of convenience, by which she had become Madame Colin.

But sweeping her problems under the carpet, as it were, did not curb the public's hostility towards her, and in 1938, shortly before Mistinguett and her company left for South America, Marianne and her new husband had sailed for New York. Bearing in mind that her songs were both morbid and extremely dramatic, it comes as a surprise to learn that the Americans immediately took her to their often insular hearts: both Mistinguett and Edith Piaf failed to conquer their first American audiences. Marianne's autobiography had been translated into English and the title, *One Small Voice*, had been used for her highly-successful radio series, which had been followed by the engagements in Greenwich Village.

Mistinguett telephoned her in New York and advised her to divorce her husband and stay put until the political situation had settled. This somewhat motherly advice was not unappreciated, though Marianne had already made up her own mind. Several months later she divorced Colin. Her return to France after the war brought her fiercer criticism than ever before. Though she continued to work until a few weeks before her death in 1983, and was proved ultimately never to have collaborated with the enemy, her popularity slumped practically to zero.

As for Marie Dubas, she abandoned her revue at the ABC (her place was taken by Charles Trenet) and in August 1939 sailed from Marseilles to Rio aboard the Florida, the same ship that had transported Mistinguett and her company ten years before. Keeping her company during the voyage was the American jazz singer Lena Horne, and together they gave a joint recital for the other passengers.

However, if Marie had anticipated meeting up with Mistinguett in Rio, she was to be disappointed. Mistinguett and her dancers had left the city two weeks before on the Campana, ultimately bound for France. It was whilst the ship was crossing the Atlantic, on 3 September 1939, that the news was transmitted that Britain and France had declared war on Germany.

> On the ship, everyone was crying. The Campana, with its cargo of stars, switched off its engines and the voyage seemed to go on for ever, zig-zagging all over the place to avoid the submarines and being detected by enemy planes. We kept our life-jackets on all the time . . . even in bed. We felt as though we had been destroyed already.

Towards the end of October, the Campana dropped anchor at Casablanca and two of Mistinguett's dancers – the two German girls – were forced to swim ashore under cover of darkness and seek refuge in the Convent of the Sisters of the Poor until Mistinguett decided what to do with them. The next morning they were arrested by the Moroccan police and transported to a surveillance camp. Mistinguett, finding her hands tied, was forced to hire a private plane to fly what was left of her troupe back to Paris.

> Most of the theatres, cinemas and music-halls had been closed. Because I could do nothing else, I had decided to assist my friends and boost the morale of the people of Paris . . . and of course the only way I could do this was by entertaining. I was too old to be used as a spy.

Mistinguett and the
German Occupation

Even though France was at war, Mistinguett's reign over the music-hall was stronger than ever. When she announced that she was looking for a suitable establishment to put on a brand new revue, one or two of the braver directors offered their services, knowing only too well the risks they may have been taking. In December 1939 she opened in a recital-revue at the Etoile-Palace, formerly the Folies-Wagram. Her co-stars were Lino Carenzio and Georges Lambros, and her *vedette-américaine* was Léo Marjane. Had she been able to look into the near future, Mistinguett would have steered clear of this pretty, blonde and talented *chanteuse*. It was Léo Marjane who introduced 'Septembre sous la Pluie' and 'Mon Coeur Est un Violon', which she sang in both French and English. When engaged by Mistinguett her big hit was 'J'Ai Donné Mon Ame au Diable', and this is precisely what she did during the German Occupation of France when, adopting 'Je Suis Seule ce Soir' as her theme-song, she performed regularly on German-controlled radio. This song was practically an open invitation for her Nazi officer lover.

In January 1940 Mistinguett and Carenzio left the Etoile-Palace and retired to Bougival for a few weeks. Here they began making plans to move south and Mistinguett set about stashing away her immense fortune. She had never trusted banks. Stocks and shares, she declared, were only for fools interested in losing everything they had worked for over night.

Manouche was drafted in to assist with this most delicate operation, and Lino Carenzio was kept out of the way; in spite of her jealousy, Mistinguett urged him to further a relationship with the son of her gardener. Each morning she stuffed her famous handbag full of banknotes and Manouche drove her into Paris, where the money was exchanged for gold *louis* and ingots, which the two women concealed amongst their boxes of groceries. Under cover of darkness, with Carenzio still out of the way, the gold would be buried in the garden at Bougival. If Carenzio or anyone else asked questions, they were told that the most ardent animal lover in all France had just buried one of her pets . . . initially this was believed, for one part of the garden was a mass of animal graves. This did cause the odd problem. Once when she was about to go on a rare shopping expedition, Mistinguett went out into her garden alone and accidentally dug up the rotting body of one of her dogs!

Eventually, Carenzio found out what had been going on behind his back. Besides burying the gold in the garden, Mistinguett had hidden a large cache of coins under the floorboards of her bedroom. Carenzio stole the money and hid it in trunk, which was always kept locked in the attic. Mistinguett, or possibly Manouche, saw him and their subsequent treatment of the young Italian was anything but kindly. They broke open his trunk, retrieved the stolen coins, and took the trunk into the garden and burned it. When Carenzio flew into a rage, Mistinguett threatened to have him arrested and deported! Although a big star in Britain and an even bigger one in America, Carenzio had his own reasons for wishing to stay in France, and promised to behave himself, though needless to say he did not relinquish his handsome young gardener.

This caused a number of problems. Carenzio had squandered his own fortune as quickly as he had earned it and was forced to rely on Mistinguett's goodwill in order to provide his lover with the expensive presents to which he had become accustomed. Of course Mistinguett's benevolences at this time were practically non-existent. Since leaving the Etoile-Palace she had been paying him a weekly allowance. This was reduced and a 'curfew' imposed: unless Carenzio returned to the house by the prescribed hour, he found himself locked out and forced to sleep in one of the outbuildings which housed her recently-acquired herd of wild pigs.

By April 1940 it was far too dangerous to stay anywhere near the French capital, especially if one was an entertainer such as Mistinguett with the habit of broadcasting publicly exactly what was on her mind.

Just a few days before the Germans moved in, she and several of her boys – Carenzio had been suitably demoted to the chorus – travelled south to St Jean-de-Luz, near Biarritz. Léopold de Lima and Paul Derval followed. Each drove one of Mistinguett's cars which she had asked to be filled with provisions, clothes, bags of money, and as many of her animals as she thought wise to transport to their new quarters. The wild pigs had been left to forage around the grounds at Bougival: many would end up as food for the locals. From St Jean-de-Luz the company slowly worked its way across the Pyrenees towards Antibes, picking up new or long-lost members *en route*. Mistinguett was particularly interested in spending a few days in Toulouse because she had been informed that Georges Lambros was there: he had last been seen working as a waiter in a restaurant. She managed to locate him, only to lose him again after a few days. Several months later he would turn up at her villa. Drafted into the French army he had done a swift about-turn during a march, and for his pain had been arrested and sent to prison. The young man was never Mistinguett's lover, though for some reason she always had a soft spot for him, and always predicted that one day he would become famous . . . but not as Georges Lambros. When he told her that during his flight he had hidden with a family at Guéthary, near Biarritz, this gave her an idea. She amended the name slightly and baptised him Georges Guétary.

During the war, Mistinguett should have been content with her sojourn in sunny Antibes. Marcel and Fraisette were close at hand, and she absolutely doted on her little niece, Micky. Every morning she could be seen walking her down to the market-place, or along the beach. Like all the great troupers of the music-hall, however, she was very much out of her depth when not actively engaged in her career, and in Antibes she felt lonely and dejected. Carenzio had escaped from the fold again, and in this respect Mistinguett seems to have been inordinately patient, for Antibes was suitably close to the Italian border for her to send him packing once and for all. The answer to this particular problem was proposed by Manouche, who stopped off at the villa *en route* for Corsica. Manouche had hated Carenzio since first setting eyes upon him. She had hoped that the episode with the missing gold, and his affair with the gardener might make her 'god-mother' see sense, and she advised Mistinguett to sack him before he ended up breaking her heart. 'I can't,' came the astonishing reply. 'You see, we're married!'

The Mistinguett-Carenzio 'marriage' had taken place at the time of the shooting of *Rigolboche*, and, like her much earlier 'marriage' to Mayol, had been a publicity stunt.

> In July 1936, Lino married me for one day, and everyone believed that it was the real thing. We had our photographs taken, and hundreds of articles were written about us. The journalists didn't latch on to the fact that we were taking the piss!

Manouche told me that Mistinguett was also unbelievably naive . . . a tough old woman with the heart and emotions of an adolescent girl. The fact that she was extremely demanding and always thought that the current man in her life had eyes for her alone did not diminish in Antibes, even when Carenzio began an affair with the gardener there. When she asked him why he was spending so much time in the potting shed, he replied that it was because the gardener was supplying him with cigarettes, and she believed him. She still refused to allow anyone to smoke in her company, and the slightest whiff of tobacco anywhere within the villa meant that the guilty party was immediately banished to one of the outbuildings.

Gradually, the situation around Antibes began to change. The male dancers who had deserted her during the European tour had failed to find work once they had returned to Paris: all were either Jewish or homosexual, or both. A few at a time, they turned up at the villa, and Mistinguett welcomed them with open arms, only to frighten the wits out of them by announcing that as soon as she had assembled a full troupe she would be returning to Paris to open in a new revue. Her boys were housed in the same outbuildings which contained those of her animals which were not house-trained, some of her costumes, and Carenzio and his gardener.

Being surrounded by such a wealth of homosexual talent hardly made Mistinguett the most popular woman in Antibes, and one day a group of locals presented her with a petition to get rid of her entourage because it was bringing the street – Le Chemin du Croûton – into a state of disrepute. This did not perturb her at all.

She declared, 'Whilst my boys are at it like lodging-house cats, they're harming no one. What do you want them to do . . . collaborate along with the rest of you?' The petition was taken to the Mayor of Antibes, though Mistinguett got there first. She requested that Le Chemin du Croûton – in English it translates as Crusty Way – should be re-named Le Chemin du Croupion, which means Arsehole Way, on account of the activities taking place in the out-buildings! The request was turned down, though the name has stuck. Even today some of the locals call it by no other name.

As if aware that most of her boys were taking her for a ride and using her as a convenient meal ticket, Mistinguett became parsimonious to the point of absurdity. As Manouche recalled:

> She told me, 'Don't give them too much sugar, Manouche. There's a war on, and in any case they're sweet enough already!' She was still hiding her gold coins and bars, and swiping whatever lay at hand . . . now it was food which brought her talents to the fore, and not SNCF towels and tea spoons. She took her admirers to the most elegant of the restaurants along the Riviera . . . inevitably one or more of them ended up paying, no matter who had invited whom! Miss had what can only be described as a genius for sneaking off with any butter or cheese that had been left on the plates. That handbag went everywhere . . . by the time she left a place it was too heavy for her to carry herself, and she gave it to one of her hunks. She used to coo with delight when she got back to Bougival, when we emptied her evening's pickings out onto the table. She was like a giddy little child who had played a trick on the grown ups!

Much of Manouche's tale may, of course, be pure invention, for like her famous 'godmother' she loved to spin a good yarn, and was still doing so when I met her in Paris in 1973. My meeting with her was something of a surprise, though by no means a let down. Domergue and others had painted her when young, pretty and slim. By 1973 she had piled on the pounds, and her language was as coarse as expected, though not in any way offensive. Manouche also spoke about the petition, and Mistinguett's other adventures on Arsehole Way. One of her neighbours, who prior to her taking over the villa had been one of her most ardent admirers, had developed a taste for self-sufficiency by planting his back garden with fruit bushes and vegetables. The moment he discovered that the great star had developed a different taste for scrambling over the fence and stealing them, he had purchased a pair of ferocious guard-dogs. This only amused her. With her passion for owning animals which ordinarily would have been kept in a zoo, she had an uncanny talent for soothing even the most savage of beasts. Saving scraps from the table, she began feeding the dogs. According to Manouche she also serenaded them with a few refrains from *En Douce* and, once they had got to know and trust her, she began stealing vegetables again. The neighbour, as a last resort before reporting her activities to the police, sent his wife to Mistinguett's front door with a basket of vegetables. It was sent back with a polite message of apology: it was not appropriate to accept charity when there was a war on and everyone was more or less in the same boat! The next night her neighbour caught her stealing his vegetables again!

Throughout the summer of 1941, Mistinguett pined for Paris so much that she became ill with chronic depression. Lino Carenzio, now beginning to tire of this increasingly mean and difficult woman who was, after all, more than thirty years his senior, left the villa and the gardener, and moved to Nice, where he was offered the position of artiste-in-residence at the Kan-Kan Club. Mistinguett realized that she would have to return to Paris, Germans or no Germans, for, away from the glare of the spotlights and the applause of her beloved public, she was slowly wasting away. Maurice Chevalier was staying at his villa at La Bocca, just outside Cannes, and he dropped in every now and then, though his treatment of Mistinguett was ever cautious because he was afraid that she might attempt to ensnare him again. Tino Rossi was working in Monte Carlo ... occasionally he would be invited to sing at La Cage aux Poules, whenever Mistinguett felt like making the effort to leave her room. Perhaps her greatest influence at the time was Charles Trenet, whom she had once described as 'a handsome, bumbling country-boy', and who usually turned up at her club in the company of the ageing drag-queen, Odette. Again according to Manouche, Trenet wrote Mistinguett a song:

Si tu vas à Paris,
Dis bonjour aux amis,
Dis leur qu'un jour viendra,
Où l'en retrouvera. . .

(If you go to Paris,
Say hello to my friends,
Tell them the day will come,
When we'll be together. . .)

Although Mistinguett adored everything Trenet sang, she turned this one down because singing it at a time when Paris was overrun with enemy soldiers upset her too much. Trenet gave the song to his friend Roland Gerbeau, and it was one of the biggest French record successes of the following year. Several years later Gerbeau would introduce two more Trenet classics – 'Que Reste-t-il de nos Amours' and 'Douce France' and he would sing Edith Piaf's – 'La Vie en Rose' two years before her definitive version rocked the world. Mistinguett admitted to being 'very fond' of Gerbeau, but only until he 'jumped over the fence to join up with one of the enemy'. This is not as severe as it sounds; the 'enemy in this instance was Joséphine Baker, with whom the young singer began a series of world tours. As for Charles Trenet's beautiful song, listening to it made her more and more homesick and determined to return to Paris. She telephoned Henri Varna, who informed her that a new season would be waiting for her the moment she set foot in the capital. She began packing at once. Two days later she and most of her boys were installed in the apartment on Boulevard des Capucines. This, she declared, was preferable to living at Bougival because, surrounded by so many tall buildings in the midst of a big city, she felt that much safer.

Mistinguett was deeply shocked and hurt by the changes which the occupying Germans had inflicted upon Paris. When she observed the Nazi swastika fluttering over the Arc de Triomphe, she wept. Marshal Pétain, the hero of Verdun, who had returned to power at the age of eighty four, she dismissed as an 'old wanker and a tired fart who would blow no good'. She became angry when, on a visit to Enghien to place a wreath on her parents' grave, she watched two of her old school chums ripping down the sign Liberty, Equality and

Mistinguett's final performance in New York, April 1951. She wears the Guyarmathy gown, and is partnered by Lino Carenzio. (*Popperfoto*)

Allegedly the greatest love of her life, Mistinguett congratulates Maurice Chevalier after his come-back performance at the Folies-Bergère, 1954. (*Topham Picture Source*)

Fraternity and replacing it with one which read Work, Home and Family. The worst insult of all, however, came when the former prime minister, Pierre Laval, issued a proclamation that if need be he would collaborate with the Master Race if it meant assisting them towards a speedy victory over the British. Mistinguett loved England almost as much as France. She vowed that if she ever got her hands on Laval, she would personally castrate him. Knowing her character and her famous bad temper, she would have done exactly this.

Throughout the German Occupation, Mistinguett remained fiercely patriotic. Others did not. Léo Marjane could be seen riding through the streets of Paris in an open-topped carriage, flaunting her affair with a senior Nazi official. Suzy Solidor, whose cool Aryan looks made her a natural favourite for the supporters of the jackboot, transformed her nightclub, La Vie Parisienne, into an establishment which some people regarded as a miniature Berlin. Manouche told me, 'Poor old Suzy sang surrounded by so many of her portraits that it made some of the customers sea sick!' Whether Suzy actually collaborated with the Germans is not known: on what evidence we have, it would seem unlikely. Maurice Chevalier was suspected of 'gross misconduct', though Mistinguett was still so wrapped up in her memories of him that she refused to listen to anything that was said against him. Tino Rossi, on the other hand, received the sharp end of her tongue. She declared, 'That man would collaborate with his embalmer for a song!' In the world of the cinema and the music-hall there were others. The author neither condemns nor condones, but transcribes what was written in the newspapers of the day.

The first of the great film directors to accept patronage from the Germans was Marcel Carné . . . as did his most famous star, Arletty. Carné's contemporaries, Henri Decoin, Robert Bresson and Jean Delannoy, quickly followed suit, taking the actresses Suzy Delair and Danielle Darrieux with them. Tino Rossi played Don Juan in the German-backed *Fièvres*. Viviane Romance (Mistinguett's old enemy from her Earl Leslie days) and Jean Marais, who was Cocteau's lover, all worked for the other side, either through fear or goodwill.

There were, of course, many artistes in Paris who, like Mistinguett, nurtured a fierce ambition to inflict as much damage as possible on the German nation. Joséphine Baker was spying for the Resistance – one of her activities involved smuggling messages in her sheet music – though this did not make her any more popular with Mistinguett. Lucienne Boyer, that most delicious and feminine of charm-singers, was contributing to the German downfall by assisting French parachutists to drop in Britain. Edith Piaf had, figuratively speaking, gone straight to the fountainhead by securing a tour of the German prisoner of war camps. The prisoners in Stalag III had adopted her as their 'godmother', and she was helping dozens of them to escape by getting them to pose for photographs whenever she made an appearance. The photographs were then taken to Paris, enlarged, cut up and mounted onto false identity cards. The German officers were so besotted with the Piaf voice and her larger than life personality that apparently they never realized that whilst she entered a camp with eleven musicians, she always left with seventeen. Many of the men she helped to escape were homosexuals who would have been given short shrift by their captors. Piaf also chartered a ship during an engagement in Marseilles, which transported a large number of prisoners to England. When Mistinguett was informed of this by one of her 'spies', she insisted that Piaf should be told that she was 'more than a little bit proud of the funny little bugger in the widow's weeds'.

Like all entertainers, Mistinguett had to report regularly to the Nazi Propagandastaffel on the Champs-Elysées to have the lyrics of her songs vetted by the German authorities: had she refused, she would not have been allowed to perform at all. Like Piaf she fared well under the Germans. This was not because she succumbed like many others, but because when speaking to them or being questioned she had the guts to speak her mind. Neither did she encounter any problems in delivering messages to the Resistance whilst on stage. Some of her songs were so full of Parisian argot that even some of the Parisians could not work them out. When she opened at the Casino in the winter of 1941, many of her songs were also sung in English and the asides, containing the valuable messages, were delivered in Cockney! There was also a most dreadfully insulting version of 'Je Cherche un Millionnaire', sung in English with the Führer in mind!

> I'm feeling like a million,
> And when I get lots of cash,
> I'll grab old Adolf by the tash,

And kick him in the conker!
Yes, I'm feeling like a million,
And I know just what to do,
With the fucking monkeys in his zoo!

The Germans who happened to be sitting in the audience, and there
were many, laughed along with the song without knowing that she
was offering the supreme insult to their leader. The song only became
more vulgar as it progressed, and ended with a dance sequence and
a tirade of filthy words which only Mistinguett could have got away
with. And yet, in the German-controlled press, her performances were
revered to such an extent that those who did not come to see her at the
Casino actually accused her of collaboration.

One of the boys engaged by Mistinguett for her new revue was
Roger Normand, whom the author is proud to count amongst his
friends. Roger was born in 1920, and subsequently became one of
the youngest, and smallest, dancers she ever had. This is something
which he considered a blessing.

> Being small meant that I always had to stand at the top of the
> staircase . . . I always pitied the ones who had to wait for her at
> the bottom. Everyone reckons she was a difficult woman . . . she
> was extremely tough to work for, but this is because she was a
> perfectionist of the highest order. If you kept on her good side she
> was the kindest person in the world, but if you crossed her . . . her
> handbag was lethal and her fist even more so, but those eyes!
> I've seen her look at the biggest, toughest man in the troupe
> and reduce him to tears without saying a single word. Our time
> together at the Casino taught me all I know about the music-hall.
> I wouldn't have missed it for the world. Mistinguett, setting off
> on one of her many outings, was a sight not to be missed. Yet
> beneath it all, she was a little lost girl.

Another of the author's friends, Michel Guyarmathy of the Folies-
Bergère, who had already worked with her, told me,

> Miss was extremely rich, and extremely famous, yet in spite of
> this she never forgot that she had been born working class.

She was only interested in the working classes . . . she played to the galleries, never the stalls. What I remember with especial fondness are her eyes. They were beautifully blue and always smiling, even when she cried on stage, which she did often. She had guts, she had a heart. Not enough of her critics have said that. For me, she was Titine . . . La Titine des Rues! I've been in this business for more than fifty years, and I've yet to meet her equal. That is a fact!

Mistinguett was not, however, earning the money she had been accustomed to before the war and she now had a sizeable troupe to support at her apartment. Since most of her boys were so nervous of the Germans that the only time they stepped outside the building was when they left for the theatre, always to return immediately afterwards, she began what she referred to as her 'victuals campaign'. Manouche told me,

> She really was in her element, for this time she had come up with the most brilliant way of scrounging. The orchestra would play a melody of her songs . . . very quietly . . . and she would walk in front of the curtain with tears in her eyes and begin, 'Look at your poor little Miss! She is shivering with cold because she has no coal to keep her bones warm! So, please help her to keep warm. And if you would like her to keep warbling like the poor little sparrow she is, please send her any grub you have left over when you've finished stuffing yourselves! You know, any little titbits you'd normally put in the bin! A nice bit of scrag-end, perhaps! And a pot of real coffee instead of that bloody awful stuff they make by grinding their nuts together! Remember my address . . . it's Twenty-Four, Boulevard des Capucines . . . just up the road from the Olympia. And now, if you'll excuse me for a moment, I'll go and eat a biscuit . . . it's all I've got to keep my strength up whilst I'm singing tonight!'

The response to her pleas was so great that Mistinguett had to employ a young man to handle the supplies as they came in. The same man then drove the supplies to specified locations in and around Paris, where they were sold on the black market for several times their value. Contrary to what many people have said, Mistinguett always donated the money to the war effort.

The Resistance fund was further enhanced by the money collected by Mistinguett whenever she went out on the town. At Chez Tonton or Chez Liberty she would often sing one or two songs before passing the tin around, and she would never take it back until it was full.

More often than not, she and Manouche were accompanied on these occasions by the drag-queen Odette, who had been allowed to call his club Chez Liberty because, when interrogated by the officers at the Propagandastaffel, he had informed them that the name had come from the famous fashion shop on Regent Street, in London, from which he bought most of his dresses! For a while, Odette had lived near Mistinguett on the Riviera, but boredom had forced him to bring his bizarre collection of friends back to Paris. The artiste in residence at Chez Liberty was a large, filthy-mouthed comic singer known to her friends in Paris as Milady Patate, and to the English visitors as Mrs Spud, owing to the fact that she had amassed a considerable fortune by selling potatoes from her Breton farm on the black market. Manouche told me,

> When Odette turned out in full drag, linked on each arm by Miss and Milady Patate, you had one hell of a job working out which of them was the prettiest. God, they were as common as common could be. Miss always looked very fetching as Cleopatra, but you'd never seen anything until you'd seen Odette's Brünhilde! He would sing . . . and the moment he hit a high note, let out a rasping fart. It was great fun!

The fun ended, however, towards the end of 1942 when Manouche's mother died suddenly. Mistinguett was one of the mourners at the Cimetière de Vincennes, and immediately after the memorial service her little friend announced that she was returning to the Free Zone. This was not an easy task; getting a visa involved a lot of red tape, and although Mistinguett was the first to admit that she hated being left alone, she still did all she could to enable Manouche to leave the capital. Several of the young men who had elected to stay on at the villa in Antibes had been arrested and transported to prison camps, where they had been compelled to wear the pink triangle of the so-called deviant. One or two never returned. Manouche herself decided to boycott the villa and rented a hotel room in Cannes. When the situation there became dangerous, she moved to Monte Carlo, where for a while she was taken in by Tino Rossi. The fact that he had recently completed another film with German backing was not mentioned. It was Tino who introduced her to the Corsican gangster, Paul-Bonaventure Carbone, the young man who became, without any doubt, the greatest love of her life.

Ultimately, Manouche would become fêted as the Madonna of the Corsicans, though she was already aware of the fact that besides worshipping the conventional deity the average Corsican idolized two more – his mother and Napoléon Bonaparte.

Back in 1940, before becoming Carbone's mistress, Manouche had been asked to participate in what the Corsicans called the Ceremony of the Eaglet. The Duc de Reichstadt, otherwise known as the Eaglet, had been Napoléon's only legitimate son. He had died of consumption at Schöhbrunn in 1832, and in 1940, to honour the centenary of Napoléon's reburial in Les Invalides, Hitler had allowed Reichstadt's bones to be taken back to Paris and placed next to those of his father. Since this time, each 15 December Corsicans everywhere had held all night vigils to honour the young man whom everyone else had ostensibly forgotten. The one in 1942 was of particular importance because Carbone and Manouche had decided to observe it in Les Invalides, with Mistinguett as guest of honour. She turned up at the church, dressed from top to toe in black and leaning upon the arm of a young dancer whom she had just purloined from Odette. His name has never been divulged, though he must have been high up in the affections of the drag-queen, who had left Paris immediately and who, after the episode, would never speak to Mistinguett again.

Once the necessary prayers had been dispensed with, Mistinguett walked around the 'mourners' with her massive handbag wide open, so that everyone could contribute to the war effort. And then,

> One of her heels caught in a huge spray of ferns and those million-dollar legs skidded past the honorary guard. Her handbag, which was a deadly weapon these days, careered high into the air and landed on the stone floor with such a clatter that I'm sure all four

Napoléons lying within the church must have been brought back from the dead. . .

During his clandestine visits to Paris, Paul Carbone had often met up with Mistinguett, though she only befriended him because of his association with Manouche. She always maintained that he would come to a sticky end, which is of course exactly what happened a few years later. Though he performed many acts of benevolence during the last war (most of them were for his own people) nothing could sway her way of thinking that Carbone was, above all, a gangster and deeply involved with many shady characters who condoned and assisted his dealings in drugs, contraband and prostitution of both sexes. She also knew that he was collaborating, albeit indirectly, with the Germans.

Shortly after the ceremony at Les Invalides, she and Manouche went with him to a private screening of Marcel Carné's latest masterpiece, *Les Visiteurs du Soir*, which was released in Britain and the United States as the aptly-titled *The Devil's Envoys*. The two stars of the film were Alain Cuny and Arletty. Mistinguett was neither impressed by the film nor their performances. Only a few days before, she had listened to the famous actress impersonating her on the radio – the song had been Maurice Yvain's '*J'En ai Marre*', and the take-off wickedly accurate – and needless to say she had been intent on giving her a piece of her mind. Arletty had wisely kept out of her way. A few years later, in spite of the collaborationist charges laid against her, the actress and the ageing star would become the best of friends. Arletty's tears, at Mistinguett's funeral, would be very real.

It was around this time that Mistinguett founded her rest home for retired animals: these were the ones she could not house train, or the ones who were too old to travel with her between Bougival and Antibes. The estate, Walnut Trees, was set in the picturesque countryside between Bormes-les-Mimosas and Cogolin, not far from St Tropez. The first 'residents' were the masturbating monkey, now old and nasty-tempered – some said like its mistress, the wild pigs which had not been devoured by the residents at Bougival, and a dozen assorted cats and dogs. That Mistinguett loved her animals more than any of her men, including Chevalier and Pilcer; and that they were better-treated than most of them, goes without saying. Closing her memoirs, she wrote:

> At Bougival there are fourteen dogs, a parrot and a shoal of goldfish, a tame cockerel, a parakeet, a ram called Rothschild, and a pig which I named Léon after Léon Volterra. Whenever one of my animals was ill, I turfed the man of the moment out of my bed in order to keep it warm. My animals have never let me down, which is more than can be said for some of the men! My animals have also proved more intelligent!

Although she returned to Bougival after the Casino revue, taking most of the boys with her, Mistinguett gave only a handful of memorable performances during what remained of the German Occupation. Perhaps her finest was during the summer of 1943, when she opened at the Alhambra in a series of recitals where the songs and their propagandist content took priority over her costumes. She also had something else to occupy her mind. Manouche, that seemingly ever-faithful companion who so often reviled her in her memoirs . . . and who was not mentioned at all in Mistinguett's own . . . informed her that she was pregnant.

The baby should have been an important one. Paul Carbone's wife had borne him no children, and under the 'laws' of his country, Manouche was carrying his heir who, should the Resistance carry out their threat and kill him for selling contraband to the Nazis, would end up a very rich heir indeed. Mistinguett, it seems, knew only half the story, and even this had been 'coloured in' by Manouche, who now asked if she could move into Bougival. Carbone's Paris office was an apartment building teeming with his fellow Corsicans, on the rue du Colisée, just off the Champs-Elysées. He was also liaising with Mendel Szkolnikov, a Polish Jew who was working for the S.S. in Paris. This made Manouche's position doubly dangerous, and would have caused innumerable problems for Mistinguett, had she been aware of the fact. Fortunately, as soon as Manouche informed Carbone that she was pregnant, he left Paris and moved to Cannes, where he set about purchasing a number of hotels with the fortune he had amassed. The hotels were not for himself, but for Szkolnikov. Had Mistinguett known this, Manouche would have been evicted from Bougival, in spite of her condition. That Mistinguett no longer trusted Carbone was evident, for shortly before he left for Cannes she had a confrontation with him in her Paris apartment, and there was a violent quarrel, so violent that Carbone told her that as soon as his 'business' in the south had been wrapped up, he would be sending for his 'wife'.

On 15 December 1943 – and the date was apt, for it was the anniversary of the Eaglet – Carbone turned up at the railway station in Marseilles, hoping to catch the Nice-Paris express. He and his fellow passengers were informed that there would be a two hour delay because the Americans had bombed one of the viaducts between Cannes and Saint-Raphaël, as a result of which only one side of the track was being used for trains travelling in both directions. When the train arrived it was understandably crowded. Carbone had booked a sleeper, but when he boarded the train he found that there had been a mix-up over the tickets, and that his sleeper had been given to an elderly restauranteur. Rather than argue, he accepted another in the next carriage, and this act of compassion, apparently rare, cost him his life. What Carbone did not know was that a Maquis suicide-squad had trailed him to Marseilles. A few hours later there was a massive explosion. The carriage containing Carbone was blown off the rails and plummeted to the bottom of a ravine. The elderly restauranteur was thrown clear and escaped with a few cuts and bruises. Two Corsicans, who had been travelling in another carriage, rushed to their leader's aid. Carbone's right leg had been severed above the knee. He was taken to a hospital in Lyons, where subsequently he bled to death. The *commissaire de police* in Lyons could not have been more indifferent. He immediately gave orders for Carbone to be buried in a communal grave on the outskirts of the town. Carbone's brother handed over what amounted to a small fortune, a coffin was acquired, and the body was secreted back to Paris under a cartload of potatoes.

Mistinguett received first-hand information of what had happened and broke the devastating news to Manouche, whom she asked to leave Bougival. When Carbone's brother met the 'widow' at a secret Paris location, he handed her Carbone's suitcase containing a quarter of a million francs. This, he said, was for the upkeep of the child. According to Manouche she never touched it, which makes one wonder what happened to it. Manouche telephoned Mistinguett, who advised her to return to Bougival. For some unexplained reason she herself went with Tino Rossi to Carbone's apartment on the Boulevard Péreire to console the real widow where, though she was not a Corsican and thus nothing to do with the family, she was asked to assist in the all-night vigil around the coffin.

Even Carbone's funeral was paid for by illegal means. The church of Sainte-Marie-des-Batignolles had neither heating, electricity nor candles on account of the Occupation, but these were supplied right under the noses of the Germans, many of whom attended the funeral or sent wreaths. Amongst the more important mourners were the German ambassador, Otto Abetz, Paul Marion, the Vichy Secretary of State, and Mistinguett . . . she sat at the back of the church, heavily disguised so as not to be recognized. Carbone, before expiring, had asked to be buried in the churchyard at Propriano, but this had been out of the question, and he was interred amongst the famous and the infamous within Père Lachaise. At this stage of the proceedings Mistinguett had returned to her apartment, where she had earlier deposited a grieving Manouche. 'The next time I visit a graveyard, it'll be as a customer!' she told her protégé. What she did not add was that she had been told, from a reliable source, that Manouche was now high on the Resistance hit list. A few days later, pretending that she was acting in the interests of the young woman and her unborn child, she secured her an apartment in the Square Malherbe. For the time being at least, she must have been pleased to be rid of her.

This freedom of a kind did not last for long. Towards the end of March 1944 Manouche gave birth to a son in the clinic at Boulogne-Billancourt. Mistinguett, who was almost as fond of babies as she was of animals, was the first of Manouche's friends to arrive on the scene. She was so moved when the young woman asked her to be the baby's godmother that she had an attack of the vapours and had to be revived by one of the doctors. Once she had recovered she announced that, as godmother, she should have the right to choose the baby's name, and that as he had been fathered by a Corsican who had taken patriotism to the point of absurdity, he should be baptised Napoléon!

Manouche was no more surprised at this than she was when Mistinguett introduced her to her new lover. Odette's dancer-toyboy had been dispensed with for a handsome, athletic hunk who was one of the handful not to have come from her side of the show business fence. His name was Louis Gerardin though he never answered to anything but Toto, and he was the most famous racing-cycle champion of his day.

It is not known how Mistinguett met Toto, though she was of course herself a very keen cyclist, and did admit to having physiotherapy for her injured knee. Her own story, that Toto was in the shop when she bought a new bicycle may or may not be true. The fact is, she fell for him in such a big way that many people believed that loving him had driven away, once and for all, the spirit of Chevalier. Toto also belonged to that rare brigade of Mistinguett-lovers who were exclusively heterosexual, and for which he should be given at least a little credit. He was, naturally, the idol of many thousands of women, who were utterly disgusted by the fact that he had taken up with a woman who, at seventy, was more than forty years his senior, even if she did not look it. Discreet investigations have proved, unequivocally, that it could only have been love, and not Mistinguett's name, which had attracted him to her in the first place. He was already very rich and as renowned in his world as she was in hers. He knew that her meanness and ferocious temper were bywords in the music-hall profession, and that if ever they went out socially he would be the one picking up the tab at the end of the evening (the only man capable of getting her to part with her money had been Harry Pilcer). When Toto Gerardin confessed, some years later, that he had fallen in love with Mistinguett because she had been 'one hell of a woman', he can only have been speaking from the heart. And when Mistinguett told Manouche that Toto was going to be her son's god-father, the young woman quietly acquiesced, though she did refuse to have the boy saddled with a name like Napoléon.

He was baptised Jean-Paul-François Germaine on 30 April 1944 ... these were the first names of the Carbone brothers. The photographs taken after the christening are both interesting and amusing: it is Mistinguett who is seen holding the baby, with Toto looking on as if the child is his, and with the mother standing nonchalantly in the background as if she had had nothing to do with the event!

Several weeks later on 6 June 1944, Mistinguett, like everyone else, delighted to the tidings that the British and American allies had landed in Normandy, and that the days of the Nazi jackboot were ostensibly over. By the beginning of August, most of the buses and metros had been halted in order to save fuel, though this did not bother Mistinguett, who was not averse to cycling all the way from Bougival to see what was happening in Paris, especially on 25 August when she was amongst the thousands of excited Parisians turning out to welcome General Leclerc and his army. For so auspicious an occasion she modified one of her revue costumes: she could be seen in a huge red, white and blue picture hat, a flowing skirt, and matching tricolour, sequined gloves. Not content with standing with the onlookers lining both sides of the Champs-Elysées, she cycled alongside the marching soldiers and yelled: 'Vive de Gaulle!' The crowds and the soldiers bawled back: 'Vive la Miss!' The emotion, however, was too much for her. Half-way up the Champs-Elysées, her front wheel hit the curb and she careered over the handle-bars, wrenching the knee which had caused her almost constant pain since her fall from the staircase at the ABC. Even so, she refused to be taken to hospital, for after the parade she had planned to visit the platforms which were being set up in preparation for the head-shaving of those women who had been found guilty of cohabiting with the Germans. One of these, she had been told, was the actress Arletty.

According to Manouche, and several eyewitnesses, Arletty was arrested and when confronted by her captors screamed: 'My fanny may have been German, but my heart remained French, which is more than could be said for some!'

Arletty was not the only artiste accused of collaboration. Mistinguett was alleged to have been delighted upon hearing of Maurice Chevalier's plight, whilst attempting to flee from liberated Paris:

> He ran straight into the hands of the Périgord Maquis. Not content with beating him up, they were about to shoot him when Maurice, his sang-froid totally abandoned, offered them a large sum of money, which of course they accepted. Maurice, whose stinginess was more notorious in music-hall circles than his talents, was for once only too happy to cough up millions of francs. . .

Manouche was perhaps over-scathing when writing of Maurice Chevalier and Mistinguett. Though many people have spoken of his meanness, and though he did later attempt to exonerate his wartime activities by appearing in a piece of newsreel film which may or may not have been contrived, there seems to be no evidence, one way or the other, that he actually collaborated. Those close friends of the singer to whom the author spoke during the preparation of this book maintain that he did not, which is probably firm evidence that over the years Chevalier's character has been needlessly maligned, and it would seem doubtful that he would have been able to pursue his career with such verve and success, virtually until the end of his life, had such charges possessed any foundation.

The same may be said for Arletty. Though she did have her head shaved, few things were actually proved against her, and immediately after the Liberation she went on to star in Marcel Carné's *Les Enfants du Paradis*, arguably the best film either of them ever made. It also starred Jean-Louis Barrault, yet another artiste who had steadfastly accepted German backing for his work.

It has to be said that whilst many of these artistes worked or performed for the Germans, it was not simply a question of choice. Most of them had only their careers to support them, and the Germans were, of course, everywhere: it would have been impossible to even think of avoiding them. What is interesting to note is that the poet Jacques Prévert, who had supplied the script for *Les Enfants du Paradis* and the earlier *Les Visiteurs du Soir*, had his name omitted from the credits of the original prints. This remained so until recently, when they were restored. Prévert had also been the first to criticize Marianne Oswald for her pro-Nazi attitude several years before the outbreak of war. Another legendary figure of the film world, Sacha Guitry, was accused of having dined with Goëring. The actor Pierre Fresnay, then married to Guitry's second wife Yvonne Printemps, was also charged with collaboration. Tino Rossi and Suzy Solidor were arrested, questioned, and allowed to go free after some deliberation.

In March and April of 1945, Mistinguett was guest of honour at two parties thrown by Manouche, now very rich but widely distrusted since she had been formally charged with working with Paul Carbone against the interests of the Resistance. The first of these was to honour the first birthday of her son, Jean-Paul Germaine . . . the François had been dropped because his mother had found three names too much of a mouthful. Mistinguett brought Toto Gerardin, who by this time was sleeping at Bougival, though not in the same bed as the boss. With them was Madame Brigitte – or Madame Billy, as she liked to be known – the proprietress of the famous brothel on the rue Villejuste, the quaint little street now known as the rue Paul Valéry. Manouche, along with many others including Edith Piaf, had stayed there during the Occupation, ostensibly because a house of ill-repute is never cold. It mattered little that many of the clients had been German officers, for in reality it had been a hotbed of Resistance activity. It would also appear that the proprietress had been unaware of Manouche's involvement with Carbone, otherwise she would not have been allowed through the door. In her memoirs, the gangster's moll declared that she was a close friend of both Piaf and Madame Billy, which was, of course, untrue.

The second party, held on 30 April 1945 to celebrate the first anniversary of Jean-Paul's christening, suddenly became a magnificent feast when, half way through the proceedings, Manouche switched on the radio and everyone learned that Adolf Hitler had committed suicide that very day.

'I felt rather sad,' Mistinguett said, later. 'I'd rather hoped to get hold of the bastard myself!'

'It's What's Called Living
on Borrowed Time!'

Mistinguett's mighty career, it may be said, was almost over. She said, 'I've lost count of the men I've loved . . . and the ones who used me and deceived me. Even Chevalier only wanted me for what he could get out of me. As soon as that happened he dumped me. But my public . . . they've always been there to help me over the hurdles. My real lovers are the ones I've never seen . . . the men and women sitting there, up in the gallery. They're the ones that I would give my life for, if I had to!'

In 1946, perhaps through spending too much time in bed resting her injured knee, Mistinguett began putting on weight. She was also alarmed to discover that she had begun to develop wrinkles. In order to combat the ageing process she began mixing a special foundation cream which she applied to her face and neck. Harry Pilcer had been doing the same thing for some years. Unlike Damia, who had more or less invented the single spotlight, she paid particular attention to the footlights, which were not as severe, though by now most of her performances were triumphs of mind over matter. Toto Gerardin was still her *chevalier-servante*, but on account of her hasty temper, which was always at its worst when she was not working, he had begun searching further afield. He would hang on for a few more years, and then would begin perhaps the greatest drama of his career, and Mistinguett's rivalry with Edith Piaf, which so far was limited to a few bitchy but well-aimed comments, would reach its peak.

During the summer of 1946 it was widely rumoured that Mistinguett would never work again. Though she had once said that she would only stop performing when they carried her out of a theatre in a box, she herself was sensible enough to realize that she could not go on for ever. Others had attempted to drag out the same handful of songs and the same routine well into their dotage, and had ended up making fools of themselves. When, however, a visit to her doctor revealed that her fatigue was due to heart trouble, and that being over-weight could only make matters worse, she decided she would have to do something about it.

'I don't want to end up a crotchety old hag, like some I could mention!' she declared.

A contributory factor towards Mistinguett's 'comeback', if such it was, for she had never really been away from the stage for more than a few months over the past forty years, was Marie Dubas' sensational season at the ABC, which opened on 6 December 1946. Writing for *La Marseillaise*, Pierre Barlatier said:

> This is perhaps the greatest triumph of Marie Dubas' entire career. I have never seen anything quite like it. Twenty-one songs . . . fifteen of them new! I found it impossible to contain my tears. Without any doubt, Marie is the greatest star in France today. . .

Marie Dubas remains the only female entertainer in France to have been given the Mistinguett seal of approval, which on the face of it is somewhat difficult to comprehend. It is true that for a while, whilst dancing the *chaloupée* with Max Dearly, Damia had been a serious threat to her career. Fréhel, likewise, had attempted to 'get one over' on Mistinguett by chasing after Chevalier. Her hatred of singers such as Léo Marjane needs no explanation, and her dissension over Edith Piaf, once Toto Gerardin had deserted her in 1951, is understandable. It has to be said that whilst interviewing many famous personalities or their families, the author never listened to a single discrediting word about Damia, who was perhaps the most amiable of all the French singers. Marie Dubas did gain a few enemies at the time of the last war, but through no fault of her own; she had not been able to choose her Jewish religion, and in any case she did convert to Catholicism. She did, however, come very close to parodying Mistinguett in her revue, *Sex-Appeal 1932*, and this should have incurred the older woman's wrath. All it did was draw Mistinguett towards her, which certainly must tell us something about Marie's quite extraordinary personality and stage presence.

During the early years of the war, however, the attitude of the French media towards her had been almost as horrendous as that of the Germans. The mere mention of her name had been *verboten* by the Propagandastaffel, and in Paris her records had been burned publicly. After her South American tour, unable to return to her apartment in the Square la Fontaine which had been taken over to house a number of known collaborators, she had spent some time in Portugal, where she had married her lover, Georges Bellair, in April 1941. Mistinguett had telephoned her there with the news that several of her contacts were waiting to welcome her in the Free Zone and had found her a suite in a Nice hotel, which she had used as a base for her tour with Georges Feydeau's *La Dame de Chez Maxims*, which Mistinguett had been to see.

Marie's problems had not ended there. The Free Zone had been little safer than occupied Paris, and after a brief tour of Algeria – none of the theatre directors would pay her, so she had performed for charity to keep up her dwindling spirits – she had been offered a series of engagements in Switzerland. During the next two years, separated from her husband and young son, Marie had lived in Lausanne. Though her friends, including Mistinguett, begged her to return to France, fear of reprisal for being born a Jew prevented her from doing so, and in March 1944 she had given a concert which had been broadcast not just to France, but to England as well. A new song, 'Ce Soir Je Pense à mon Paris', had made Mistinguett cry so much that she immediately made up her mind to travel to Lausanne 'to sort things out'. Only illness prevented her from doing so.

> Quand la nuit tombe sur la ville,
> Quand l'ombre descend sur la rue,
> Je suis dans ma chambre tranquille,
> Si seule, et si perdue. . .
>
> (When night falls on the town,
> When shadows descend on the street,
> I'm in my peaceful room,
> So alone, and so lost . . .)

'I will never understand the French,' Mistinguett said, alluding to the fact that she was half-Belgian.

After Marie Dubas' ABC première, the two great stars met in her dressing room. Marie was fifty years of age, and if she did not look it, she was the first to admit that she felt it. She even told Mistinguett that she was thinking of retiring. The Liberation had brought with it an American wave of entertainment which only made her highly-specialized style appear out of date. When she announced, however, that she was thinking of changing her approach, she was advised not to. 'Being different is what makes us special,' she was told. 'The public want to listen to real songs, not all this American crap!'

Listening to the applause at the ABC inspired Mistinguett to 'have another go'. She told her friends that this would be the last time, though as late as 1954 she was writing:

> The greater I become, the less time I have left to do all the things I want to do. I've seen myself working eleven months on the trot, without so much as a break. I can't afford to be ill. When I die . . . and I know I won't be lucky enough to die on stage, it will be the greatest revue of them all. The best tableau will be the fight for my soul between the Good Lord and the Devil. I know God will win . . . He's been with me all the time!

Toto Gerardin, himself probably fitter and in better shape than all the previous lovers put together, began helping her with her early morning work-outs. She always rose at seven, and usually began with several laps on her bicycle around her Bougival estate. Then there were press ups, some weight lifting and jogging, and a more cautious approach to her diet. Incredibly, she had been eating as many as six meals a day. As Roger Normand told me, 'I honestly don't know where she put it all!' Gradually, her weight returned to normal and her doctor told her that she would be able to work again, so long as she did not over-tire herself with the dancing. During her indisposition the offers had kept coming in: new revues at the Alhambra and the ABC, and tours of Belgium, Britain, Canada and the United States. She was determined to fulfil every one of her contracts; not because, as many of her contemporaries have said, she

was avaricious, but because she genuinely believed that she would
soon be dead.

'I want to see New York again,' she announced. 'And I want the
British to see me as I really am, before it's too late.'

Before any of these tours took place, there was to be a penultimate
social event of some importance. Manouche, who had refused to
touch her son's inheritance, was virtually on the bread-line and had
been for some time, though she had until now refused to consider
selling her jewellery. Most of it had been given to her by wealthy
admirers during a period of sleeping around which had only been
broken by her involvement with Paul Carbone. The collection was
said to be worth a small fortune, especially a fourteen carat diamond
which she had received for her twenty first birthday. This was sold
and the money put to good use. Acting upon Mistinguett's advice,
Manouche bought L'Atomique, a café-bar in the rue Chambiges,
tucked away behind the fashionable avenues Montaigne and George
V. Extremely popular with the Parisian gay crowd, its name was
changed to Le Chambiges, though the regular clientele never knew
it by any other name but Chez Manouche. The drag-queen Odette
travelled from the south of France for the inauguration ceremony
and of course Mistinguett, who had organized the publicity, was
guest of honour, even though these two were no longer on speaking
terms. Manouche tempted fate by trying to get them to sit at the same
table . . . it did not work and Odette was banished to a far corner of
the club, where he is said to have cringed 'at this hundred-years old
harridan, croaking out her latest pastiche of vomitable slop'. The
song which she was performing regularly at this time was in fact a
new adaptation of one of her old hits . . . 'Dans les Bouges la Nuit',
which she had performed in *Paris Qui Brille*, and which, during her
tour with the troublesome American dancer, Lad, had become 'Prenez
Mes Fleurettes'. Even at over seventy she was still playing the little lost
girl:

> Dans les boites de la nuit
> Quand les gens sont aimables,
> Gentillement j'leurs souris,
> Je vais près de leurs tables:
> 'Madame, prenez ces roses,

Prenez-les ces pour rien,
Je me souviens le temps
Où j'avais pas d'galettes!'

(In the night clubs when people are friendly,
I smile sweetly,
I go up to their tables:
'Madame, take my roses for nothing,
I remember the time
When I was without a sou!')

It was around this time that Manouche began her own career as a *chanteuse*. It has to be said, however, that she was not very good. Her range was somewhat limited, and though she possessed a better singing voice than Mistinguett, vulgarity was the name of the game, and this restricted any hope of lasting success. Two of her favourite songs were 'Mon Homme' and 'De l'Autre Côté de la Rue'. The latter was a Piaf number which she practically murdered. Many people went to Chez Manouche with the sole intention of being insulted by the star of the show, and were never disappointed. Others were grossly offended by her emulations of Mistinguett and Suzy Solidor, and never set foot in the establishment again. Mistinguett had neither denied nor been ashamed of her own vulgarity . . . her asides between songs were both witty and intelligent, and barring those directed at the Germans during the occupation, were in no way crude. As she said herself, on stage she was always a lady and as for the rest . . . well, it was nobody's business but her own. Fréhel's catch-phrase for many years had been crude, but her distinctive personality had been such that she could get way with anything. Manouche had little or no personality which was not grossly contrived, as was still evident when I interviewed her in 1973, when much of her dialogue comprised of filthy words and anecdotes, few of which could in any way be described as comical. Mistinguett warned her in 1947 that she would one day go too far, and she would. Her recipe for 'success', raucously delivered on stage and repeated during every single interview throughout the sixties and seventies, never failed to raise a laugh from 'my pansies', as she called them: these were the waiters in the bar, which by then had become little more than a gay pick-up place.

> You see, my young friend . . . it's like this. Right up to the age of twenty, a girl needs her parents to look after her morals. Between twenty and thirty she has to rely on her looks. Between thirty and forty she needs to be a good fuck, and up to the age of fifty needs lots of personality. All she needs after fifty are lots of luck, a bag over her head, and heaps of money. Nowadays when I go with a man I put a bag over his head . . . that helps if my bag happens to come off!

In October 1947 Mistinguett, tired of being seen every night at Manouche's place with the same hangers-on whom she dismissed as 'a bunch or fairies and fag-hags', accepted a contract from the British impressario Bernard Delfont, just one of the many entrepreneurs who had been trying to book her for many years, and who had almost given up hope that she would ever perform in London. Lord Delfont, as he is now, has never discussed the engagement but others have and still shudder whenever Mistinguett's name is mentioned. No fee was discussed at this early stage, and it seems that her only condition was that she would be partnered by her 'friend' Lino Carenzio, who was immediately 'dug out of retirement and dusted down'. She told reporters, 'Carenzio may be a little shit, but he's the only dancer left in the world who's up to partnering me!' The management of the London Casino must have known little about the volatile relationship between Mistinguett and Carenzio, and it has been suggested that a stand-in had been arranged . . . Harry Pilcer who, at fifty seven, was still active and had just completed an engagement in Harrogate at the time the final contracts were signed. Carenzio, short of money as usual, accepted the challenge, though he did forewarn everyone that there was no guarantee that the engagement would sally forth without its share of problems. He hated Mistinguett, he said, as much as she had once loved him.

On 5 December 1947 there was the now-familiar arrival at Croydon airport, and for the first time in her life Mistinguett was mobbed by hundreds of hysterical fans who, unable to buy tickets for her shows, had to make do with a glance and a wave. The newspapers at the time recorded that she was making her London début after more than fifty years stardom on the continent: hardly anyone remembered that her actual London début had been at the same theatre, forty four years before, and she was in no hurry to remind them. One young man who ought to have known better, asked her her age. 'Fifty nine,' she quipped. 'How old are you?' Cautiously descending the steps of the plane – her knee was still playing up on her – she temporarily disappeared under a sea of flowers and even sang a few bars of 'My Man'. Lino Carenzio, for his part, smiled a lot and said little . . . the 'boss' had warned him not to give anything away.

On the eve of her London première, Mistinguett met and was entertained by her English friends . . . these included Charles Cochran, Noël Coward, the Duff-Coopers, and the journalist Beverley Baxter. During her 'walk-abouts' she never tired of showing her legs, which were still remarkable and still insured for several million dollars. Cynics laughed, of course, and regarded her as some sort of joke, and so it appears did some of the audience on her opening night, 6 December. An article published in *The Times* began:

> Mistinguett, whose music-hall reputation became for our week-ending fathers one of the symbols of Parisian gaiety, made her first appearance in London last night. Curiosity was perhaps the emotion uppermost in the mind of the audience. Beneath an immense mushroom of feathers, and somewhat precariously balanced on very high thin heels she sang in a voice that is still pleasantly firm a few songs that cynically, if a little conventionally, link love with money . . . songs in praise of Paris in which 'la, la, la' serve well enough for the missing words. And with 'la, la, la!' the sympathetic audience helped her out. . .

She had received a personal introduction from Delfont, and age had added an unmistakable quality to her voice . . . when she sang 'J'En ai Marre' there was a touch of Lotte Lenya. The programme was perfectly arranged, proving yet again that only the great continental *chanteuses* know exactly how to present their works in the correct order. There was also more than a hint of coquettish titillation: for 'I'm Feeling Like a Million' she brandished a long cigarette holder and made her descent into the auditorium, where Charles Cochran and Noël Coward were sitting in the front row. The problem arose when, during 'Mon Homme' which she had intended singing in French and English, she allowed her emotions to get the better of her. The orchestra had begun the introduction when someone in the audience shouted, 'Miss, show us your legs!' Not knowing if the man was joking or not, Mistinguett obliged and in doing so forgot the words of the song. This had never happened before. She burst into tears and left the stage in such a hurry that Bernard Delfont actually thought she was going to have a heart attack. He had been told, as had many people, that she had already suffered a mild attack before leaving Paris, though Mistinguett herself had dismissed any such indisposition as 'just a load of balls'. Drying her eyes, she returned to the stage and yelled to the orchestra, 'Okay, sunshine. Let's have another go . . . get it right this time!' During the second stanza of the song she dried up again and stopped the music. Carenzio ran on from the wings and put his arms about her. This was the worst possible thing he could have done, for she had always hated being touched, even more so by a man whom she apparently despised. The curtain was brought down and Carenzio appeared again to explain what had happened. 'Miss is very tired. She's had a bad day and she's suffering from first-night nerves!'

Throughout the next thirty minutes or so, the audience was kept amused by the quick-wit patter of Billy Milton, one of the dancers who had first appeared with her in *Paris Qui Brille*. Milton went on to better things as a singer-songwriter, but the episode at the London Casino, with Mistinguett alternating between fits of rage and weeping, must have been one of the most harrowing events of his career. He still shuddered when recalling what had happened, on and off the stage, a few months before his death in November 1989.

In her dressing-room, Bernard Delfont pleaded with her to give it all up as a bad job. The spectators, he told her, would be given their money back. The thought of this only horrified her. She retorted that in fifty years, she had never had to cancel a show and that she would not do so now. Carenzio, temporarily demoted to errand boy, was asked to fetch her a drink. The photograph taken at the time shows her with a glass in her hand, but it was nothing stronger than water. Carenzio was then sent back to tell the audience that she was changing her dress, and that she would make her entrance 'presently'.

A few minutes later the curtains opened to reveal the celebrated staircase. Still suffering terribly from stage-fright, Mistinguett descended to the stage, supported by her partner, and singing 'C'Est Vrai'. In spite of the speed of the song and its difficult argot, she managed to finish it and received a standing ovation. No one knows to this day if this was out of pity, or out of genuine admiration. The rest of the evening was, however, an unqualified success. Mistinguett sang fourteen songs . . . these included 'Sous Les Ponts', 'Au Fond De Tes Yeux', and 'Avez-Vous Vu Hubert', which was her duet with Carenzio. The final song was 'Ca C'Est Paris', which earned her more than a dozen curtain. calls. Both her diction and delivery, after her disastrous start, were spot-on, and the dance routines were nothing short of excellent. She later said that she had felt no pain whatsoever in her injured knee, though by the end of the show she did find it difficult to walk across the stage, which was on account of the sea of flowers strewn at her feet. The critics, along with that scurrilous section of her audience who had turned up to watch her make a fool of herself (most of them had been given complimentary tickets) could only agree that in Mistinguett's case, age had not diminished the fact that she was the best in the business.

During the press conference after the show, Mistinguett attributed her 'cock up' to the fact that she had not been wearing her 'lucky' jewels at the time of her entrance. The following night this mistake was rectified and she appeared in a fabulous diamond collar valued at millions of francs. Not content with singing 'Mon Homme' all the way through without faltering, she repeated it in English. More than forty years after her first London appearance, Mistinguett had finally been accepted by the British public . . . not as an exotic ornament, but as an artiste.

Public acclaim, however, had arrived a good ten years too late. In spite of her insistence that she was 'fighting fit', the great star was ill. When she was offered a full-scale British tour at a fee considerably higher than for a contemporary British star, she politely declined. Her son Léopold, now acting as her doctor, advised her that the damp, mid-winter climate would be detrimental to her health. 'I'm sorry, folks,' she said. 'Popol knows best!'

In January 1948 Mistinguett bid a tearful au revoir to her British admirers and returned to Bougival. She was met by a French entrepreneur who offered to buy some of her costumes for fifteen million francs. 'I can't sell them yet,' she told him. 'I need them!' Léopold drove her down to Antibes, where she rested for a while with Fraisette, Marcel and their five children. Lino Carenzio, who had told British reporters that their 'marriage' had in fact been the real thing, had left her again, though he still insisted that he loved her. Mistinguett may have been feeling the same way. The London revue had begun with a number of violent quarrels but had ended amicably enough, though Carenzio had refused to travel with her to the south, probably anticipating that Toto Gerardin would be there. He was, though not for long. Manouche arrived from Cannes, and sent him packing.

Mistinguett had now been singing and dancing professionally for fifty five years, and with such relentless enthusiasm, energy and passion that she had always refused to allow herself the luxury of a break even whilst on holiday, she had always given recitals or appeared in revues. She knew now that if she followed the advice of her doctors and friends who nagged her constantly to hang up her feathers for good, then life would hold no meaning. In London she had almost succeeded in turning the tables on herself and making herself look a fool, but in the end she had triumphed. The demand for more and more performances in France, in spite of her advanced years, had increased rather than diminished, and many of her admirers really did think her capable of going on for ever. Mitty Goldin telephoned to say that he had arranged a tour of Morocco, if she was interested, but that he would give her several weeks to think it over. 'There's nothing to think over,' she declared. 'You'd better bring Carenzio down from the shelf and dust him down . . . he isn't getting any younger, you know!'

The tour began in 1948, and Mistinguett's fortitude proved nothing short of remarkable. Though some of the dance routines had to be removed from her act, including the athletic ones which had made her famous, she insisted that new ones should be added, including the jitterbug. She also withstood the intense heat better than any of her co-stars, several of whom were grounded by sunstroke. In Casablanca and Aîn Seba the temperature soared to more than one hundred degrees, yet she persisted in staying on her feet for up to ninety minutes, accepting any number of curtain calls. After each show, when everyone else had staggered to their beds utterly exhausted, she attended parties and danced away until dawn.

'It's called living on borrowed time,' she said.

The tour was so successful that before leaving Morocco Mistinguett received another telephone call from Goldin to offer her an open contract with the ABC, for what would be her last French revue, *Paris Qui S'Amuse*. There was no hesitation. Her friends and family, who firmly believed that she would one day drop dead on stage, which was, she told them, what she had always wanted did not try to stop her from giving what they considered would be her swan-song. In spite of the open contract, everyone, including Mitty Goldin, reckoned upon her lasting for just one fifteen-day season, especially when they watched some of the new dance routines which she had devised. Mind over matter or not, Mistinguett stayed at the ABC for more than a year: her troupe of young dancers, unable to keep up with her, was changed several times!

The story line of *Paris Qui S'Amuse*, which opened early in 1949, was not too complicated; it was the semi-autobiographical tale of an ageing star who is teaching a newcomer the tricks of her trade. There was just one problem . . . Mistinguett's co-star. She told Mitty Goldin, 'I want to know who's going to play the old wreck. I hope it's not going to be me?'

Though she cracked jokes and was expectedly difficult during rehearsals (some of the dance routines were practised with Harry Pilcer, in Antibes), Mistinguett was in considerable pain throughout the rehearsals and the revue. One hour before curtain-up, she found it impossible to get out of the arm-chair which had been installed in her dressing room. A doctor was sent for, and promptly dismissed. Her bad knee had almost doubled in size and Mitty Goldin, still thinking himself responsible for the injury in the first place, begged her to cancel the générale (the night prior to the première, when most of the front stalls were filled with the high society of Paris and members of the press). Again, the director was 'evicted' from his own theatre, though she did agree to be treated by a chiropractor, and this allowed her to hobble as far as the wings. It was then that the miracle occurred . . . the moment the curtain rose. Yvan Audouard, then working as a reporter for France-Dimanche, wrote:

When she appeared, it represented one of the greatest moments in the history of the music-hall. The public rose, as if greeting the President himself. But there was something else in the eyes of the public: Would she be capable of staying on her feet? In fact, she never made a single mistake. The songs were the ones she had been singing for years, with the same absence of voice. But she had become immune to age . . . she had become eternal!

Audouard, famed for observing the unseeable and writing about it fearlessly in his column, failed to detect Mistinguett's agony during the first half of her show. During the interval her knee seized up again . . . this time she agreed to return to the stage only if her doctor gave her an injection to kill the pain. She had also developed a temperature, and Léopold believed her to be on the verge of pneumonia. During one sketch she recreated her celebrated role, Titine, but the most astonishing side of Mistinguett was seen during the finale, when she be-bopped for twelve minutes with a young dancer less than a third of her age, without so much as pausing for breath! The young man, it has to be added, retreated to the wings for a moment, during the frenzied applause, where he had to be treated for the stitch. 'That's the trouble with the youngsters of today,' she declared later. 'They don't know how to keep up with us old ones!'

Yvan Audouard continues his story:

> They were frightened of dropping her, or that she might have broken in their arms. She kept telling them, 'It's all right. I'm not fragile!' La Miss is a monument . . . more than that, she's an institution. She was born at the same time as the Third Republic, and she has survived it. She gives confidence to the nation. Show business fits her like a glove!

Paris Qui S'Amuse ultimately revived Mistinguett's failing health, but it did not cure it completely. When the revue closed early in 1950, she turned down the offer of another and returned to Antibes, where every now and then she gave an impromptu performance at her club, La Cage aux Poules. In music-hall circles, the rumour quickly spread that she had retired for good, and she was content to allow them to believe this. There was another mild heart attack, which she dismissed as 'just another bout of flu', and a not-unexpected attack of pneumonia which left her with a bad chest. When her son Léopold told her that it might do her good to sip a small glass of pastis each night before going to bed, she in turn warned him of the perils of getting addicted to absinthe, which was of course an entirely different substance. Also, she did not like the way in which the liquid changed colour when water was added. It took her until the end of 1950 before she decided to take the plunge . . . a precipitous plunge for a woman who had endured seventy five increasingly difficult years without so much as taking a single sip of alcohol or even an aspirin.

By January 1951 Mistinguett was sufficiently cured to give out the news that she was going to make a come-back. Most of her troupe, unable to find work with anyone else, were dispersed along the Côte d'Azur, and they were immediately summoned back to base. Lino Carenzio was already with her. She declared, 'He's only hanging around hoping to inherit my money . . . not that I would leave him so much as a single franc!' Carenzio, however, cared sufficiently for the woman and not for her fortune to advise her against over-tiring herself, and Léopold added that wherever his mother went, he would go too. 'It mightn't be as easy as that!' she quipped. Mitty Goldin and several of his colleagues had offered her contracts in Paris, though after playing for a whole year in the capital, she announced that she was looking for a change of scenery: even the offer of three million francs each night did not tempt her on this score. 'Paris can have me any time,' she declared. 'Paris'll always be there when I'm too old or too infirm to travel. I want to go to the States again . . . this time, you can throw in a tour of Canada!'

There were no rehearsals; instead of appearing in a revue, Mitty Goldin thought it would be safer if she appeared on the cabaret circuit, though he was cautious enough to leave the choice of material to Mistinguett herself. Pressures of work prevented Léopold from travelling with her, which came as a relief, for though she loved her son more than anyone else, she did find him over-protective, and declared that this only cramped her style. Lino Carenzio, then aged about fifty and perhaps well past his peak, agreed to travel with her, though she had given him no inclination that he would be asked to partner her, once they arrived at their destination.

The tour began in Montreal. Though Mistinguett looked a good thirty years younger than she really was, and though her figure and her legs were as fabulous as they had always been, the Canadians expected too much of her, and she tried too hard to please them. Her performances, though to packed houses, were attended mostly out of curiosity by the critics and the public alike. Opinions and reviews ranged from 'absolutely brilliant' to 'pathetic', though the star herself did not take much notice. The fact that she received a standing ovation each night was all that mattered, and even her taste for 'le fric' took a back seat.

The costumes for the North American tour had been suitably toned down as Mistinguett no longer possessed the strength to carry fifteen pounds of feathers on her head, or drag an enormous train around with her. One of her favourites (she had made it herself) was a flimsy silk ballet costume, the skirt of which barely covered her thighs. It made her look neither common nor ridiculous. Perhaps the best was the last costume designed for her by Michel Guyarmathy of the Folies-Bergère. It was a floor-length gown of crimson velvet, which Guyarmathy had trimmed with a wide fur belt, and was complimented with a simple single-crest head-dress of egret plumes. Her hair was longer than it had been for some time, and her voice, probably now more important than her dancing, had improved for the better by dropping an octave. Mistinguett no longer 'squawked' her songs, but delivered them in deep, sensually dulcet tones which were no longer mocked but envied by her so-called American and Canadian peers. One critic was so amazed by her vocal abilities, once the 'curiosity' element of her opening night had been dispensed with, that he described her as a réaliste, 'in the very best of the tragédienne tradition'.

Tragedy was, unfortunately, lurking in the wings during the Canadian tour. On 22 February 1951 Mistinguett received a telephone call from France: her friend, the great chanteuse Fréhel, had been found dead in her Paris apartment of a suspected heart attack. For Mistinguett the news came as a double blow. She was reminded of her own vulnerability where her health was concerned. Fréhel had been just fifty nine, though grossly overweight, and like Mistinguett had been constantly warned about over-exerting herself.

A few days later, more details came to light. Fréhel had staged a come-back in 1949, whilst Mistinguett had been appearing at the ABC, and their paths had crossed but briefly. Fréhel had been paid a large fee for her recitals, but instead of investing her money she had frittered it away on her friends ... friends, it had since been proved, who could not have cared less. Her last few months had been spent in abject poverty: she had received a modest royalty cheque for her record sales, but instead of spending the money on herself she had lavished it on her collection of cats, dogs and exotic fish. The doctor carrying out the post-mortem had diagnosed heart failure due to self-neglect. Her funeral, which took place in sub-zero temperatures at the Cimitière de Pantin, remains the biggest there has ever been in Paris with the exception of that of Edith Piaf. Thirty thousand people turned out to pay their last respects. Mistinguett sent a representative, and later would visit the singer's grave.

Fréhel is regarded by many, even to this day, as the finest French singer of her generation. What is curious is that many of her admirers were not even born when she died. Her life had been nothing but a catalogue of disasters; the penultimate had taken place during the war when, singing an anti-Hitler song in a Hamburg theatre, she had found herself on the receiving-end of an incendiary device. Mistinguett said,

> I really loved that woman, in spite of the episode with Chevalier. That affair ended happily one night when our paths crossed in a restaurant. Instead of bawling me out, she sang a song, just for me. We became close friends. Her end was most distressing. . .

On 10 April 1951 Mistinguett opened at another cabaret in New York, on Broadway. Many Americans have subsequently said that this was the finest season of her entire career. Unlike the Canadians, they were only ever interested in her art, and not in queuing for tickets just so that they could poke fun at her. Mistinguett sang twenty songs, and looking resplendent in her Guyarmathy robe, danced with Lino Carenzio. Observers sitting close to the stage noticed that, though she made her entrance with a long cigarette holder, she only pretended to smoke. When one elderly gentleman was seen 'lighting up', one fierce glance from the star told him to extinguish his cigarette at once! Several days after her première, she was surprised by the management . . . someone had 'leaked' that it was her birthday. A huge cake was wheeled in and the audience sang happy birthday to you! When someone bawled, 'What does it feel like to be twenty one?' she retorted, 'I don't know. You'd better come back and ask me next year!' After the show she told a reporter that she was seventy six – probably the first time that she had admitted her age to anyone, even her family. When asked if there was a current man in her life (Carenzio, it seems, was not regarded as such by the American public) she said that she was working on it. Such questions would never have been posed in France, where reporters knew better than to get too familiar. In America, as in England, Mistinguett seems to have had no reservations at all about opening up. Perhaps she thought the revelations would never reach the ears of the inquisitive French, who for most of the time had been forced to make do with rumours, or 'exclusives' leaked by former friends and acquaintances. The most lethal question of all, however, was put to her by a young reporter from a women's magazine: who, amongst her many lovers, had been her favourites. Again, there was hesitation. 'Chevalier, of course. Each time I've been in bed with anyone else, I've always been thinking about my Maurice. He was a lousy lover, but one hell of a man!'

Towards the end of 1951, Mistinguett returned to France, where the welcoming committee at Bougival observed, for the first time, the vast change in her appearance. She looked frail and old – something which she attributed to the fact that she had forgotten to put on her make-up and her gloves. 'I thought about having a face-lift whilst I was over there,' she quipped. 'It would have cost too much money. The only part of me that was lifted was my legs!'

There was also another drama, of sorts, once her family had settled her in her room at Bougival. Manouche informed her that Toto Gerardin had finally got the message . . . the young cyclist had moved out and was currently living with Edith Piaf at her farm in the country. Mistinguett was livid: according to Manouche, she immediately burned the presents which her lover had given her, and attempted to get in touch with Piaf via the telephone. The singer refused to speak to her, which did little to curb her anger. She bought another monkey and baptised it Toto. She admitted she would have loved to call it Edith, had it not been for the fact that she had taken an oath never to mention Piaf's name again. Piaf reciprocated: during a tour of North Africa she was asked to 'adopt' and name a baby camel. 'You'd be better calling it Mistinguett,' she joked. 'By the time it grows up it'll be just like her . . . ridden by thousands of arabs!'

The Piaf-Gerardin affair was in effect short-lived. When he moved in with Edith, he took most of the family valuables with him; these included a number of championship trophies, jewellery, precious porcelain, most of the money from the safe, and eighteen gold ingots which, Mistinguett later claimed, he had stolen from Bougival. In December 1951 Toto's wife, Alice, hired a private detective and had the pair followed. Piaf was used to having her name splashed on the front pages of newspapers, but this was going too far. She threw Toto out into the street, and flushed the jewellery he had given her down the toilet. Mistinguett was said to have been delighted that Piaf had done exactly what she should have done in the first place. Even so, she still accused her of 'purloining' Toto Gerardin and hit the roof whenever one of Piaf's records was played on the radio.

This little drama had enabled Mistinguett to build up some of her strength. According to the crude-mouthed Manouche, 'There was nothing like a bollocking good argument for dragging her back from a fit of the doldrums! She thrived on trouble, and always went out of her way to find it, if it wasn't there already!' She knew, however, that there would be no more revues, and little chance of ever opening again even in a minor series of recitals. After spending just a few days at Bougival with Manouche and her young son, she was driven down to Antibes for the rest of the winter. On mild days, she could be seen walking through the streets or along the sea front with her niece and nephews: of the four boys, François was said to have been favourite. Occasionally, she visited her club, where there was a reunion of sorts with Harry Pilcer. She told him, 'I don't think I'll ever leave Antibes again. From now on I'm going to call the Villa Mistinguett the Terminus-Antibes.'

'My Whole Life!'

Prior to Mistinguett's American tour, the villa at Antibes had been teeming with her 'gay boys'. There had been so many that they had overflowed from the house, to set up camp in the outbuildings. Her interpretation of what she expected in a man has been often discussed. Obvious machismo had always taken a back seat. A man had to be beautiful, spiritually and physically, and these were qualities, or so she believed, which could only be found in the homosexual; added to which was the fact that if one of her boys was homosexual, this would lessen the risk of him falling in love with her. This was not always the case. Harry Pilcer had begun by working as a male prostitute, and in spite of his passionate affairs with Gaby Deslys, Jenny Golder and Mistinguett, seems to have continued with his fascination for the male body. Both Earl Leslie and Lino Carenzio were bisexual; only Lad and Maurice Chevalier seem to have been exceptions, and even the latter was accused of having brief affairs with Maurice Yvain and his young butler.

This fascination between the siren and the homosexual will remain eternal. The audiences who flocked to see Damia, Fréhel and Yvonne George were predominantly gay. In recent generations, the trend has been continued with Judy Garland, Marlène Dietrich and Barbara, who still figure prominently in female-impersonation acts throughout the world. It may well be that during the thirties and forties, when homosexuality was not as accepted as it is today, a sense of guilt brought with it a form of neurosis which was expressed as artistic licence . . . Jacques Brel once said that this was so. Recent critics of Mistinguett's seemingly bizarre way of life have accredited her with the title of 'fag-hag', which may be cruel, but which is in no way inapt. Many of her boys proved to be little more than leeches and scroungers . . . this was all too evident once she announced, upon her return to France, that she had decided to retire, for most of them left her to sponge off someone else. Of course, the faithful clan remained. Chevalier and Tino Rossi called in regularly to pay their respects, though Mistinguett was not really interested in their impromptu visits because she had decided to devote what remained of her life to her loved ones . . . in other words, her family. There were two exceptions: Manouche and Harry Pilcer.

The great dancer was now in his sixties, and himself ill with heart trouble. Mistinguett had once said that Pilcer would always remain the love of her life, though the statement was made in the heat of the moment, probably after she had had an argument with Chevalier. In one respect, Pilcer was very much like Mistinguett; in spite of his poor health he refused to compromise, and was still working up to the day of his death. The love of his life, however, had never been anyone but Gaby Deslys and Mistinguett was amazed, when she visited his villa in 1951, to find portraits of the young dancer still hanging everywhere. 'He's still got her hanging over the altar,' she told friends, referring to the chapel which Pilcer had constructed in Gaby's memory. 'Pilcer never prays to God . . . he prays to Gaby Deslys. He spends so much of his time with the dead, he has no time for the living!'

It was probably Pilcer who suggested that Mistinguett put pen to paper, when he visited her villa during the summer of 1952. Her earlier memoirs had in fact been little more than a series of personal recollections which she had recounted, for want of something better to do, during the winter of 1937–8, when her attitude towards life had been far different to what it was in 1952. Many of her friends, of course, were against the idea of another kiss-and-tell story whilst they were still alive; Chevalier and Frédéric Rey were just two, for they both expected her to bring her true vindictiveness to the fore.

However, her treatment of Chevalier was, by and large, much kinder than it could have been, though there was the odd lapse of bitterness. Some of the tawdrier aspects of Frédéric Rey's life were not discussed, though Mistinguett delighted in telling the world about his affair with Ramon Novarro. Earl Leslie and Léo Kok suffered most of all, and Pilcer was hardly mentioned; like her age, he was a subject not to be discussed, and she even had the audacity to suggest that he had never been a good dancer, which was of course untrue. Lino Carenzio, on the other hand, is presented as a somewhat neo-medieval character, chivalrous to the point of absurdity, and extremely likeable . . . a man who only had eyes for the woman in his life, which was again untrue. During an interview, a few years before his death, Carenzio admitted that he had always hated women, and Mistinguett more than most. This only points to the fact that, like most of the others and including Chevalier, he regarded her as little more than a means of achieving his own success.

Damia, who apart from Joséphine Baker, was Mistinguett's most dreaded enemy, is dismissed in a few condemning sentences. In 1969, on the eve of her eightieth birthday, she was asked about her 'enmity' with Mistinguett and called her 'an evil woman who never tried to understand me'. Edith Piaf, who admired her but is not mentioned at all in her memoirs, always spoke of her with great reverence. Manouche, who apart from her family was her best friend during the last two decades of her life, is not mentioned either. For these reasons, Mistinguett's memoirs were dismissed by some of her critics as false, and little better than those recounted to Maurice Verne. Even so, the dates are never anything but accurate, even going back to the turn of the century, which suggests that until 1952 Mistinguett may have kept a diary. So far as is known, no such journal has ever been found: it may even have been destroyed by the star, who would not have had any particular desire for it to fall into unscrupulous hands.

Mistinguett confessed, during a British interview of 1955, that whilst dictating her memoirs she had not consulted any back up information. 'Everything came out of my head. What's so remarkable about that?'

There were two volumes. The first was begun at Antibes in April 1953. Reclining in the garden, Mistinguett dictated the story of the first fifty years of her life to Fraisette, once again her 'secretary', who typed it all up at Bougival during the Christmas holidays on the machine which Mistinguett had been given when she had toured Switzerland with Earl Leslie. The second volume appears to have been dictated between stays at Bougival (now signed over to Fraisette and Marcel) and the Boulevard des Capucines apartment. Both volumes were taken to the offices of René Juillard, probably by Mistinguett herself, on the rue de l'Université in April 1954. Orders for publication were issued immediately and the memoirs were launched on 21 June, without the usual massive blaze of publicity. Both volumes were dedicated to Marcel Bourgeois, who with his wife and children was now living at Bougival.

Though Mistinguett gave a number of interviews in France to coincide with publication, she was not interested in the fact that she had probably penned a best seller. She declared, 'I couldn't care less. I've got it all off my chest . . . that's all that matters!' When asked why she had used the title *Toute Ma Vie*, when certain aspects of her private life had been purposely omitted, she added, 'The title *All My Life* doesn't apply to myself. It applies to the ones I loved the most, more than any of my men. It applies to my public!'

What is somewhat unusual is the fact that large portions of Mistinguett's memoirs were not directed towards French admirers, but British and American ones who had not, she claimed, always readily understood the French way of life. Several chapters were dedicated to her adventures in Britain and the United States, and whilst the two volumes were being edited by René Juillard, she insisted on their being translated into English. *Mistinguette by Mistinguett* was launched concurrently on both sides of the Atlantic in October 1954, and the seemingly erroneous name of the author was deliberate . . . this was how she had signed her programmes during her 1947 season at the London Casino. Though it would seem likely that even at almost eighty she was planning yet another tour of the United States, her doctors advised her that, on account of her fragile health, this would be totally out of the question, and she settled on one final trip across the Channel to London. She arrived at Croydon on 10 October 1954, and was driven straight to Hatchette's Bookshop, on Regent Street. With her were a small group of retainers, including Jean Robert, one of her 'boys' from her last Paris revue: he is frequently seen in photographs taken at the time, ostensibly standing guard over her, or carrying her handbag. Though she still did not look her age, those admirers who clustered around her whilst waiting for her to sign copies of her book observed that she looked wan and tired. She had also put on a little weight. She was offered a chair, which she refused. The sprightly charm and the quick temper were still evident, however, when a young man politely asked for a kiss. Though she threatened to hit him with her handbag, the kiss was delivered once the young man had parted with his money for the book! Immediately after the signing, she paid courtesy calls on her friends in and around London, and the following day she returned to Bougival.

During the next few months, Mistinguett almost became a recluse. There were fewer friends in Paris than there had been in the south, and she admitted that she was missing the visits from Pilcer and Chevalier. Though there was always talk of a new revue or tour, everyone knew that this would never be, though vocally she was in fine form. In April 1955 she celebrated her eightieth birthday. Fraisette and Marcel arranged a party – the chief guests were Léopold and his wife, Mistinguett's butcher, Monsieur Styger, and Simone, her housekeeper! Many photographs were taken and the smile was eternally evident, though Mistinguett did later confess to a journalist that it was often put-on.

It's been hard, putting on an act twenty-four hours every day. I've lived life to the full . . . my foot was always pressed down hard on the accelerator, whilst everything roared around me like at a racing-track. That smile was plastered to my face like a carnival mask twenty-four hours every day! I was happy, and I was sad . . . I always smiled! People envied me because I was happy and because I had loads of money, but I don't know whether I was really happy or not. I had everything, it's true, but there were still times when I felt like being the same as everyone else . . . eating chips in the street, or going to the fair and scoffing gingerbread! My career was my private life, my private life my career. I belonged to the public because I owed them everything. The public was the most exacting of all my lovers!

In July 1955 Mistinguett received an unexpected but welcome visit from Marie Dubas, now over sixty and herself ailing. Bruno Coquatrix, who had re-opened the Olympia in February 1954, had proposed a new series of recitals: *Chansons d'Hier et d'Aujourd'hui*, and Marie was worried about taking on the new challenge. Since her last season at the ABC, her career had slumped somewhat. Because they considered her a little old-fashioned, few orchestras would agree to work with her and she had taken to performing with the solitary accompaniment of a piano, mostly reciting poems to classical music. She was told, by Mistinguett, to keep at it and to accept Bruno Coquatrix's offer; Mistinguett even promised to attend the première. She later changed her mind when someone told her that Damia had been signed up to share the bill: the old hatred had not diminished over the years! The recitals went ahead and were tremendously successful, even if Damia did announce her retirement soon afterwards, largely due to the increasing intervention of the microphone. 'That horrible lump of metal's finally taken over! Time to call it a day!' the singer growled. Mistinguett was prompted into agreeing with her, though she did add acidly, 'The old cock with the Christmas pudding stuck on the end . . . I always said it would have some use, eventually. After all, it's got rid of Damia!'

Mistinguett's final 'performance' (the exact date is not known), took place towards the end of 1955, when for personal pleasure she accompanied herself at her piano on a number of her old hits. A tape recording of 'J'En ai Marre', with an English introduction, has survived. The voice, maybe a little cracked and worn, sounds sincere. The photograph, taken side-ways whilst she was not looking, is equally moving . . . an old lady, working like an indefatigable war-horse, almost until the end.

On Friday 23 December 1955, Marcel Bougeois called in to see his sister at her Paris apartment and found her curled up in an armchair, shivering. She had earlier announced that she was going to spend the Christmas holiday at Bougival and, wrapping her in a blanket, Marcel drove her straight there and carried her up to her beautiful, swan-shaped bed. Simone, the housekeeper, telephoned for a doctor and he arrived within the hour. By this time Mistinguett appeared to have recovered from her indisposition and was back to her usual self, cracking jokes and demanding to see the children. Marcel could not prevent her from getting up and going downstairs, once she had taken a short nap. For as long as anyone could remember, whenever she had spent the Christmas at Bougival, Mistinguett had always decorated the Christmas tree and set up the crib. The doctor had diagnosed a slight stroke, but neither he nor Marcel had dared tell her the truth, and the two men stayed with her in the lounge, where they helped her with the decorations. At around six in the evening, Léopold de Lima arrived with his wife, and not even he could persuade his mother to rest awhile and take things easy. At seven – she was still decorating the crib – she suddenly clutched at her chest, and Léopold caught her as she fell. This time when she was carried up to her room, she was told what was wrong; the stroke had been followed by a heart attack, and she was also suffering from pneumonia. Early the next morning she was placed in an oxygen tent and the family gathered around her bed, anticipating the end.

On Christmas Day Mistinguett still possessed sufficient strength and temper to argue with everyone that in spite of her 'cold' they should still go downstairs and enjoy their Christmas dinner. As usual they did as they were told, though the meal was eaten in silence and dread.

The news that the greatest star in the history of the music-hall was dying was broken to the media. During the next two days there were radio and television bulletins on the hour, every hour. Telegrams and letters arrived by the sackful and the telephone never stopped ringing. Friends were encouraged not to visit because Léopold feared that even the least excitement might kill her; instead they sent flowers, and in next to no time these overflowed from her bedroom into the passage outside. On the Wednesday her condition actually improved. She told Léopold to take away the bouquets and leave only the small bunches of flowers which had been sent in by her fans, who turned up at the gates of the big house every day, in spite of the cold, to pray for her recovery. There was a telephone call from Maurice Chevalier, and another from Harry Pilcer. Even the Queen of England had expressed her concern: shortly after her coronation in June 1953, Mistinguett had written to her to wish her a long and prosperous reign. There were messages of condolence from Jean Sablon and Suzy Solidor, the godparents of Marcel and Fraisette's two younger sons. Lino Carenzio spent much of the day sitting in an armchair next to her bed, sobbing, and probably telling himself that without his benefactress he would have little future.

On New Year's Eve a telegram arrived from Chevalier. It read: *Have Courage, Great One*! Léopold thought that it might not be a good idea for his mother to be reminded of him, but Fraisette showed it to her all the same. She began crying and said, 'When I do die, I'll be thinking of Maurice. He was the best of them all!' She then asked to see Manouche, and her eleven years old 'godson', Jean-Paul. By the time they arrived she had taken a turn for the worst . . . Léopold diagnosed a cerebral haemorrhage, and she lapsed into a deep sleep from which she never emerged. On 5 January 1956, at 11.45 am, Mistinguett slipped away from us.

Maurice Chevalier said, 'I've lost the great love of my life. My poor Miss. . .'

Mistinguett was embalmed and laid in state within the Madeleine, where a solemn high mass was sung. For several days, thousands of her grieving admirers filed past her coffin. Fraisette had dressed her in a pink, silken robe and her hairdresser, Jean Clement, had fashioned a head-dress out of rose-coloured plumes. As the funeral cortège left the church and moved at a snail's pace along the rue Royale towards the Place de la Concorde there was a deathly silence as the many thousands of people gathered there fell to their knees, making the sign of the cross. Many of the shops and bars had closed out of respect.

Within the churchyard at Enghien, the little town where she had only been known as Jeanne Bourgeois, Mistinguett was laid to rest in the vault which she had commissioned, some time before, to house the bones of her parents. It was a far different scene from the one in Paris. There were few show business personalities: Manouche and Arletty, perhaps, were the only ones, along with a handful of Mistinguett's boys. The family were burying the woman they had all called 'grandmother' . . . though never to her face.

With her they were burying the French music-hall. Though she would be often emulated, Mistinguett would never, never be replaced. She had been the first. She would be the last.

Epilogue

The family, friends, colleagues and retainers . . . and the hangers-on . . . are now mostly gone. Carlos Machado, Léo Kok and a number of others had faded into obscurity long before Mistinguett's death: the latter is only remembered when one reads the small print under the title of one of her most famous songs, 'Je Cherche un Millionnaire'. Lino Carenzio and Earl Leslie continued to give the odd performance, but age and the absence of their *patronne* prevented them from achieving further recognition, and both men died feeling unwanted and embittered. Frédéric Rey made futile attempts to rekindle the glories of the *époque*, and died practically forgotten. Lad simply disappeared.

Harry Pilcer, often plunging into the very depths of despair, contined to mourn the two great loves of his life – Gaby Deslys and Mistinguett. He never stopped working and never lost his appeal and popularity. His last performance took place in Cannes, on 16 January 1961, where he executed a dance which he had devised to commemorate the fifth anniversary of Mistinguett's death. Two hours later he himself collapsed and died of a heart attack, aged seventy five.

Jean Sablon and Georges Guétary, already big names in the French music-hall, became famous in Britain and the United States where, besides thrilling their audiences with large numbers of romantic songs, they made a number of important films. After a very successful career on both sides of the Atlantic, Pills and Tabet split up: the latter, after his divorce from Edith Piaf, remained popular until his death in 1970. Jean Gabin, of course, became the greatest of all the continental film stars.

Shortly before Mistinguett's death, Maurice Chevalier had been seen in the company of Patachou . . . Mistinguett had never called her anything but Patamerde. Though Chevalier would endure a number of relationships, he would not marry again; many said because, in his heart, he had always been married to Mistinguett. Between 1956 and 1962 much of his time was spent making films in Hollywood, including the phenomenally-successful *Gigi* and *Cancan*. In 1968 he told his admirers that he was retiring; he was eighty, and his final season at the Théâtre des Champs-Elysées was one of the most triumphant of his long career, which had spanned, incredibly, almost seventy years. In 1971 he swallowed an overdose of barbiturates, and though his doctors managed to save his life, he finally expired in February 1972 when he was eighty one.

And the 'rivals'? A few years after Mistinguett's death, Joséphine Baker suffered extreme hardship which coincided with a lengthy period of ill-health. During the course of her marriage to the bandleader Jo Bouillon she had adopted twelve children of differing religions and ethnic cultures. Evicted from her sumptuous home, Les Milandes, she was rescued by Princess Grace of Monaco, who had announced her engagement to Prince Rainier on the day of Mistinguett's death. Like her greatest rival, Joséphine continued to pack out Parisian theatres almost until the day of her death . . . she collapsed of a cerebral haemorrhage only hours after her première at the Bobino music-hall in April 1975, and died a few days later. Damia, though she had officially retired in 1956, gave a few privileged performances in and around Paris: the last was to commemorate the centenary of the Pacra music-hall in 1967. She died, aged eighty eight, in January 1978.

Marie Dubas, perhaps the only woman in the entire music-hall whom Mistinguett confessed to respecting as well as admiring, gave her final performances at the Pacra, in 1958, after which she was diagnosed as suffering from Parkinson's Disease. She died in 1972.

Marcel Bourgeois, Mistinguett's brother, died at Bougival in 1968, aged eighty six. His wife followed him to the grave five years later. That other Jeanne Bourgeois, Mistinguett's beloved 'Micky' died in 1984, aged just forty eight. The photographs taken of her during the seventies reveal that, as far as looks were concerned, she was a real chip off the old block.

Michel Guyarmathy continues to direct the Folies-Bergère, and Roger Normand still lives in the heart of Pigalle, very active and eternally eager to continue promoting the name of his idol. The author acquired their friendship during a recent visit to Paris and will always remain grateful to them for their reminiscences. Manouche, that 'demon spirit' so influenced by Mistinguett during the last twenty years of her life, and the woman who was only too ready to try and discredit her in her memoirs, had died only a few weeks before our scheduled meeting.

So far as is known, there have been no film or theatre tributes to the Queen of the Music-Hall. In 1989 I wrote a musical-play, *Miss*, which told of her relationship not with Chevalier, but with Pilcer . . . it was based on fact, but most of the dialogue had been repeated to me, second-hand, by Manouche. Some of Mistinguett's songs were loosely adapted into English and others were added, songs which I feel she would have liked to perform, had she still been around. The play is still waiting to be produced.

In France, most of the 'tributes' to Mistinguett have been little more than grossly inadequate, and often crude and cruel caricatures . . . mostly by female impersonators. In England, she appeared as an essential character in a television drama, *Miss Bluebell*. The actress who played her, Thelma Ruby, was nothing short of exceptional. Apart from her obvious acting abilities, Thelma danced almost as well as Mistinguett at this stage of her career, and her songs – these included 'There's Something About a Soldier', which Mistinguett had once sung in English – proved perhaps that she had a better singing voice. What was really astonishing, however, was Thelma's ability to portray the star's 'bitchiness' without going over the top. She told me,

> I did all the research I could. I read two or three books by or about her, and several books by and about Maurice Chevalier. An interesting thing happens when you create a character. Like you, I had read that she was a difficult personality . . . let's not mince words, 'a right bitch'. But as I started to work on her, I started to feel that her so-called bad behaviour was just an insistence on excellence and a desire to be in complete charge of every aspect of the shows which she appeared in. Miss Bluebell herself came over from Paris to visit the rehearsals and to watch the recording of the Folies-Bergère scenes . . . in Halifax! She told

me what a cow Mistinguett was, how impossible she was to work with. I was furious and deeply offended . . . I forgot she was only insulting the character I was playing. I took it to heart and defended Mistinguett passionately! As you can tell, I loved playing the part! When my agent telephoned me about the part he said: 'The director wants to know, how are your legs?' I replied: 'The rest of me has gone to pot, but the legs are still sensational!' I was sure that the days of flashing the legs were well past, when along came Mistinguett. I have a lot to thank her for!

And, the author may add confidently, the music-hall has a lot, quite a lot, to thank Thelma Ruby for.

Mistinguett is gone, leaving an empty space, a few broken hearts and a host of indelible memories. One can only add, finally and lamentably: 'Miss . . . Je Vous ai Reconnue!'

Appendix:
The Recordings of Mistinguett

In spite of her immense popularity and appeal, very few recordings of Mistinguett have appeared after her death, either in Britain or France. Her recording career, which spanned the years 1920 to 1945, produced around fifty 78 rpm shellac recordings. Most of these are now extremely difficult to find, and almost half of them were considered so technically sub-standard that they were never transferred to microsillon. The following is a very rough guide to what exists today, or what did exist, though of course one is never sure what is stored in archives and rare collections around the world, and one hopes that in the near future many elusive items will come to light.

FRANCE

78 rpm shellac recordings were issued by Columbia between the years 1920 and 1942. Because of the time limit imposed on such recordings, around three and a half minutes, many do not have satisfactory endings, and there are quite a lot of re-takes, especially of Mistinguett's duets with other artistes, when through problems of a personal nature alternative artistes sat in on the recording sessions. Thus it is not usual to find recordings of Mistinguett and Earl Leslie after the break-up of their relationship, or of Mistinguett and Lino Carenzio, even though several recordings of on-stage performances were made. These 78 rpm records have been re-issued on microsillon as follows:

Du caf' conc' au music-hall: Volume 17 (CO54–15291)

C'est vrai (Oberfeld-Willemetz) 1935
Oui je suis de Paris (Oberfeld-Bayle-de Lima) 1936
Pour être heureux, chantez! 1936
Avez-vous Hubert? 1938 with Lino Carenzio
Je vous ai reconnue (Oberfeld-Lelièvre-de Lima) 1938
La tour Eiffel est toujours là
Les barbus
Mon homme (Yvain-Willemetz-Charles) 1938
Tu m'aimes, dis chéri?
Je cherche un millionnaire (Brown-Cab-de Lima) 1938
Fleur de Paris
Tout ça n'arrive qu'à moi
On le joue pour nous
C'est moi Mélie

Mistinguett (C178–15422/3) Dates as above, unless specified
Mon homme
Je cherche un millionnaire (with Léo Kok) 1938
Sous les becs de gaz (Pipon-Lelièvre-de Lima) 1938
Je vous ai reconnue
Mon gangster (Cambier-Bayle-Cab-de Lima) 1938
Toute petite (Doloire-Decaye) 1938
J'ai des touches (Sylviano-Varna-Lelièvre-de Lima) 1931 possibly with Harry Pilcer
Garde-moi (Yvain-Varna-Lelièvre-de Lima) 1931
Dans les bouges la nuit (Bixio-Marino-Lelièvre-de Lima) 1931
Un boy c'est gentil (Marf-Varna-Lelièvre-de Lima) 1931
Qu'est ce que j'ai donc? (Forrester-Lelièvre-Varna-de Lima) 1929
Moineau de Paris (Padilla-Lelièvre-Varna-de Lima) 1929
Pot-pourri sur les airs de la Miss 1936:
    L'faubourg Saint-Denis (Sylviano-Lelièvre-Varna-de Lima)
    J'en ai marre (Yvain-Willemetz-Arnould)
    La java (Yvain-Willemetz-Charles)
    En douce (Yvain-Willemetz-Charles)
    La belote (Yvain-Willemetz-Carpentier)
    Mon homme
    On me suit (Pearly-Chagnon-de Lima-Lelièvre)
Oui, je suis de Paris

Au fond de tes yeux (Oberfeld-Bayle-de Lima) 1936
C'est vrai
Nuits de Paris (Varna-de Gredos-Lelièvre-de Lima) 1931
A travers les barreaux de l'escalier (Yvain-Lelièvre-Varna-de Lima) 1931
Gosse de Paris (Sylviano-Lelièvre-Varna-de Lima) 1929
C'est tout ce que j'ai (Borel Clerc-Gold-Varna-de Lima) 1929
On me suit (with Jean Gabin) 1928
Il m'a vue nue (Pearly-Chagnon) 1927
Ca, c'est Paris! (Padilla-Pearly-Boyer-Charles) 1927
Valencia (Padilla-Boyer-Charles) 1925

Bravo à Mistinguett et à Marie Dubas
Features ten titles each of the two stars:
C'est vrai
Gosse de Paris
On me suit (without Jean Gabin) 1931
Sous les ponts (Scotto-Varna-Lelièvre-de Lima) 1931
Ca, c'est Paris
Il m'a vue nue (1938)
A travers les barreaux de l'escalier
J'ai qu'ça
Garde-moi
Prenez-mes fleurettes ('Dans les bouges la nuit' with different text)

GREAT BRITAIN
A large number of Mistinguett 78 rpm records was released here between 1931 and 1950, and are again elusive. Perhaps the easiest to find are:

Columbia DF 1988: Oui je suis de Paris/Au fond de tes yeux
Columbia DF 1989: Oui je suis de Paris/Pour être heureux chantez
Columbia DF 1987: Pour être heureux chantez/Pot-pourri

Mistinguett at the Casino de Paris (Parlophone GEP 8659)
Though this extended 45 rpm was alleged to have been recorded on stage at the Casino, it was not. The titles are:
Ca c'est Paris

C'est vrai
Garde-moi
Sous les ponts

To date, no albums of Mistinguett have been released in the United Kingdom, though it is hoped to rectify this by a 'companion' album to this biography. The titles, at the time of going to press, are not known, though they are not expected to be any of the 'lost' pressings. Mistinguett songs have, of course, been issued regularly on compilations of the French *chanson*. The most interesting was in 1989, when Conifer Records issued *La Vie Parisienne* an album of 'rare' songs including works by Edith Piaf, Fernandel, Jean Sablon and Mireille. There were two songs by Mistinguett: 'C'Est Vrai' and 'Oh! Que J'Aime Paris' (Stanley-Varna-de Lima). The latter song, so far as is known, has never been commercially released in France. It is also believed that Mistinguett made a number of records during her visits to Britain. 'Mon Homme', 'Je Cherche un Millionnaire' and 'Valencia' were often sung in English, and a photograph of one of these 'sessions' appeared in a British newspaper in 1933.

The following songs, which were recorded often on 'test' 78 rpm records between 1933 and 1954, are in the author's private collection, though it is hoped that they will be put on general release in the near future.

Mary (sung in English/French) with Harry Pilcer, c. 1936

I'm on my way home (sung in English) with Carlos Machado, Léo Kok and Georges Guétary, possibly 1942

J'en ai marre (English introduction) with Jean Sablon, 1954

Je suis nature c. 1938

Parisette c. 1936

Paname n'est pas Paris c. 1933

C'est un p'tit rien, with Lino Carenzio, c. 1940

Mitsou c. 1930

C'est un p'tit rien, with Harry Pilcer, c. 1940

Tu m'aimes dis-cheri? with Harry Pilcer, c. 1930

The songs were probably written by the regular team of de Lima . . . in other words Mistinguett herself . . . and Lelièvre, Cab, and Henri Varna.